Also by the author

The Big One: An Island, an Obsession, and the
Furious Pursuit of a Great Fish

THE
DYLANOLOGISTS

Adventures in the Land of Bob

DAVID KINNEY

SIMON & SCHUSTER
NEW YORK   LONDON   TORONTO   SYDNEY   NEW DELHI

Simon & Schuster
1230 Avenue of the Americas
New York, NY 10020

First Simon & Schuster hardcover edition May 2014

SIMON & SCHUSTER and colophon are registered trademarks of Simon & Schuster, Inc.

For information about special discounts for bulk purchases, please contact Simon & Schuster Special Sales at 1-866-506-1949 or business@simonandschuster.com.

The Simon & Schuster Speakers Bureau can bring authors to your live event. For more information or to book an event contact the Simon & Schuster Speakers Bureau at 1-866-248-3049 or visit our website at www.simonspeakers.com.

Designed by Jill Putorti

Manufactured in the United States of America

10   9   8   7   6   5   4   3   2   1

Library of Congress Control Number: 2013008574

ISBN 978-1-4516-2692-6
ISBN 978-1-4516-2694-0 (ebook)

For Monica, Jane, and Owen

FAN
You don't know who I am, but I know who you are.

BOB DYLAN
Let's keep it that way.

CONTENTS

THE
DYLANOLOGISTS

INTRODUCTION

It starts with the voice. One day we hear its strange, broken glory, and before long everyone else in our lives would rather jam ice picks into their ears than listen to another Bob Dylan song. We know what you're thinking. That the man cannot sing, that he yelps, grunts, and caterwauls, that he sounds like a suffering animal or a busted lawn mower, that his throat is a rumbling, grating cement mixer. How can we ever explain this so you understand? Dylan's voice, so reviled and ridiculed by you heathens, is a wonder of the world to us. It's human, real, and above all *expressive*. It embodies rapture, heartbreak, rage, bitterness, disdain, boredom. It can be by turns biting, sarcastic, and deeply funny. It's freighted with weirdly spellbinding magic. It's what pulls us—the faithful—to the foot of the stage, and keeps us there for a lifetime.

We who listen too hard are compelled to do things that are difficult to talk about. We devour millions of words of scholarship on his life and work. We spend hours arguing about the songs. We celebrate new albums as important events; they help us mark time in our own lives. We manage towering collections of bootlegs and hunt down underground tapes. We find ourselves identifying with him, and quoting his choice lines in conversation. Some of us have been known to wake up in the morning and wonder what he's eating for breakfast and how he takes his coffee. We go off on pilgrimages: stomping through the timeless Greenwich Village streets where he first made it in 1961; trekking to Big Pink in Woodstock, where he set down beloved reels of classic Americana with the Band in 1967; popping into a café linked to Dylan in Santa Monica; driving past his estate in Malibu; peeking down the long driveway to his farm in Minnesota. We go to concerts by the dozens, and wait in lines all day so we can dash to the front of the stage. We bet on which songs he'll perform at the show tonight.

We keep track of everything: every recording session and every tour date, every song on every bootleg, every word ever caught by a recording device. We are preoccupied with facts and dates, as if cataloguing these things will solve the mysteries of his life, and ours. We investigate the unanswered questions of his career. We pile up pages for Dylan books and Dylan fanzines and Dylan blogs, or just for our own private circles of Dylan friends. We go to conventions and tribute shows and meet-ups and lectures. We figure out how to play the songs on our guitars. We track down all the literary, musical, and cultural allusions in his work. We collect the things he left behind: scraps of writing paper, guitars, harmonicas, books, cigarette butts. One day we discover with a flash that more than a few of our closest friends, sometimes even our spouses, are fellow fans.

I first found Dylan in the dusty basement of my childhood home. In the summer before my junior year in high school I was flicking through a pile of vinyl left behind by my older brother. I found a heavy box with five records inside. The man glowering on the front cover looked like he didn't take orders from anybody. I liked that. I pulled off the top of the box, slid one of the records from a sleeve, fitted the vinyl onto the turntable, and dropped the needle into the groove. The music started, and a switch flipped in my head. The album was called *Biograph*, a retrospective of the first two decades of a recording career still very much in progress. Dylan's folk ballads were jumbled together with wailing mid-1960s rock classics; his gospel songs shared space with tomfoolery. A maid is beaten to death. A good man is sent to jail. A husband abandons his wife to hunt for treasure with a shadowy figure, and all he finds is an empty casket. There were songs about girls, and war, and politics. I didn't know who all of the characters were: Johanna, Ma Rainey, Cecil B. DeMille, Gypsy Davy. I couldn't honestly say I knew what Dylan was saying half the time. But the lines were riveting. I wore out those five records. I learned every word and made them mine, and Dylan grew into an outsize figure in my universe.

I preached the gospel to anyone who would listen. I loaned *Highway 61 Revisited* and *Blood on the Tracks* to friends, or played Dylan for them in my car. I expected them to see the light and join the congregation. But it wasn't 1965 anymore. Dylan's Ray-Ban cool had worn off. When I tried to play "Subterranean Homesick Blues" on the boom box during a school bus trip, my classmates yelped in protest. They couldn't get past the voice.

For the longest time, I felt alone in this addiction, and a little crazy. No one in my world took Dylan as seriously as I did. But it also seemed as though I was in on a secret. In time I came to realize that there were many others like me—an entire underground nation of unreformed obsessives. I had a people.

One day not long ago, I set out to meet them.

1

PILGRIMS

The little Minnesota town that Bob Dylan fled in 1959 is a hundred miles shy of the Canadian border. From the Twin Cities, it's three and a half hours by car, due north past fields and silos and a hundred lakes. Maps show crossroad towns, Sax, Independence, Canyon, but look out the car window and there is little proof they even exist. The thick woods are remote enough to hold moose. In the winter, when temperatures can drop below zero overnight, a stranded driver has reason to fear that frostbite will arrive before the tow truck.

Dylan's followers make the pilgrimage en masse to mark his birthday each year, and lucky for them he was born in May. They only have to deal with a heavy splattering of bugs on the windshield. The capital of the Land of Bob is Hibbing, quintessential iron-mining town, population sixteen thousand or so. They know they've made it when the off-road ATV shops, biker bars, and broken-down rural miscellany give way to the regional airport and other markers of modern civilization: Super 8, Walmart, KFC. A commercial district encircles a grid of avenues lined with modest houses and tidy lawns. Howard Street, broad and bedecked in two-story red brick, is the major artery of a drowsy downtown well past its prime. It has a jeweler, a bookseller, a bank, the Moose lodge, a knitting shop. Every other block seems to have a vacant storefront standing out like a missing tooth. The drinking crowd is liable to make a scene outside Bar 412 in the wee hours. Otherwise, *hush*.

Bob Zimmerman skipped out of town a half century ago, adopting a stage name and becoming a singer, an icon, and a millionaire many times over. Storefronts have changed hands and a lot of his family has passed away or moved, but in many ways Hibbing has barely changed since he left, and the quiet tells the pilgrims what they need to know about why he did. Dylan made a name as a teenager by jumping up in front of crowds and making noise, a lot of noise, amplified noise. *Infernal* noise, the respectable crowd said. He hammered on pianos and screamed like Little Richard at volumes his listeners considered uncomfortable. A photograph from 1958 shows him standing on a stage behind an Elvis mic, wearing a striped suit, his hair swept into a pompadour, his mouth open, his right foot poised to crash down on the boards to the beat with a resounding *crack!* At one of these wild-eyed performances, the principal switched off the microphones and yanked the curtains shut. Years later, the man was still shaking his head. "He got so crazy!"

"Hibbing's a good ol' town," Dylan wrote not long after he departed once and for all. And it was. A perfectly fine, respectable, middle-class, civic-pride sort of place, a burg where you could be content to settle down with a steady job and your girl from high school. Hibbing was conventional, mainstream, solid. Most of all it was quiet. There was no chance in the world that it could have held on to this, its most famous son, a man who would make a career out of upsetting the peace, and changing and changing and changing again. "There really was nothing there," he said later. "It couldn't give me anything."

A lifetime on, the boy these pilgrims hoped to find was a ghost. Still they trekked all the way up into the North Country to look for traces of his past life. As it happened, so did he.

2

On September 23, 2004, a Thursday, one of those golden mornings in early autumn, a social worker named Bob Hocking was at his desk in the Hibbing employment office when the telephone rang. It was his wife, Linda. Ordinarily, she would have been over at Zimmy's, her Dylan-themed bar and restaurant on Howard, where the pilgrims can order a "Hard Rain" hamburger while they chew on the delicious idea that as a teen Bob bought LPs just up the street at Chet Crippa's Music Store. But this morning Linda was three blocks south at Blessed Sacrament for a funeral. Myrtle Jurenes, ninety-two, was dead. Hibbing being Hibbing—that is, Dylan's childhood hometown, and the sort of place where everybody knows everybody else—Myrtle was the mother of a Hocking family friend, and she was Dylan's brother's mother-in-law.

"Bob's here," Linda told her husband. She suggested he get over to the restaurant just in case. Maybe Dylan would hang around after the service. Maybe he would want lunch. Maybe he would come by their joint, finally. One of them ought to be there, you know, just in case. Hocking jumped into his pickup truck and was at Zimmy's five minutes later.

They had not been expecting Dylan to make an appearance. He

spent a quarter of every year playing dates in North and South America, Europe, Asia, and Australia. He had homes around the world. But he also owned a farm on the Crow River just north of Minneapolis, and stories circulated every now and then about local sightings. He had been spotted at Minnesota Twins baseball games, and in Duluth. Once, decades ago, he drove up to Hibbing in a station wagon with an enormous dog and pulled right up to his boyhood home. The owner invited him inside. Dylan, wearing a leather jacket and boots, asked after some teachers, noticed where he'd carved his initials onto a basement wall, and marveled about how *small* his bedroom really was. Now, on the day they sent Myrtle off to the hereafter, Bob Dylan was back.

Linda was sitting in the back of the church when she spotted that legendary nimbus of hair halfway to the altar. *That can't be Bob*, she thought at first. But she kept watch, and when he turned his head, she had no doubt. He was sitting beside a woman with long, straight blonde hair and a skirt that went down to her ankles.

Afterward, he milled around with other mourners on the patio in front of the church. Linda noticed that his suit was well made, and he looked rested and healthy. He made his way over to speak with his high school English instructor, B.J. Rolfzen. The Hockings had become very close to the old retired teacher, so Linda sidled up as if she belonged.

"Robert," she heard the teacher say, "so nice to see you. Do you remember me? Room 204?"

"Yes," Dylan replied. "You taught me a lot."

He looked at his Italian leather shoes, then over at his old house down the street. His aunt came by and reminded him to stop in on his uncle, who was ill. Linda was just about to introduce herself and invite Dylan to lunch at Zimmy's when she saw him peer over her shoulder. A stunned look crossed his face.

A local TV crew had appeared, and they were racing over with their camera and microphone. She turned back and Dylan was gone—running across the lawn. He jumped into the driver's seat of his Ford pickup and disappeared. In a flash, Linda's moment with the singer was shot.

Meanwhile, over at the restaurant, Hocking paced the floor, chatted with the waitresses, looked out the window. Zimmy's was on the corner of Howard and 6th Avenue East, right in the middle of downtown. In the 1920s, the building housed trolley cars that ran along Howard Street; original tracks are still there in the basement. Around Dylan's time it was a Shell station. Now it had the exposed brick and always-on televisions of an Applebee's in Anywheresville, except that the cartloads of bric-a-brac were authentic Dylan artifacts. Hocking, who had a ramshackle gait and was more than capable of holding up both ends of a conversation, went to Hibbing High a decade after Dylan left, but he grew up taking the celebrated alumnus for granted. It wasn't until he left that he realized how revered the man was everywhere else. In St. Paul, his first stop out of high school, other students spoke of Dylan like a minor god. Just being from Hibbing made Hocking a person of interest. So he listened harder to the records, and soon he caught the bug.

If he comes, Hocking thought, *I'm here.* He had never run into Dylan, and now, with the possibility hanging in the air, he was anxious. His mind raced. He worried about what he would say. He ran through the scenarios in his mind. He didn't want to be one of those tongue-tied fans. Hocking was well versed in local history and knew just about everybody in town. He could fill Dylan in on the times gone by. He figured he'd play it cool. *Welcome to Hibbing, let me buy you lunch, if you have any questions about anything, I'll be around.*

It was a long shot, of course. He knew that. Given Dylan's half century of public churlishness, you would have to assume he would never go near a place named after him, that had a faux Hollywood

Walk of Fame star on the sidewalk and a menu featuring a "Simple Twist of" Sirloin ($15.99). A place that was liable, any day of the week, to have some crazy Dylan fan on the premises, some all-knowing Dylanologist ready to pounce and pepper him with questions. Still, crazy things happened, and Hocking couldn't help but imagine it. Bob Dylan *inside* Zimmy's.

Gazing from photographs on a towering billboard sign out front were Bob Zimmerman, age seventeen, holding an electric guitar, and his high school girlfriend, Echo Helstrom, posing for a glamour shot. A cardboard cutout of sixty-ish Dylan greeted diners inside the front door. He had a thin mustache and a white cowboy shirt open three buttons from the collar. On the walls were guitars and posters, a Highway 61 road sign, and images of Dylan from the 1940s and '50s. Bob on a motorcycle, Bob at his mother's feet as a toddler, Bob holding a drum he made in middle school. In one photo, a first-grade class portrait, every child looks at the camera except him. He had turned his head at the moment the shutter clicked open.

Across one wall was a sign spelling out, in vintage yellow light-bulbs, the name LYBBA. It's an obscure name that only locals should recognize, but the pilgrims who go to Hibbing with Dylan on the mind, the ones who wander around Zimmy's like they're at the Metropolitan Museum of Art—staring, pointing, their mouths agape—these people know the name straight away. Lybba Edelstein was Bob Dylan's great-grandmother, and her husband, B.H., named one of the family's movie theaters after her. Zimmy's has bits of Dylan's childhood house. The most recent owners replaced nineteen windows and passed along the original ones to various Dylanophiles. "It's like the four thousand fragments of the true cross," one fan said. Here and there around town you find the windows, as if they could reveal what went on behind them when they were in Bob's house. One sash went to a guy up the highway who named his sons Bob and Dylan. A Minnesota folksinger got one, the library got one. Zimmy's had to have two, and the Hockings wanted theirs to be the windows that hung in the boy's bedroom. They also owned bits of bathroom tile from the house, and the bathroom sink, and the door to his high school English classroom. These old things were a concrete link to the real Bob Dylan, and the Hockings still felt a tiny charge when they thought about him walking the streets of the town they called home.

Bob Hocking and Linda Stroback met as art students in Missoula, Montana, in the early 1980s. Not long after they arrived in Hibbing, he landed work with the state and painted, mostly abstracts. She got a job as a manager at Zimmy's. Only it wasn't Zimmy's yet. Back then it had an instantly forgettable name, the Atrium. A few years after Linda arrived, the owners decided they needed to rebrand or else they would struggle like any other downtown restaurant. At a brainstorming session, Linda brought up Dylan. Surely, he would be a better draw than other celebrity Hibbingites, like attorney-author Vincent Bugliosi, or Jeno Paulucci, the man behind Chun King canned Chinese food. "I don't think you realize how big Bob Dylan is everywhere *but* Hibbing," Linda argued. The owners were sold, and the new name went up on the signs.

Linda got an informal green light from Dylan's office, but she worried that people would say the business was cashing in on a superstar's celebrity. Sure enough, a couple of local women appeared to scold them. *Beatty would not approve.* Beatty Zimmerman was Dylan's mother. She had moved out of town after her husband's death decades earlier, but she returned regularly. A few months after the name change, she was in town visiting friends. They stopped into Zimmy's for lunch. Linda watched Beatty go from table to table greeting people. She seemed to still know everyone in town. After Beatty sat down to eat, Linda walked over. The Zimmy's manager is round-faced and perpetually smiling. She grew up in a big city—Philadelphia—but she has the warmth of a small-town girl, a workaholic's industry, and the mind of a natural-born marketer. She introduced herself and asked Beatty what she thought.

"Honey," the woman told her, "it's about time somebody did something nice for my son in Hibbing."

Dylan was an eccentric and sensitive kid. Perhaps he wouldn't have fit anywhere, but growing up, he surely didn't fit in Hibbing. Later on, after he became famous, writers and critics used to wonder: How did a cultural giant as smart and original as Dylan come from a nowhere sort of place like *this*?

Hibbing sits in the center of an eighty-mile constellation of settlements that were founded atop a narrow band of low hills called the Mesabi Range. Prospectors began mining iron there in 1890, and soon it become clear they had tapped into one of the richest veins in the world. Within two decades the once-isolated region of forest and bog had sixty-five thousand inhabitants and an array of nationalities: Scandinavian, Finnish, Bohemian, Italian, Polish, Russian, Greek. With miners came hucksters and gamblers and prostitutes and saloons by the dozens. But tax revenues boomed, and the new settlements did not remain bawdy frontier camps for long. Hibbing in particular aspired to greatness, and in short order it touted a fine school, a Carnegie library, a courthouse, a three-story town hall, a hotel, a racetrack, and a zoo with lions and buffalo. What the mines gave, they soon took away. Turned out, ore lay beneath Hibbing's foundations, and the townspeople had barely settled in when the decision was made to move almost two miles south. Starting in 1918, some two hundred buildings were hoisted onto wheels and inched off the mother lode. A new town hall went up with a clock tower. Howard Street came alive with national chain department stores, a theater, and a plush hotel. North of Hibbing, the strip-mined canyon grew until it sprawled as far as the eye could see. From the ground, it's a four-mile moonscape. On satellite maps it looks like a spill, something pouring out of the town's borders. Mining spoils now encircle the city in towering red-earth ridges.

Bob was born in Duluth, an hour and a half's drive southeast, on May 24, 1941. When he was five, his father, Abe, was struck with polio and housebound for six months. In 1947, having lost his job as a Standard Oil manager, he moved Beatty, Bob, and his second son, David, then one, to Hibbing. They wanted to be closer to their extended families. The Zimmermans were middle-class and Jewish in a town that was predominantly working-class and Christian. Abe was president of the B'nai B'rith lodge and Beatty of the local Hadassah chapter. After he recovered, Abe worked at the appliance business with his brothers, and Beatty worked at a downtown department store, Feldman's. She was the sort of saleswoman who would call her customers when a new dress appeared that she thought they'd like. *It's perfect for you, come check it out.* The Zimmermans did well enough that Beatty had a fur in her closet, and as a teenager Bob had a convertible and his own motorcycle.

Like a lot of kids growing up in the 1950s, Bob fell in love with music through a new lifeline to the world: the transistor radio. In Hibbing, polka ruled. Accordions filled the front window of the town's music store. But over the airwaves at night, Bob could hear early rock, rhythm and blues, and country on radio stations out of Little Rock and Shreveport, Louisiana. He listened to Elvis, Buddy Holly, Hank Williams, Chuck Berry, Little Richard. Banging away on the guitar and the family piano, he learned how to play what he heard, and then launched a succession of rock bands. Some of Bob's gigs were at Hibbing High School, a granite-and-limestone colossus that cost nearly $4 million to construct in 1920–22. The hallways were finished in intricate, hand-painted molding and decorated with oil paintings. The doorknobs were brass. The gemstone of the school was an auditorium modeled on New York's Capitol Theater. It seated eighteen hundred in red velvet seats and boasted a pipe organ and a grand piano, an ornate proscenium, and crystal chandeliers from Europe. Playing on a stage this majestic could plant ostentatious ideas in a teenager's head.

Over the years, pilgrims to Hibbing were surprised that Dylan was not hailed as a local hero. A visitor could come and go and never realize the connection. Wear a Dylan T-shirt in Hibbing and you were liable to get an earful from the locals about how much they wanted to pummel that no-good weirdo when they were growing up. After Dylan landed his record deal—only two years out of high school—he fabricated a new biography for himself. He told interviewers he'd run away from home repeatedly. He'd lived in Gallup, New Mexico, and Marysville, Texas, and Sioux Falls, South Dakota. He'd been a "roustabout" for carnivals. In Hibbing, people couldn't understand why Dylan went to such lengths to deny growing up middle-class in their respectable city.

Decades later, he was still less popular locally than Kevin McHale, the basketball star who won three NBA championships with the Boston Celtics. McHale kept a hunting lodge north of town and always spoke highly of the place. "It's rough up here," said David Vidmar, a mining industry consultant whose aunt bought the Zimmerman house after Dylan's father died. "You could probably understand why a lot of people didn't care for him. Myself included. I hunt and fish. Poetry? Sorry. People worked in the mines. They're not listening to poems." When Aaron Brown was growing up in Hibbing in the 1980s and 1990s, he had no idea that Dylan was any more important than any other rock star on the radio. "The fact that Dylan was a big deal? We got sex ed before we got that," said Brown, a columnist for the *Hibbing Daily Tribune*. "If we had a mayor's election between Kevin McHale and Bob Dylan, Kevin McHale would win with eighty percent of the vote."

Eventually, Dylan spoke warmly about his hometown. "I am proud to be from Hibbing," he said when he was thirty-seven and a father himself. He saw something mystical in the North Country. "You can have some amazing hallucinogenic experiences doing nothing but looking out your window."

What his high school girlfriend, Echo Helstrom, remembered was being bullied for something like twelve years. She spent a lot of time being angry at the world. She had to laugh when she thought about the glamorous photo of her up on the sign at Zimmy's. There she was, looking down at all the people who were mean to her growing up. After school, after moving to California and finding a job in the film business, Helstrom never considered going back. Yet, weirdly, Hibbing still had a hold on her. "My heart just can't leave it and be done with it. It's still *home* to me." Although they did not stay in touch, she suspected Dylan felt the same.

Still, she couldn't imagine Dylan coming to Hibbing for some grand homecoming, where he could be feted as a hometown hero. Bob Hocking's grand fantasy was that Dylan would visit for a farewell concert at the high school theater, but it's safe to say something like that is not going to happen. It's a crazy idea—as crazy as thinking that Dylan would drive over to Zimmy's one day, stroll in the front door with a smile, and order up the "Slow Train" veggie pizza ($8.49, gluten free!).

But that afternoon in 2004 after Myrtle's funeral, Hocking could not help himself. He had to hope. Maybe, maybe, maybe. Maybe.

Then he saw it: a news truck parked right next to the restaurant. He saw it, and he knew.

No way Dylan would run that gauntlet. The cameramen were inside eating lunch, but Hocking didn't ask them to move their van to a less conspicuous spot. Customers were customers. Instead he hung around until one, watching and waiting, then gave up and went back to the office. He shrugged it off. If it wasn't meant to be, it wasn't meant to be, and anyway, sometimes the fantasy was better than the reality.

Later, word came back that Dylan had stopped in on his uncle before departing. There was some excitement at Zimmy's when Dylan's nephews walked in for lunch and hung around for a couple of hours. Linda, just as she had done with Beatty a decade earlier, chatted and handed over a bunch of Zimmy's swag. When she offered them a shirt to give to their uncle, they laughed. *You should know something about Bob, they explained to her. He doesn't wear shirts bearing his own likeness.*

Six years on, Dylan turned up again, and this time the Hockings had no clue he might appear. He arrived with a woman nobody recognized. They looked at the school and the family movie theater and some other sites. But, again, Zimmy's was not on the itinerary. On the outskirts of town, Dylan and the woman stopped into a coffee shop. A friend of Bob Hocking's happened to be there. "I know who you are," he told the singer. "You're that Bob Dylan guy." He left with an autograph on a napkin.

By the time word got back to Hocking, Dylan was gone—just a rumor.

3

At least the Hockings could count on the pilgrims to show. On a warm spring night, one day after Dylan turned seventy, an out-of-town couple ducked into Zimmy's and took a couple of stools at the bar, where they ordered hoppy beers and watched for fellow travelers.

All over the world, fans were celebrating with tribute shows and symposiums. The press and the blogosphere were filled with plaudits from writers who grew up on Dylan. Hibbing was hosting its annual Dylan Days arts festival, a tradition that began with informal birthday bashes the Hockings started at Zimmy's in 1991. The Dylan freaks were descending on the town in waves for a long weekend—by motorcycle from Ontario, by car from Fargo and Minneapolis, by jet from Australia and the Netherlands. They wanted to see the sights, breathe the North Country air, and raise their glasses to their hero, the Bard of Hibbing, Minnesota. He had been invited.

The couple, Nina Goss and Charlie Haeussler, newlyweds at age fifty, had flown in that day from New York. They checked in to a hotel on Howard and left on foot to make the rounds to some of the key Dylan landmarks before retiring to the bar for the duration of the evening. This was their second visit to Hibbing, and it felt a little like a homecoming. Linda Stroback walked by their bar stools and, recognizing them, swept in for hugs. The restaurateur was hoarse and overbooked, and the festivities were only beginning. But Linda looked ebullient as ever, and so did Nina and Charlie.

Ever since their first trip, they'd told every Dylan fanatic who would listen, "You *must* go to Hibbing." The last time, Charlie had welled up at the sight of the piano Bob had banged away on at the high school. Nina had spent hours at Zimmy's talking about William Carlos Williams and Walt Whitman with Bob's charismatic English teacher.

Nina left town convinced of one thing: It was wrong to think of this place as too small, too parochial, to have spawned a genius of Dylan's stature. She found the town to be a time capsule, a little community that encompassed the whole sweeping story of American growth. Immigrants drawn west, finding jobs and fresh starts, flourishing and assimilating. How different was that from the story of her big city back home? Hibbing had labor riots as the miners went to war with the big steel companies back east. It had a mayor whose advocacy for the workers and antagonism toward big business won him comparisons to the great populist Huey Long. It was the quintessential melting pot, and it had a vibrant Jewish community. It was more confining than a big city, of course, but more bustling than you'd expect from a little flyspeck up in the middle of nowhere. So yes, sure, Dylan had fled Hibbing, but by Nina's way of thinking, it was only "the very first of countless places" he had spurned. He ran away from New York City, too. Only a fool would think he didn't take a dose of Hibbing's history with him in his veins. Now that she knew the place, she heard it in Dylan's songs.

She and Charlie had returned to Hibbing because if you're a Dylan maniac, then being in the places where he became what he became is thrilling, if irrational. You could see the coffee shop where he ate cherry pie with his girlfriend. You could meet the guy who played drums in his high school band. And what hard-core fanatic wouldn't want to drink beers surrounded by a hundred photographs of the man? "That," Nina said, "is my idea of heaven."

She was an overachiever among the pilgrims, a recent convert who proselytized with zeal. Nina, who has a doctorate in literature and taught English at the college level, speaks and writes about Dylan in thickly layered sentences that unfurl like frantic attempts to grasp the truth. In 2005, having never listened to the singer before, she read his engaging and unconventional memoir, *Chronicles: Volume One*. She fell, and hard. "If anybody can say a book changed their life," she allowed, "I would join that rarefied list of eccentrics." It did not escape her notice that in 1961, she and Bob Dylan both shivered through their first New York winters. He was nineteen and on the make. She was a newborn. A few weeks after reading the book, she found herself in the eighth row of a theater in Manhattan thinking she had gone entirely crazy. Why was she falling in love with this old man's music? She was strangely nervous, sitting there that night. Nina is a wisp of a woman with brown hair that bunches in tight coils. When she is engaged, her eyes don't focus so much as penetrate. You can just about see the synapses firing. That night, she was no passive audience member. She concentrated, she *worked*.

Dylan came on stage. He had the inscrutable look and the piercing blue eyes that have intimidated armies of admirers, and he swept away the woman in row eight. She told me later that she was "completely and utterly unprepared for what an extraordinarily expressive and communicative presence he was onstage." She had been a lifelong opera aficionado, but Dylan killed her interest in it. It felt artificial, mannered, shallow. She had seen the best, but "they're *trained animals* compared to what Dylan does," she said. "My mother would probably put her head in the oven to hear me say that."

In the handful of years after her discovery, Nina's life began to revolve around Dylan. She loitered on the Internet forums. She went to an adult-education class, dozens of shows, and a meet-up group, where she met Charlie. It made sense that she would find love in a Dylan circle: It was inconceivable for her to be with a man who was not equally consumed. She felt a burning need to write about Dylan, so she prepared a paper for a conference, and edited a book of academic writing, and started a thoughtful, earnest blog. She launched a journal, recruiting fresh voices to write for it in hopes that they would bring something new to the study of his music. She showed up at just about anything Dylan-related. When he played in New York, she waited in the long lines. When Fordham Law School hosted a day-long symposium about Dylan and the law, she sat and listened to every presentation.

And now this week she was in Hibbing with Charlie. They tucked into the cherry pie à la mode (Bob's favorite, honest) and Beatty's banana chocolate-chip loaf bread ("a wonderful recipe and to make it is so easy, dear," Mom said). They went to the basement cafeteria at the Memorial Building Arena for a rock 'n' roll hop headlined by one of the guys who played guitar with Bob in high school. They rode on a tour bus to see the synagogue and the hotel where Bob had his bar mitzvah, and the lodgings of the rabbi who prepared him for it, and the shop where his father, Abe, worked, and the railroad crossing where Bob and his motorcycle were nearly jackhammered by a passing locomotive. They saw the old Zimmerman place. They visited Echo's house, where people stood out front and snapped photos of the remains of the tree swing, so evocative of teen romance.

Nina knew that nothing about these Dylan-themed adventures made her particularly unique. "There are all kinds of people who would lay claim to being the greatest Dylan fan in the world," she said. "I would say I am. But the world is full of us."

The world was also full of people who looked at Dylan and were puzzled. They might have heard they should appreciate him as they would Shakespeare, Homer, Mozart. They might have heard that Dylan was a towering figure who changed the course of music, influenced everyone who followed, revolutionized songwriting. But they watched and they listened and they didn't understand. Dylan appeared on television and he seemed entirely out of place, all peculiar mannerisms and gnomic pronouncements. Accepting a lifetime achievement award at the Grammys in 1991, he looked at the camera and said, "My daddy, he didn't leave me much, you know he was a very simple man. But what he did tell me was this. He did say, 'Son,' he said—" He paused for a few interminable seconds, grinning and playing with a funny hat. "He said, 'You know, it's possible to become so defiled in this world that your own father and mother will abandon you, and if that happens, God will always believe in your ability to mend your ways.'" (It took some digging for Dylanologists to discover that he'd borrowed that from rabbinical commentary on Psalm 27.) Twenty years later, when he returned to the Grammys to sing "Maggie's Farm," his voice was a croak, his face an eroded monument, his clothing antique. He gave off a vaudevillian vibe. He could have been teleported from the 1920s.

Even in person, Dylan left people baffled. He didn't look like a cultural icon; he looked homeless. One day in 2009, a homeowner in Long Branch, New Jersey, called the police to report that an "eccentric-looking old man" had just wandered onto his property, which had a for-sale sign out front. A twenty-four-year-old beat cop reported to the scene and stopped the man for questioning. It was Dylan, and he told the officer that he was in the area to play a concert that night. But he didn't look like the photographs she had seen of Dylan in his prime, and he was acting "very suspicious." He was wearing two raincoats, the hoods up, and his sweatpants were tucked into his rain boots. She wondered if he'd walked out of the hospital. He also didn't have identification with him, so she put him in the squad car and drove him to the hotel where he said his tour buses were parked. To her great surprise, the buses were there, and his people rustled up a passport and she let Bob Dylan go free.

Nina and the faithful saw what the world did not. They had placed an epic wager: Their man was not simply a songwriting giant, a performer par excellence and a figure of extraordinary literary merit. He was a man of lasting importance, unique in this epoch, an artist whose songs would be heard and discussed a hundred years from now. Future generations would laud them for their foresight. *They got it.*

When the world was bewildered by Dylan's many costume changes—the angry protest singer (1962), the hung-up, lovesick troubadour (1964), the electrified composer of entire albums of surreal poetic masterpieces (1965–66), the missing rock star (1966–67), the rough-hewn sage from the dark woods (1967), the country singer with the sweet voice on "Lay, Lady, Lay" (1969), the heart-broken man from *Blood on the Tracks* (1975), the Christian convert (1979–81), the lost soul (1981–91), the traditionalist (1992–93), the man obsessed with the past (1997), the raunchy bluesman from *Love and Theft* (2001), the memoirist cribbing lines from ancient books, old magazines, and everything else (2004), the elder states-man worthy of an honorary Pulitzer Prize and a Presidential Medal of Freedom (2008–12)—*they got it.*

While heathens and fools complained about the voice, that wreck of an instrument "you could scour a skillet with," as the novelist John Updike put it—*they got it.*

All weekend, Zimmy's was crammed with the people who got it. They paraded up to a stage in the corner to perform songs by Dylan and songs that he inspired them to write somewhere along the line. One was Mark Sutton, a PhD student in from Sydney who wore a scraggly red beard and a T-shirt reading WHAT WOULD AHAB DO? He was on a cross-country trip to research a dissertation zeroing in on Dylan's latter-day work. Mark had met a lot of Dylan freaks at the Sydney fan club, where they discussed their hero and drank their beer the Australian way—in great volume. Inspired after one outing, he wrote a lampoon of the prototypical Dylan tragic, and as he took the stage at Zimmy's with a borrowed guitar, he knew his composition was perfect for this crowd and this moment.

The protagonist in the song goes to hundreds of concerts, has every last bootleg, has memorized all the lyrics and tattooed some of them to his back, has followed Dylan's supposed spiritual jour-ney by becoming a Jew, then a Christian, and then a Jew again, has learned how to crash his motorcycle just like Dylan did in 1966 . . . all of which was to say, as the kicker went, "I'm a bigger Dylan fan than you." His knowing roast of Dylan freakery, and the competitive streak lurking just under its surface, brought down the house.

As Sutton finished, a man sitting at a table near the stage stood up and walked away. He wasn't smiling. He had a thin face and close-cropped white curls, and he wore a denim jacket over a button-down shirt. He had been milling about the edge of the scene at Zimmy's all weekend. He spoke quietly with a few people he knew. Mostly he kept to himself. Nobody would have guessed it by looking at him, but if anybody could one-up the braggadocio in the parody, this was the man.

His name was Bill Pagel, and he was the ultimate Dylan pilgrim. He showed up in town one day in 2006, and he didn't leave.

4

The short story is that Bill was a Dylan collector, and he wanted to buy the Zimmerman house. The stout Mediterranean, plastered over in stucco, was in a tranquil neighborhood of maples and neat hedges. The Zimmermans brought it in 1948 and stayed until Abe died two decades later. Beatty sold the house and some of their furniture to a local couple with young kids, the Marolts. She left a lot of random stuff behind, silver salt and pepper shakers, Bob's ice skates, some poems her sons wrote. Angel Marolt gave them away or sold them for almost nothing or threw them out. ("If I knew now!" she cried years later.) Another two decades passed, and the Marolts were ready to move. Their Realtor decided they should tap the global market of Dylan fans. *People* ran a feature. A Californian came with a plan to turn the house into a museum, but the town stiff-armed him.

So instead the Marolts found a local buyer. The Frenches, expecting their third child, were in the market for a bigger place. Gregg French, a Frito-Lay delivery driver who had spent most of his life in Hibbing, was not a particularly avid Dylan fan but he did like saving money, and he noticed that the utility bills were cheaper at the Zimmerman homestead than at the other house the Frenches were considering. When he was asked about it later, he'd tell you it wasn't the Dylan tie that sealed the deal; it was the insulation. The Marolts accepted a $50,000 offer. The Sunday after the Frenches moved in, it hit them that what they thought was a house, others considered a shrine. Three fans pulled up in a car and got out to gawk. One broke a twig off a tree in the front yard as a keepsake. Another struck the *Thinker* pose on the front stoop while his friend took pictures. Then they jumped into their car and headed off down the road. "It's been somewhat nonstop ever since," French said.

The Frenches had lived there for a decade and a half when Bill arrived from Wisconsin in 2006. He took a pharmacy job in Hibbing, in part because he figured it would be easier to buy the Dylan house if he already lived in town. He introduced himself to the Frenches and, in a friendly way, expressed interest in the place. Were they thinking of selling anytime soon? He didn't get a firm answer. According to the local gossip, a Realtor once told the Frenches that the house might be worth $1 million after Dylan's death, five to ten times the value it would have without the celebrity backstory. Anyone who actually spoke with French would realize he wasn't pie-eyed enough to expect that kind of Dylan premium in his lifetime. But it was clear to Bill that the Frenches weren't ready to sell yet. He rented an apartment next door and set about waiting, and when the wait stretched still longer, he bought the property immediately behind his dream home.

In Hibbing, insular as any small town, they weren't exactly sure what to make of Bill Pagel. Around friends, he was full of left-field wit and cracklingly dry Midwestern sarcasm. Around those who didn't know him, he was guarded, as if when they turned their heads he might just make a break for it. Some locals wondered, was he just another Dylan collector here to snap up artifacts? What did he want to do with that house? And exactly *who* was he again? Bill liked to keep his private life private, so it took time for them to figure out the answers to those questions.

He grew up in the suburbs of Chicago. As an undergraduate at the University of Wisconsin in Madison, he spotted Dylan's debut record and bought it. He got in on the ground floor, 1962. The record sold only five thousand copies initially. He took to the music, bought album after album, then got the bootlegs and started going to the shows. As the years went on he earned a reputation in Dylan circles as a collector of paper. Like a lot of music fans, he bought the concert posters and programs, and he saved tickets and newspaper clippings and photographs. But he didn't pick them up in ones and twos. He collected in bulk. When he saw a flyer he would take all of them, and when others asked for a copy he would refuse to part with the extras. He started to document what songs Dylan played each night. He had vague ideas of publishing this information, but mostly he did it because he enjoyed the work. (Later, he launched a website, Bob Links, that tracked Dylan's tour and published set lists and reviews; as of 2012, it had had more than thirty million hits.) In the early 1980s, he quit his job and for two or three years dedicated himself to this task full-time. While following the tours—in 1981, he saw every show—and during visits to cities where Dylan played earlier, he would go to the library and pore over old newspapers for reports of concerts past. He logged many thousands of miles in his Volkswagen Rabbit and returned with reams of photocopies.

He saw all of America this way. There aren't many places Dylan went that Bill didn't. He was like a shoe-leather reporter running rumors to ground. He stopped in on promoters, club owners, anybody whose path had crossed Dylan's over the years, and in the process turned up all sorts of information, tapes, photographs, and ephemera. "He's a bloodhound," Bob Hocking said. "He could work for the CIA." Just the suggestion that something existed was enough to keep Bill searching for years.

Eventually, unable to physically fit all of this paper in his home, he rented climate-controlled storage units for the overflow. He had lived in a number of places over the years, and he'd rented containers for his stuff in Minnesota and Wisconsin and Arizona. Once he leased a unit somewhere in Nebraska, if he remembered correctly, where his truck had broken down while he tried to transport some of the paper back east. (He later consolidated his treasure, but he was vague about his current document storage situation. He had at least eight four-drawer file cabinets, banks of hard drives, and towers of archival-quality scrapbooks at home. But he also kept hundreds of boxes in undisclosed locations.)

Over time, his collection grew more varied. He spotted an out-of-print book on Dylan at a New York shop, and when they told him they had a whole box, he brought every last copy home. He acquired not the best prints a photographer made, but entire sets of negatives. He found a ticket from Bob's prom. He bought armfuls of 1957–59 *Hematite* yearbooks from Hibbing High. They can sell for $5,000 if Bob penned an inscription, no matter how vapid. "Best wishes to you an' Dick in the future. Good luck in whatever you do," reads a typical one. He paid for old Hibbing phone directories from some of the years the Zimmermans lived there, 1941, 1952, 1956, 1958, 1961, 1965. He came to own a ceramic candy bowl that once belonged to Dylan's grandmother. It sat on a faux-gold stand, and guitar-strumming dandies serenaded fair maidens on the cracked lid, which was messily glued back together after, Bill was told, Bob busted it.

In 1993, Bill was in Hibbing for the town's centennial, and thumbtacked to a board in a historical display was a photo he had never seen before. It was a shot of young Bob that belonged to a woman who used to live next door to the Zimmermans. Attached was a handwritten letter from Beatty to her neighbor. Bill unfolded the note and read it with growing excitement. Then he ran to the nearest pay phone to call the woman.

According to the letter, Beatty had given the neighbor the family highchair—Dylan's highchair. When Bill called up, the proud owner invited him over to take a look. It was wooden, with a tray, wheels, and a seat back done in red Naugahyde. It was unclear whether she realized the chair might be worth money someday, but either way, she told Bill she actually used it to feed her own grandchildren. Now she was willing to sell it.

To someone who lacked the collecting urge, this opportunity might have raised several existential questions. Would it cross some kind of weirdness Rubicon to own this piece? What would another Bob Dylan collector do? What if it were, say, Shakespeare's? Wouldn't a museum curator snap *that* up in a second? Bill had no second thoughts. He was thrilled to discover it. He paid the woman and took it home. It's not on display; he tucked it under the eaves, hidden in the back of a crawl space facing a wall.

Once you own Bob Dylan's highchair, it becomes easy to rationalize any other purchase, which possibly explains how Bill ended up with the *other* Zimmerman house, the original one in Duluth, where they lived when Bob was born in 1941. By the turn of the century, it was beginning to disintegrate. The roof sagged. The front porch had rotted. The pipes were rusting. The structure looked unsound, perched high on a steep avenue that careened, straight and true, all the way down to Lake Superior half a mile to the east. This section of the city had turned rough. Drugs, gangs, prostitution, home invasions. Once, a Molotov cocktail had been tossed onto a porch across the street. Everything about the Duluth house said caveat emptor.

But when Bill saw the house put up for auction on eBay in 2001, he bought it. In fits and starts, he set about restoring it. He wanted to list it on the National Register of Historic Places, like the birthplace homes of other important figures. Relying on photographs unearthed from the 1940s, he had the metal railing on the balcony torn out and rebuilt to look like it did during the Zimmerman stay. For precision's sake, he counted each wooden tine in the photos. Workmen shored up the roof, repaired the stairs, reconstructed the skirt around the porch, and caulked the cracked wooden siding. The old photos being black-and-white, Bill had to guess on the color. He had the exterior painted a jaunty yellow with white trim.

Back in Hibbing, people snickered about all this. Even in Dylan circles, Bill's peculiar collection was regarded with awe, and some alarm. (One regular on a Dylan online discussion forum called the purchase of the Duluth house "creepy.") Bill was aware of how his acquisitions appeared in the real world. "It doesn't look good," he told me once. "Kind of makes me sound obsessive, doesn't it? That's the final phase, when you start collecting houses. Maybe that's when they should lock you up."

Bill said he was not obsessed but *dedicated*. He was an archivist, a preservationist. He loved listening to Dylan, whom he considered a musical genius, and he was driven to save all this material for later generations. He explained that there was talk of a Dylan museum in Hibbing or Duluth, or perhaps one of the homes would be restored to its 1950s glory and opened to the public. Placed in that context, his lifetime of accumulation would make sense. Even the highchair. He said a lot of people would have bought Dylan's old houses if they had the money, if they didn't have wives or children or obligations. He was salvaging the things Dylan left behind. "My heart is in the right place," he said. "I think I'm doing it for the right reasons." All of that was true, as far as it went. But mainly, it seemed Bill wanted these things because he wanted these things. He couldn't help himself. It was written in his code.

As the revelers at Zimmy's ushered in Dylan's septuagenarianism, Bill had a new acquisition on his mind. He had discovered that Dylan's aunt and cousins still owned a delivery truck from the Zimmerman appliance shop. He went to take a look. It was a dark-blue Ford pickup with wooden railings that kept the merchandise from tipping out. He could just make out the name of the old family business under the paint on the door. Bill left a note under a windshield wiper. When he didn't hear back he called. "We don't want to sell it," came the curt reply.

He did not give up. Sometimes missions like these took years.

5

It was a Friday in May 2009, and Colin Hall had just finished showing tourists around John Lennon's childhood home in Liverpool, Mendips, for the nineteenth time that week. One more showing before the weekend. Usually at the end of a tour, Colin sent visitors outside to wait for the shuttle bus to take them back to their cars, but it was a bit chilly out, so he let them stay inside this time.

The phone rang: The bus driver was calling to say he was dropping off the next batch of tourists. "If you don't get those people out of the house," he said, "Bob Dylan isn't going to wait any longer."

The curator figured the man was having a joke at his expense, or, as they say in England, taking the mickey. Dylan was performing that evening in Liverpool. But when a friend had asked Colin whether he thought the singer might stop in, he had laughed and laughed.

Now Colin led the tourists out of the house to the gate, and there he was.

Dylan had appeared unannounced at the Tudor manor house where the minibus picks up tourists for the three-mile trip to Mendips. He'd gotten on at the last minute with an entourage of three. Two women from North Wales on a shopping and sightseeing trip were in the back row of the bus, and they hadn't gotten a good look at Dylan, who was wearing a leather jacket and a sweatshirt with the hood pulled up. But the bus driver recognized him immediately.

At Mendips, Dylan and the others got off and the previous group filed on. A few recognized him. *Oh my God, is that . . .* , they tittered. *No. No, couldn't be.* Hearing them, the two women from North Wales buttonholed Colin. "Who is it? We know it's someone."

"It's Bob," he told them. "Bob Dylan."

He was as dumbfounded as they were. Colin, a retired schoolteacher, was a Dylan fan. But he also had done some music writing, and he had met a few big musicians, so he quickly resolved to be a professional. He was not going to let himself disintegrate and become a gushing fanatic. He would treat Dylan like every other paying customer and give him a standard group tour. But the women stopped him. *You should show him around privately,* they said. *We've got a story we can dine out on.* So for about forty minutes, he walked the special guest through the home where Lennon lived from ages five to twenty-three with his Aunt Mimi.

Dylan remarked how much the place recalled his own home in Hibbing. He wanted to know where Lennon and Paul McCartney would play, and Colin led him to the living room where the Quarrymen were allowed to rehearse on Sundays, and to the tiny glazed porch where the echoing acoustics pleased the kids. Dylan did a sideways shuffle-hop into the kitchen and then back. In the kitchen the floor was tiled in small black and white squares. The gas cooker and the crockery and the washing powder were all straight out of the late 1950s. "This kitchen, it's just like my mom's!" he said. A lot of visitors felt that way. Mendips was restored to look the way it did the year Lennon and McCartney met, so for people of a certain age, the place brought them back sharply to childhood. Many people cried. "Their own past comes up to meet them," Colin said.

The group went upstairs to the bedroom where Lennon read, drew, wrote poems, and played his guitar. Looking at those single-pane windows, the Minnesotan imagined how cold it must've been up there, just as it had been in his bedroom. Dylan asked about the books on the shelves and on the candlewick bedspread, and Colin told him about *Just William*, an English children's series Lennon loved about the misadventures of a troublemaking child. For a moment, it was dizzying. Colin could hardly believe it. He was standing in John Lennon's bedroom talking to Bob Dylan about a book that was as English as cricket.

Back downstairs, Dylan decided not to board the minibus; his driver had come to pick him up. Colin couldn't resist saying something—*thanks for the music, I have so many of your records*—and though Dylan had heard that thousands of times, he was gracious. He invited him to the show that night and left some free tickets at the box office. The last thing Dylan asked was how to get to Strawberry Fields, and Colin directed him around the corner. He had to resist the urge to turn it into a deeper question. "How *do* you get to Strawberry Fields?"

Every Dylan appearance in the real world generates discussion in fan circles, and this sighting seemed to say something surprising: Dylan understood! Surely, he understood what his fans were feeling. Surely, he got the sentiment that sent Nina Goss and Charlie Haeussler and the rest of the pilgrims to his hometown time and again, that drove Bob Hocking and Bill Pagel to save the artifacts of his life. He'd felt it himself.

Dylan had spoken many times about the heroes who moved him, and what was striking was that he used the same words as Dylan fans. "People have told me that they've heard a song of mine, and it's changed their lives," he told an interviewer once. "Now, I can only believe that or disbelieve it. But I know what it is to feel that because I've felt that way myself about some other people's work." Chunks of Dylan's memoir are devoted to beautifully crafted testimonials to the musicians he loves. He once ran into 1950s singer Johnnie Ray and was starstruck. "He was like one of my idols, you know. I mean, I was speechless," he said. "There I was in an elevator with Johnnie Ray. I mean, what do you say, you know?" Onstage at the Grammys to accept an award, Dylan described being a teenager and seeing his hero Buddy Holly play in Duluth. "I was three feet away from him . . . and he *looked* at me." The year before he went to Mendips, Dylan appeared at the door of Neil Young's boyhood house in Winnipeg. "Oh, oh, Neil Young fan alert," the owner said, thinking this man in the leather pants and very expensive cowboy boots was another obsessive. At Sun Studios in Memphis, tour guides say Dylan strolled in one day while tourists were being shown around. He bent down to kiss the spot where Elvis stood while recording "That's All Right" on July 5, 1954. Then he walked out. Someone chased after Dylan to gush about how much he loved him. "Well, son," Dylan answered, "we all have our heroes."

When Dylan set out for New York in 1961, it was as much as a pilgrim as a budding musician. At nineteen, he had fallen under the spell of Woody Guthrie, the Oklahoma drifter who penned "This Land Is Your Land" and more than a thousand other songs, the dust bowl radical who agitated on behalf of the downtrodden and sometimes played with a guitar that bore the words THIS MACHINE KILLS FASCISTS. Listening to the records for the first time felt "like a million megaton bomb had dropped," Dylan would write, ". . . like the record player itself had just picked me up and flung me across the room." He read the book (Guthrie's autobiography, *Bound for Glory*), perfected the sound (Okie), adopted the appearance (work clothes), and swiped the stories (*ridin' the rails*).

Then, learning that this mythical folk hero was actually still alive, Dylan hitched a ride east to meet him. But their encounter opened the young upstart's eyes to something, an uncomfortable truth about fandom. What he learned from Guthrie in the flesh was that heroes were not gods. They were just men, as flawed as anyone.

A few years later, when the tables were turned and Bob Dylan became famous the world over, sought after, idolized, labeled a prophet and a guru, he tried and tried to get his flock to see things his way.

From the very start, it was a losing battle.

2

HOSTILITIES

On a windy night in January 2011, Nina Goss and Charlie Haeussler took the train from their home in Brooklyn into Greenwich Village, where they had beers in the back room of the Kettle of Fish, the latest incarnation of a bar where Dylan and the rest of the folkies hung out in the early 1960s. Draining their drinks, they walked a few blocks south to a run-down brownstone on MacDougal Street. A neon sign hung over the door, with a moon and a guitar beneath cartoonish bubble letters reading CAFE WHA? As they walked down the stairs to a basement space, they passed pictures telling the story of the club—Jimi Hendrix, Bill Cosby, Bruce Springsteen. They found a booth and ordered another round.

The Monday-night house band, Brazooka, was due onstage at eight-thirty, but Nina and Charlie were here for something more ethereal. Fifty years ago this very night, Dylan first crossed the George Washington Bridge, found his way to the Village, and strode down the same stairway to the same basement. He introduced himself to the manager and asked if he could perform, and the next thing he knew he was onstage playing a couple of songs. He said something to the unsuspecting crowd about how he was followin' in the ramblin' footsteps of Woody, travelin' the country with just his guitar and his knapsack.

Nina and Charlie had come to the club on the anniversary of Dylan's first appearance in New York because they wanted to experience that flickering sense of history that haunts certain rooms. They were listening for an echo. But the space felt entirely without soul, and as the Brazilian outfit started shaking, Nina looked sour. She didn't really connect. The past was the past. She could not reconstruct 1961; it was too far gone.

Dylan arrived in a Chevy Impala. He had been hanging around Madison, Wisconsin, that January, and a friend knew a guy with a car who needed relief drivers for a road trip to New York, 950 miles away. Dylan eagerly signed on, and they made it without incident, though somewhere in New Jersey the car's owner had heard more than enough Woody Guthrie from the kid with the acoustic guitar, the severe voice, and not a shred of common courtesy. "Shut the fuck up!" he finally said.

He'd been at this Woody act for some months now. The transformation astounded those who knew him. He had *become* his idol so quickly; it seemed to happen in a couple of days. To be honest, the act got annoying, fast. Dylan would show up somewhere and drown out the partiers with his caterwauling. He would play the Guthrie whether you wanted him to or not. He would keep singing and strumming into the small hours when everyone else wanted to go to sleep.

He was earnest, embarrassingly so. He would talk and talk and *talk* about traveling east, meeting Woody, making it big. Nobody believed he would do it.

Guthrie had Huntington's disease, and he had been decaying inside the walls of a depressing hospital in New Jersey, an asylum where
the great folksinger was just another nut. Not long after Dylan arrived in New York, he took the bus an hour and a half south to the
hospital. Guthrie suffered from debilitating spasms. He struggled
to even light a cigarette. His voice was a rasp; he could barely be
understood. But Dylan brought his guitar and sang Guthrie's songs
for him. Soon after, he sent a note to friends back in Minnesota. "I
know Woody. I know Woody. I know him and met him and saw
him and sang to him. I know Woody—Goddamn."

As much as he loved Guthrie's music, what tipped it over into
obsession was the book. *Bound for Glory*, the fictionalized autobiography Guthrie wrote in the early 1940s, begins on a train crammed
with brawling stowaway hobos rolling across Minnesota. In the
book, he gave voice to all sorts of ideas that would, in the 1960s,
come to be called "Dylanesque." "Things was starting to stack up
in my head, and I just felt like I was going out of my wits if I didn't
find some way of saying what I thinking," Guthrie wrote. He dismissed every "-ology" and "-ism." His simple mission in life was to
sing "songs that said what everybody in that country was thinking."

Guthrie tells a long yarn about being mistaken for a sort of shaman after giving a few people common-sense solutions to their most
vexing problems. Soon he finds a mob of roughnecks at his door.
They want him to share some wisdom. He walks out onto his porch
and says, "I ain't no fortune teller. No more than you are. But I'll tell
ya what I see in my own head. Then ya can call it any name ya like."
Then he delivers his grand ideas for a better world—good jobs for
every able body, better houses, more oil fields and more factories.
The crowd hoots and snorts. That would not happen, no chance.
"You ain't no prophet!" they cry.

Dylan was mesmerized. "Guthrie divides the world between

those who work and those who don't and is interested in the liberation of the human race and wants to create a world worth living in," Dylan wrote decades later in his own memoir, recalling how, after finishing the book, he decided that he would become "Guthrie's greatest disciple." Dylan bought in to the whole program. It felt to Dylan as though this folksinger, this man he had never met, was telling him and him alone, *I'll be going away, but I'm leaving this job in your hands. I know I can count on you.* Dylan felt called.

He spent 1961 honing his music and his act in Greenwich Village, as eccentric a neighborhood as any he could find. In the nineteenth century it had been a fashionable quarter with shops and Greek Revival townhouses. By the turn of the century it had changed as Irish, German, and Italian immigrants arrived to work in warehouses and breweries and manufacturing lofts. In the 1910s the Village was a bohemian center, home to avant-garde art and experimental theater, a home for radicals, poets, and literary luminaries. In the 1950s and 1960s, the Village hosted the "New York School" of modernist poets and abstract expressionist painters. The beats flitted through. In 1953, poet Dylan Thomas spent his last days drinking, quite heavily, at the White Horse Tavern on Hudson Street. A few years later when the other Dylan showed up, the Village was still a big tent, crammed with the weird, the hip, and the talented. He walked in on an eclectic music scene populated with jazz cats, bluesmen, bluegrass pickers, bongo players, and folksingers.

Especially folksingers. Folk was having its moment, and the Village was ground zero. On Sundays, the musicians convened on Washington Square, a former potter's field, and jammed for themselves and the crowds and the ghosts. In April 1961, the city tried to ban their weekly gatherings and the beatniks rioted on free-speech grounds. (They won.) Artists of every persuasion played at coffeehouses like the Gaslight, a former basement speakeasy and coal cellar that was filthy, dark, hot, and crawling with cockroaches. They watched and learned, borrowed and stole. They cross-pollinated. Everybody was on the make. Dylan happened to land at a moment when there was money in folk music.

"He was a rough little pixie runt with a guitar," singer Ramblin' Jack Elliott said. He looked so young. Maybe malnourished. His leg twitched, always. Onstage he carried himself like Charlie Chaplin. But he had ambition and uncanny instincts. He absorbed what was in the air. Folk buffs put him up and fed him while he played coffeehouses, and soon he was making an impression on his fellow musicians. Things started to happen. Not right away, but just about. In April, he opened for Mississippi blues singer John Lee Hooker. In September, the *New York Times* reviewed a show at Gerde's Folk City and reported that Dylan was "bursting at the seams with talent." In October, he signed a record deal with a big-league label, Columbia.

He started writing songs by the bunches, wherever he was, on whatever he had at hand. One night in April 1962 he was sitting in a coffeehouse on MacDougal Street when he came up with the idea for the song that would make his name, once and forever. In the public mind, it would overshadow everything else he would ever do. He was twenty.

At the café, there had been a long debate about civil rights for blacks in America. Dylan was not considered a political thinker around the Village, but he listened closely, and, as he told friends later, a thought flashed through his mind. The problem was not just racism, but the fact that most people didn't speak out against it. Even those who meant well were guilty. As they went about their daily lives, their silence implicated them. He went home and dashed off some verses.

The song asked a series of societal questions. How long before all men are free? How long until war ends? And most pressing, how long can people act like they don't see the injustice? The answer, as anyone with a pulse would hear in the coming years, and for decades after that, was "blowin' in the wind." The song sounded timeless, world-weary, like an ancient hymn. The older folksingers griped that it was naïve, too simple. But it had subtle power. It was a big song, bottomless. It left it to listeners to find the answers, which were there for anyone to grab, and yet, paradoxically, always swirling just out of reach. The central image seemed to grow out of a brief passage in Guthrie's *Bound for Glory*, when he stands in a skyscraper window watching a scrap of newspaper fluttering outside, "curving over backwards and sideways, over and over." Guthrie prays for it to survive long enough ("blow little paper, blow!") to be picked up by someone and read. "I'm blowing," he goes on, identifying with this piece of litter, "and just as wild and whirling as you are, and lots of times I've been picked up, throwed down, and picked up; but my eyes has been my camera taking pictures of the world and my songs has been messages that I tried to scatter across the back sides and along the steps of the fire escapes and on the window sills and through the dark halls."

Dylan dashed off the first draft of "Blowin' in the Wind" in a hurry. Quickly realizing what he had, he rushed over to Gerde's Folk City on West Fourth Street near Washington Square, where folk-singer Gil Turner was hosting the evening hootenanny. Dylan did a rendition for Turner, who loved it and asked if he could sing it himself, right then, immediately, when he went on stage. So Dylan showed him the chords, jotted down the lyrics, and watched proudly as Turner debuted the song to a stunned audience. A year later, Peter, Paul and Mary released it and, bolstered by heavy radio play, the single sold 320,000 copies in eight days and peaked at number two on the charts.

It was a song perfect for its time. The youth movement was

blooming. The teens and twentysomethings of the early 1960s were soaking in new music, experimenting with mind-altering drugs, and raising their voices in a politically tumultuous age. These kids were shaking off the buttoned-up confinement of the 1950s and demanding social change. In a few months they would spend thirteen days fearing nuclear annihilation. In a year they would hear Martin Luther King Jr. say "I have a dream." Later, they would protest the Vietnam War. Behind it all, "Blowin' in the Wind" played. It was an iconic anthem that tapped into the zeitgeist, and would came to define it. And the song branded Dylan, once and for all, as a folkie, as some sort of political activist, as a man who knew something that eluded everybody else. Like Guthrie before the rabble in *Bound for Glory*. By asking the questions, he implied that he had the answers, that he carried some special knowledge, some hidden truth about the world.

From then on, everybody wanted to know what it was.

2

He was a kid, only twelve, when he first heard the name Bob Dylan and discovered that this was the new folk hero behind the anthem floating in the air. In the summer of 1963, Peter Stone Brown plunged into Dylan's deep well of words. Now here he was, almost an old man, into his sixties, his face craggy and his frizzy hair gray, and still he hadn't drunk it dry.

He lived in Philadelphia on a street of brick row houses between Broad and the Italian Market. His walls looked like they had never seen a fresh coat of paint. The place had the feel of a crash house, with amps, guitar cases, and power cords running in every direction, piles of videos, a bike in the dining room. He was single; he never got close to marriage. He couldn't say he loved his job. He had dreamed of a music career and put in the effort: writing the songs, assembling the bands, releasing a proper record. But it never took off, and he settled for whatever he could find to pay the bills. So he was the record store manager who could tell you anything about music, or at least about the sort of music you wanted to hear if you had taste. Folk, blues, country, rockabilly. The good shit. He was a courier, which had its adventures. He was once tasked to deliver a human heart. It looked like an artichoke. For years he wrote a music column for one of Philly's alternative papers. He survived for a time by transcribing raw reality-show footage for producers, which paid ten cents a line. On the good days the strangers on his videotapes said "Okay!" a lot. But even in the reality-television industry there were cutbacks, and soon he was hunting for work again.

If it paid to know Dylan backward and forward, Peter would have been a wealthy man. When he was growing up, everybody liked Dylan in his circle of teen friends. But Peter distinguished himself with his freakishly detailed knowledge. Later, on Internet forums and private chat rooms and Facebook, he established himself as a knowledgeable correspondent. (It didn't hurt his credibility when people found out that his brother, Tony, a talented bassist, had played on Dylan's *Blood on the Tracks* in 1974.) Unlike other Web correspondents, he usually knew what he was talking about, and he was not at all shy about letting people know it.

In a way, Peter had no say in the matter. It seems inevitable that Dylan would have caught his attention. Peter was raised by secular, ultraliberal Jews. His great-grandfather was part of a wave of Russians who fled after brutal pogroms sparked by the 1881 assassination of Tsar Alexander II. He emigrated to an agricultural colony established and funded by a railroad magnate in rural southern New Jersey. Peter's mother was deeply involved with the Anti-Defamation

League. His father was active in Democratic politics in Philadelphia, and the household subscribed to the *National Guardian*, a radical liberal newspaper founded after World War II to oppose McCarthyism and advocate for the expansion of New Deal policies. When the first black family moved onto their street, the Browns went out of their way to welcome them. The family was so left-wing that his mother and father once called their boys together to instruct them what to do if the FBI came knocking: "Say nothing." The Cold War was on, and it was a scary time to be a dissenting voice.

Of course, the Browns listened to folk. Peter's mother had an f-hole acoustic guitar that she played a little, and she counted among her college friends Bess Lomax Hawes of the folklorist Lomax family, who in the 1940s sang with Guthrie in the Almanac Singers. For the Browns, going to a Pete Seeger concert was like a high holy day: The entire family would dress in their best clothes. Peter played his parents' 78s over and over and over again, Leadbelly, the Weavers, Paul Robeson, the Almanacs. *Oh, you can't scare me, I'm sticking with the uuu-nion!*

His mother died when he was ten. Peter's father remarried— "another left-wing Jew"—and Peter went off to the sixth grade in the alternative school where she taught, Miquon School. It was a very different place from the public schools he had attended. For one thing, some of the teachers had been blacklisted by the city schools when they refused to sign loyalty pledges in the McCarthy era. The students were allowed to wear jeans, which was not the norm at the time. They led the school assemblies and called the teachers by their first names, erasing the usual boundaries of authority. No grades were issued. They debated current events in the classroom. Miquon taught kids to think, not memorize. Peter remembered a field trip to the docks to watch the stevedores work. On the way back, the bus took the kids through the slums.

But the next year Peter's father got a job working at Bell Labs and he uprooted the family. They ended up in the suburbs of north Jersey. Peter was back in public school, and it felt like he had been demoted. He hated it. He was a cog again. Rather than argue about issues of the day, students were expected to focus on straight school-work. Teachers lectured, kids listened. Peter did what any bored, intelligent kid would do in the 1960s. He grew his hair long and started looking for ways to show his contempt. He tucked a minia-ture American flag into the pocket of his sport jacket like a handker-chief and used it to wipe his face at lunch. ("That," he said, "got the shit beat out of me.") He wore a tiny yellow button reading IT SUCKS to school one day, earning him a visit to the school disciplinarian's office. "What does this mean?" he asked. Peter tried to explain, but what could he say? When the man said he would be keeping the but-ton, Peter refused to leave. He sat there for hours. Finally, his father was called. This impromptu sit-in concluded when the administra-tor agreed to mail the disputed button back to the Browns.

One day, hanging around the house, Peter decided to shout something at the world. He picked an unconventional canvas: the family lawn, which the Brown boys had allowed to grow as long as their hair. He sent a friend inside to an upstairs window. Outside, Peter fired up the lawn mower and started to form a message in giant letters, like his own twisted crop circle. His friend's job was to shout directions so Peter could get it exactly right, and he did. When he finished, the Brown lawn in the respectable suburb of Millburn, New Jersey, read FUCK YOU. He thought it was just about the fun-niest thing. If anybody had asked him what exactly he hated about that town, he would have said, *Everything*.

His parents sent him to a therapist in East Orange. Peter and the man spoke a few times but they weren't really getting anywhere. So Peter asked a friend if he could borrow his portable turntable. He set the player up in the therapist's office, pulled Dylan's *Bringing It All Back Home* out of its cardboard jacket, and stuck the needle to the vinyl on side two, song three. He hoped the therapist would listen closely.

3

All through those early years, Dylan visited Guthrie in the hospital. His star was rising while his idol's condition was deteriorating. Once, when Dylan was having a rough stretch, he stopped in hoping to have a real conversation. But as he tried, it struck him that it was hopeless. Whatever he had come all this way to find from Guthrie— inspiration, validation, the truth—this broken-down man could not provide. Dylan had gone to the hospital that day the way a supplicant goes to a priest. "But I couldn't confess to him," he said in an interview a few years later. "It was silly. I did go and talk with him, as much as he could talk, and the talking helped. But basically he wasn't able to help me at all. I finally realized that."

Dylan also realized in a hurry that he did not want to be pigeonholed as the new Guthrie. In the year and a half after he crashed into Gerde's with "Blowin'" in his hands, that was a real possibility. Dylan wrote more than fifty songs during that stretch, good ones and so-so ones, sweet love songs ("Tomorrow Is a Long Time") and bitter breakup songs ("Don't Think Twice, It's All Right") and tender songs of heartache ("Boots of Spanish Leather"). But first impressions are hard to shake, and Dylan's public image hardened like plaster. This was a writer of songs aimed squarely at the powers that be. "Masters of War" wished for the death of the men who build bombs. "A Hard Rain's A-Gonna Fall" conjured up Revelation with its numbered signs of apocalypse. "Oxford Town" contemplated segregationist mobs who fought a black man's admission to Ole Miss. And then came "The Times They Are A-Changin'," written after civil rights activists filled the National Mall for the March on Washington in 1963. Over a relentlessly pounding guitar, it captured America's boiling political and cultural wars in five bristling verses. It drew battle lines.

Then everything did change, with President Kennedy's shooting. Within a few months Dylan was telling interviewers that everybody had him wrong. He didn't write "finger-pointing songs." He wasn't going to be the mascot for a social movement. Politics was a bunch of bullshit. The timing seemed curious. A few close friends told Dylan's first biographer that he had been freaked out by the assassination. Would he be in the rifle's crosshairs next? Around this time Dylan told a friend that prominent people who stood up and spoke the truth were doomed. "They're going to be *killed*." The change looked more sudden than it was. Dylan apparently had been growing more and more uneasy about the political bent of his work for some time, even as he wrote and performed fresh "topical" protest songs.

By 1964, Dylan began working to distance himself from the political agitators. But it was too late. The politically engaged songs he wrote in 1962 and 1963 were pitch-perfect for a radical new generation. Though Dylan could say he was no spokesman, he could not unsing the songs. Now they belonged to the dissidents—people under thirty, full of vigor, bursting with fresh ideas about how the world should and should not be. Dylan's elusiveness only fed his reputation as a cult leader of the mutineers.

Folk purists were upset, but Peter was too young to be bothered. He mainlined *The Freewheelin' Bob Dylan* and *The Times They Are a-Changin'*. He went to see Dylan in concert; the first time was in Newark eight days after the Kennedy assassination. *Times* gave him a line to end every argument with his parents: "Don't criticize what you can't understand." He began devouring every article about Dylan and buying every new LP.

In early 1965, the new record was *Bringing It All Back Home*. It had Dylan's absurdist sensibility stamped all over it. On the cover, Dylan was pictured on a chaise holding a gray cat in his hands, surrounded by blues records, a fallout-shelter sign, and an issue of *Time* magazine naming Lyndon B. Johnson its Man of the Year. On the back was a surreal poem in which Dylan is accosted at a parade by a middle-aged druggist running for office who accuses him of causing antiwar riots and vows that, if elected, he would have Dylan electrocuted publicly on the next Independence Day. The opener, "Subterranean Homesick Blues," is a study in paranoia. He warns kids to watch out for cops and be wary of anybody holding himself up as a leader. "They keep it all hid!" The songs howled that the world was twisted and corrupt, unfixable by politics or any other tool at the hand of man. For all the talk of Dylan shaking off the mantle of generational spokesman, Peter heard a singer taking protest to sweeping heights.

This was the album Peter brought into his therapist's office. The track he played was "It's All Right, Ma (I'm Only Bleeding)," Dylan at his scorched-earth finest. "Money doesn't talk, it swears," he spits. The world is filled with phonies, and nothing is sacred. The authorities would execute him if they knew what he was really thinking.

"*This* is how I feel," Peter told the shrink. "Everything that I'm trying to tell you is on this record. It's all there."

The therapy sessions ended. Peter kept buying Dylan records.

In 1965, Peter attended a summer camp near Poughkeepsie founded by Jewish socialists. Camp Kinderland got teens thinking about social justice, peace, and equality. In 1958, Dylan's future New York City girlfriend, Suze Rotolo, had been a counselor at the camp; by the time Peter arrived, Dylan was spoken of like a minor deity.

In between swimming and hiking and plays, the kids sang Yiddish labor songs. They didn't wage color wars, but instead competed in the Peace Olympics, during which teams prepared presentations on far-off nations. In months and years to come, every Vietnam War protest Peter attended felt like a camp reunion. They would take the train down to Washington singing folk songs.

Camp broke up that year the day Dylan was scheduled to play a tennis arena in Queens. Half the campers had tickets. Peter jumped off the bus at Union Square, dumped his duffel of dirty clothes on his dad, and bummed around the city for a while with some other Dylanheads before heading out to Forest Hills. It was a cloudy day, raw for August. They were excited: They knew this was going to be different from any Dylan show they had seen before. Standing in line, they heard a full band, electric and amplified, doing a sound check.

One month earlier, Dylan had appeared at a music festival in Newport, Rhode Island, held at a city park that had hosted open-air vaudeville shows at the turn of the century. The festival, three days of workshops and concerts first staged in 1959, had evolved into the most important event on the folk calendar. Dylan went on with a full electric band. This was not what traditionalists expected from their young hero. He had already stopped writing protest songs. Now he was pairing his lyrics with rock music? This was not a mere question of aesthetics. Folk was music of the people, created and handed down anonymously over generations. It aspired to a return to simpler times and values. Rock was juvenile, temporary, and, worst of all, commercial. Dylan was supposed to be a nonconformist, outside the mainstream, bucking the system. That's why his admirers loved him so. That's what had given him such power.

He wore a black leather coat—"a sell-out jacket," one observer called it—and carried a sunburst electric guitar. In a set that began and ended in a few short minutes, a brief summer squall, Dylan proceeded to cause a controversy of such epic proportions that nobody could agree exactly what happened. It passed into mythology so quickly that nobody had time to nail down the facts. If you believed the most incendiary accounts, Dylan caused a near riot. Men fought around the soundboard. *The great Pete Seeger was so angry he threatened to chop the power lines with an ax.* The crowd booed Dylan from the stage. He left in tears. By all accounts, some people did jeer Dylan, but it was unclear why. Were they upset by the electric band, or by the poor sound quality that made Dylan impossible to understand, or by the brevity of the performance? No one could say for sure. What's interesting is that if you listen to the recording, you will hear, of all things, cheering. Raucous, enthusiastic cheering. "I don't hear *any* fuckin' boos," Peter says. "Where they booed was Forest Hills. That's where they fucking booed. I was there, and *they booed.*"

Word about Newport had filtered down through folk circles, and Dylan's rocking "Like a Rolling Stone" was in heavy rotation on the radio. So as Peter and the other kids packed onto the benches in the concrete stands at Forest Hills, they had a sense of the spectacle they were about to witness. They were euphoric but surly. The atmosphere was tense. The courts, broad expanses of perfectly manicured grass, separated the kids from the stage. Cops stood watch.

As showtime approached, cold gusts whipped around the arena. A reviled disc jockey from commercial radio gave an introduction during which he appealed to the kids to keep an open mind about Dylan's new sound. "I would like to say this: There's a new, swingin' mood in this country, and I think Bob Dylan perhaps is the spearhead of that new mood. It's a new kind of expression, a new kind of telling it like it is, and"—here he slipped in a plug for the pop music special he had hosted on television earlier in the summer— "Mr. Dylan is definitely what's happening, baby."

The kids in the audience booed with glee.

A spotlight followed Dylan onto the stage. He came on alone with his guitar and harmonicas. The wind whipped his hair. He played a long new song, one the audience had not heard before. Cinderella looks like she might be "easy" as she slips her hands into her back pockets. Ophelia wears an iron vest. Einstein dresses as Robin Hood. The fans didn't catch all of "Desolation Row," but they loved what they could make out. They laughed and laughed at the hip reinventions of characters they knew from school. *This* was their man.

Then, intermission. Backstage, Dylan told the band to stay cool. Anything might happen. Just keep playing.

The band came on and the crowd made noises that, to music critic Greil Marcus, sounded like "someone being torn to pieces." A *Village Voice* correspondent described a riotous throng split evenly between nascent rock fans, who cheered, and folk purists, who chanted, "We want Dylan!" "The factionalism within the teenage sub-culture," he wrote, "seemed as fierce as that between Social Democrats and Stalinists."

"Scumbag!" somebody screamed between songs.

"Aw, come on now," Dylan said.

Peter watched it all in astonishment. "It was insane!" Kids jumped the barricades and scrambled across the tennis court and up onto the stage, with guards stumbling in pursuit. It was hard to tell whether the fans had foul designs or just wanted to dance. They scurried around, ducking security. Later, the musicians said they were scared because they couldn't make out what was happening in the crowd. In the stands, Peter thought there was a real chance of violence.

But the show ended and the masses streamed toward their homes unscathed. Peter hadn't joined in the chorus of discontent. It would have been perfectly understandable if he had thrown in with the traditionalists who felt betrayed by this commercial sound. He loved the folk music he'd grown up hearing. He was upset when he first learned that Dylan was going electric. But the sinking feeling only lasted for a couple of days. He was only fourteen; he couldn't be permanently disillusioned.

What changed his mind were the songs. Listening closely, he could tell it was the same man he had been obsessed with for the past two years. If the words were still uncompromisingly Dylan, what was the problem?

That night in Forest Hills, Dylan dashed backstage and into a station wagon. He sped back to his manager's apartment in Manhattan for an after-party, where he got to talking with a woman who had seen the concert. How did she like it? She demurred. When he pushed, she admitted she didn't much like the new songs. He asked if she'd booed. No, no, nothing like that, she replied. To which Dylan said, Why not? If you didn't like it, you should've booed.

Some days later an interviewer asked what he thought of the cat-callers in Queens. "I thought it was great," he said. "I really did. If I said anything else I'd be a liar." He loved the confrontations and he wasn't backing down. He had found a way to make the music he wanted to make, and it would take more than jeers for him to go back to what he had been doing before he rolled into Newport. "They can boo till the end of time," he added. "I know that music is real, more real than the boos."

4

He had been asked to explain himself before, and he'd tried. A year earlier, he had sat for an interview with writer Nat Hentoff, and the resulting piece in the *New Yorker* elegantly captured Dylan in his early twenties. He was no one-dimensional Guthrie clone, but a young man who was still growing, and evolving, "restless, insatiably hungry for experience, idealistic, but skeptical of neatly defined causes."

The magazine gave Dylan the space to voice, at length, his idiosyncratic view of the world. Hentoff asked why he stopped writing "finger-pointing songs," as Dylan called them, and instead had recorded an album almost entirely about women and love and relationships. "I looked around and saw all these people point fingers at the bomb," he explained. "But the bomb is getting boring, because what's wrong goes much deeper than the bomb. What's wrong is how few people are free. Most people walking around are tied down to something that doesn't let them really *speak*, so they just add their confusion to the mess. I mean, they have some kind of vested interest in the way things are now." There could be no change because people—individuals—were too concerned with their own status.

Dylan said he held the same views on civil rights as the youthful activists, but he couldn't bring himself to join in their work, go south, and carry a picket sign or something like that. "I'm not a part of no Movement. If I was, I wouldn't be able to do anything else but be in 'the Movement.' I just can't have people sit around and make rules for me. I do a lot of things no Movement would allow. I just can't make it with *any* organization."

He said a lot in this vein, to Hentoff and a few other sympathetic writers. But the mainstream press didn't catch on. He was moving too fast. And anyway, these were not the sorts of ideas reporters on deadline could fit into a tidy, uncomplicated newsprint narrative. He thought about the world in fundamentally different ways. He rejected what others took as given. He quickly grew tired of answering questions from reporters who were uninformed by anything more than the media echo chamber, the tabloid journalists and radio hosts who wanted to ask him about folk music and protest songs and how it felt to be the spokesman for the generation. He had moved on.

He upended journalists' assumptions and turned their questions inside out. He dismissed them as a bunch of "hung-up writers" and "frustrated novelists." He lashed out with humor, anger, sarcasm, and silliness while his entourage of knowing hipsters hooted on the sidelines. "Why should you want to know about me?" he asked one helpless journalist in England. "I don't want to know about you." He got writers to agree to spoof interviews. Hentoff did one for *Playboy* in 1966. It got to be hard, after a while, to tell what was real and what was not, which was exactly how Dylan wanted it.

In December 1965, four months after Forest Hills, he reacted incredulously to questions at a press conference to promote a pair of concerts in the Los Angeles area.

"I wonder if you could tell me," one questioner asked, "among folksingers, how many could be characterized as protest singers today?"

"I think there's about a hundred and thirty-six," Dylan deadpanned. "It's either a hundred and thirty-six or a hundred and forty-two."

"What does the word *protest* mean to you?"

"It means singing when you really don't want to sing," he said.

"What are you trying to say in your music? I don't understand *one* of the songs."

"Well, you shouldn't feel offended or anything," Dylan said. "I'm not trying to say anything to you."

"What's the attitude today among your people?"

"*Oh, God,*" Dylan cried. "I don't *know* any of these people."

Of all the questions, this last one always seemed to flummox him the most. *His* people. How to begin talking about his people? He was not willing to play along. Wasn't anybody listening to the songs? They needed to think for themselves and to wrestle free of the nonsense they had learned in school. "You don't need a weatherman," he sang, "to know which way the wind blows." He never sang, "Come along with me and I'll lead the way."

His fans seemed to grow stranger, needier. "He was paranoid to start," Village folksinger Dave Van Ronk said. "All of a sudden five million people were pulling at his coat and picking his brain, and he couldn't take it when just five people were doing that. His feeling was that the audience is a lynch mob. What he said was: 'Look out, they'll kill you.'" Everybody was trying to grab a piece of him. They wanted so much. They wanted to claim him and know him. They wanted to understand what was inside his head. They wanted explanations and facts. People would appear from far-off places—both physical and metaphysical— and ask him questions they told him they'd wondered about for years. Dylan said he found himself thinking, "Wow, man. What else can be in that person's head besides me?" He insisted that he had no message for anyone, that his songs were just "me talking to myself."

Not long after Newport and Forest Hills, Dylan sat for another conversation with Hentoff, and he ruminated about the responsibility of leaders and the weight they must carry on their shoulders. "You don't fuck around, you know, in other people's lives," he said. "To try to handle somebody else's life, you really have to, you know, to be a very powerful person." He didn't want to be that person. He didn't want to feel responsible for anyone but himself. If people wanted to listen, great, but he couldn't save their souls.

Dylan had fled New York City and was spending more time two hours north in Woodstock. He was running from the questions, making himself elusive. It started to dawn on his followers that his public persona—the singer Bob Dylan—was just a character, a myth, a front. The real man hid behind a mask, and he was not going to yank it off and stand naked before them. He didn't *want* to be known. He feared being tied down and categorized. Guthrie had

had the same idea. "There ain't no one little certain self that is you," he wrote. "I'm not some certain self. I'm a lot of selfs. A lot of minds and changes of minds. Moods by the wagon load . . ."

Dylan created personas and then demolished them, denied they had ever existed, and scorned the people who still clung to them. Almost as soon as any one image was lodged in the public's mind, he began to resist. This repeated "self-annihilation" screwed with his fans' heads, critic Ellen Willis wrote at the time. "Many people hate Bob Dylan because they hate being fooled. Illusion is fine, if quarantined and diagnosed as mild; otherwise it is potentially humiliating (Is he laughing at me? Conning me out of my money?)." The people who couldn't deal with the head games quickly dismounted from the bandwagon. The new passengers who were jumping on board—more every day—could be smug. *They got it.* Until the changeling changed again and suddenly they didn't. Dylan seemed to subscribe to P.T. Barnum's maxim: People *enjoyed* being fooled. "No other performer," Peter Stone Brown would come to decide, "fucks with his fans like Bob Dylan. There's no doubt about it. He *fucks* with his fans."

The strategy, if you could call it that, was more than a little ingenious. Controversy sold records. What better way to build your following than to tell people to go away? Dylan kept people off balance. He did the unexpected. He refused to explain himself. How did you create an obsession? You cultivated a mystique. You built something bottomless. The more people dug into the songs, or into the mysteries of his life, the deeper they went; the deeper they went, the more they dug. Everything fed the myth.

Whether he was loved or hated, he couldn't be ignored, and by 1965, Dylan was bigger than ever. But then it got out of hand. "Dylan is LSD set to music," said Phil Ochs, the folksinger. "One year from now I think it will be very dangerous to Dylan's life to get on the stage. Dylan has become part of so many people's psyches and there are so many screwed up people in America, and death is such a part of the American scene now . . . I think he's going to have to quit."

He spent the first half of 1966 on the road. In England, the crowds were nastier than the young hooligans in Forest Hills.

"Judas!" someone screamed at a show in Manchester.

"I don't believe you. You're a liar," Dylan replied.

He made it home in one piece. But in July he crashed his motorcycle on a quiet two-lane road in Woodstock. He disappeared. Rumor had it that he had been crippled, or disfigured, or paralyzed.

The wreck gave him a much-needed break from the road, the press, the hysteria, and the drugs. But it only amplified the myth. So much so that some people could not help wondering whether the injuries were exaggerated, or the wreck entirely fabricated, a ploy to advance the narrative and enhance the legend.

As he convalesced, the movement grew into the counterculture and devolved into hippie psychedelia. Dylan was anointed their spiritual leader in absentia. He was hanging around in Woodstock living the clean life. He had married a former Playboy Club Bunny and started having kids. He painted, and played a lot of music in a basement with his band—soon to be the Band—but mostly he stayed out of sight. While "his people" protested the Vietnam War, Dylan kept his opinions private and perversely suggested in one of the few interviews he gave at the time that maybe he was *for* the war.

Pilgrims besieged his Woodstock home. He found fans swimming in his pool and postcoital peaceniks naked in his bed. He came upon a guy in the living room reciting poetry. A mental case strolled in three times. Dylan and his wife once awoke to find the man standing in their bedroom, just watching them. The man who penned "Blowin' in the Wind" began to keep a shotgun by the front door. He envisioned setting fire to these crazy fuckers. "It was very dark and depressing," he said years later. "And there was no way to respond to all this, you know? It was as if they were suckin' your very blood out. I said, 'Now wait, these people can't be my fans. They just can't be.'"

Even his former girlfriends, Echo Helstrom from Hibbing and Suze Rotolo from New York, received calls from fans. They would ask what Dylan was really like, as if the man were a god. "There were a lot of weirdos," Rotolo said. "He attracts weird fans. Poor guy. I don't know how he survived." Helstrom finally changed her name after one stalker too many. One lunatic called and said he planned to kill Bob so he could take his place. "I've been hiding for years," Helstrom told me.

In 1969, the entire hippie nation descended on the Catskills for the Woodstock Festival, three days of music and peace and everything else. Or, as Dylan characterized it later, "the sum total of all this bullshit." Promoters hoped that by staging it practically in Dylan's backyard, he would show up and play. They didn't know Bob Dylan. He made other plans far away: a show-closing performance at a festival on the Isle of Wight off the coast of England. The idea was that when "his people" showed up, he would be crossing the ocean. Though a mishap delayed the transatlantic voyage, Dylan still didn't make a surprise appearance before the three hundred thousand people who turned up at Max Yasgur's farm.

Fed up with the scene, Dylan moved his family back to New York City, looking for the anonymity he had lost in 1963. He didn't find it. Instead he came face-to-face with a new breed of fan: the Dylanologist.

5

On *Bringing It All Back Home, Highway 61 Revisited,* and *Blonde on Blonde,* released in 1965 and 1966, the songs became more and more surreal, foreshadowing an era that was a lot of things, but above all else deeply strange. The new songs were filled with ambiguity, vague glimpses of unexplained characters. The best ones took on different meanings with each successive listen. His followers wanted to know what they meant. But as Dylan had sung a few years earlier, "I can't think for you, you'll have to decide."

The tribe took up the duty with relish. The pot and LSD and whatever else they were on surely didn't discourage flights of fancy. They began producing reams of song analysis. They intellectualized his lyrics, elevated them to the level of literature, subjected them to exegesis like sacred text. They tried to crack the codes. They searched for clues in whatever they could gather about his private life. They compared notes with their friends, argued and theorized and disagreed. "Hungry for a sign," *Rolling Stone* critic Paul Nelson wrote once, "the world used to follow him around, just waiting for him to drop a cigarette butt. When he did they'd sift through the remains, looking for significance. The scary part is they'd find it—and it really would be significant."

One man would outdo the rest, a wild-haired, whacked-out yippie pothead and consummate self-promoter named Alan Jules Weberman. Dropping acid while listening to *Bringing It All Back Home,* he determined that the songs were operating on multiple levels, and he resolved to interpret them. "I spent hours and hours listening to Dylan, taking Ritalin, LSD, mescaline, smoking joint after joint trying to figure it out," he said. He brought some academic discipline to the task of analyzing Dylan's writing. He drew up a chronology and set it alongside the songs. He built a concordance on an early punch-card computer. He memorized every song, liner note, and poem like some hippie hafiz.

After working at this for a while, he tried a new tactic. Dylan had moved into a house on MacDougal Street right down the block from the Café Wha?, where he got his start a lifetime earlier. One day, Weberman decided to go through the trash bins outside and search for "a piece of paper that contained a translation of his hieroglyphical poems," a clue that would help him unlock the secret codes that he was sure Dylan's songs held. Instead he found uncompleted letters, fan mail torn into tiny pieces, dirty diapers, and dog shit.

Weberman seemed to harbor as much hatred for his hero as love. It was the early 1970s, but he was still angry about what had happened years earlier when Dylan stopped writing topical protest songs. To Weberman, the man had frittered away his moral capital. He had never even spoken out against Vietnam! Weberman concluded that the singer was strung out on heroin. He founded an organization called the Dylan Liberation Front and printed up buttons reading FREE BOB DYLAN.

He had begun teaching a Dylan class, and one day he brought the students by the house for a field trip. "Hey Bobby! Please crawl out your window," Weberman shouted at the house. Just as he started demonstrating his "garbology," Dylan materialized across the street. "It looked like smoke was coming out of his head," the unhinged fan wrote later. The two men went for a walk, sat on a stoop, and had a long and remarkable conversation. Overjoyed, Weberman prepared a piece on his lucky encounter for the underground press. He had to reconstruct the discussion from memory, so he called Dylan's office and asked him to read it and check the quotes, real and imagined.

Dylan reviewed the draft, then called Weberman, who had a recorder running. It was a hilarious discussion about a half-remembered conversation. They argued over the draft. At certain points, Dylan seemed to be intently micromanaging the article. At other moments, he seemed to be just cruelly toying with the fan. Among the things Weberman recalled Dylan saying in their talk on the street was the cryptic sentiment that he "might gain a soul" if he let Weberman get into his life. Dylan denied saying this. Or did he just regret saying it? It was hard to tell. These were two men who liked their facts slippery.

"I know that's what happened," Dylan told Weberman about the remark, "but that ain't what happened, man."

"That's what you said. So fucking quotable, man!"

"It's, uh—doesn't even sound like me."

Weberman didn't tell Dylan he was taping until halfway through the second conversation. "Hang on for a second, Bob, I want to turn the cassette over," he said. When he did, Dylan lost it, predictably. "I ain't never gonna call you again, man. Never, ever, fucking again." And yet he stayed on the line and worked on the piece some more. They traded attacks. Weberman called him a millionaire sellout whose songs weren't any good anymore. Dylan said he would write a song about Weberman called "Pig"—"you go through garbage like a pig"—but he didn't want to give him the pleasure of hearing it. He said he was going to make up his own buttons with a picture of Weberman's face affixed to a pig's body. "It's okay, man," he told his stalker. "You'll live through it."

Weberman defended the Dylanological analysis he pioneered and named. "As long as you don't come up with another system that's more complicated and makes more sense, as far as I'm concerned mine stands. My system stands. You see what I mean?"

"No," Dylan replied.

The conversation ended, the story ran, and later in 1971 Weberman staged a birthday party/DLF protest at Dylan's doorstep. Hundreds of people showed up. Someone brought a cake topped with hypodermic needles. The next time the Dylanologist stopped by the house, Dylan's wife angrily chased him off. Walking home, Weberman suddenly encountered his hero. Dylan was very angry. The singer landed some punches, slammed Weberman's head on the sidewalk, tore off his DLF button, and rode away on his bicycle, the fan later alleged.

Weberman would go on to overturn the trash cans of Jackie Onassis, Henry Kissinger, Dustin Hoffman, and many others. He wrote about his discoveries, converted some of the trash into original art, and earned a measure of fame in the pages of *Rolling Stone* and *Esquire*. After their fight, Dylan moved west, and Weberman dropped Dylan for a while. He wrote a book about Kennedy assassination theories.

Then, in the early 1980s, a visitor appeared: John Bauldie, a teacher, writer, and Dylan fan from England. Bauldie had recently launched a fanzine called the *Telegraph*. The first issue was a few pages photocopied, folded, and stapled at the spine. On the cover it reproduced a note he had received from another Dylan disciple: "That's the odd thing about Dylan; he reduces me almost to the level of a screaming groupie, anxious for details about what he eats for breakfast and for the latest photograph of him and, at the same time inspires me to a contemplation of the most crucial questions about life and Art . . ."

Bauldie made a trip to New York and went to see Weberman with a friend. The three of them spoke for a while at a dog park, then Weberman invited them back to his apartment. It was eye-opening. They passed through an armored lobby with steel doors, a video camera, and tear-gas canisters. Weberman was decked out in camouflage and had a shotgun in the cupboard. "Nobody will get me in here," he remarked. They all sat there in Weberman's living room, surrounded by boxes of papers, clippings, and photos. As they looked through it all, Weberman said suddenly, "You want this stuff? Take it. I'm all through with it." They took it, but Bauldie was deeply unsettled. The original Dylanologist acted like a crazy man, and Bauldie wondered what that said about his own Dylan habit. "He scared me," Bauldie wrote later.

He returned from America to find a letter penned by a thoughtful librarian and poet named Roy Kelly asking pointed questions about the *Telegraph*. Wasn't this a bit pathetic? Dylan took his enthusiasm for words and music, and created new songs. What were we doing with what he gave us? All this pseudoacademic research seemed silly. Why couldn't they find something better to do with their time? Kelly felt foolish reading the stuff and ashamed by his fannishness. "Is no one seized by the absurdity?"

Bauldie published the letter, and it triggered a frank discussion of fandom. His readers were of two minds. One argued that it was Dylan's inspired performances that fed the cult of personality. This fan wanted the concert listings because he wanted every recording; he didn't want to miss a single "illuminative flash of genius." At the same time, "I know that, put together, my habits add up to something more than reasonable interest. What they add up to is more like a weakness, a compulsive need." But as long as he could still separate the trivial from the important, he wouldn't feel like he had lost his grip on reality.

Another correspondent took a darker view. The *Telegraph* was launched after a series of Dylan fan conventions in England. The writer found the events to be equal parts fun and "spooky." For a long time he struggled to figure out the right description for the Dylan fan community, and then it came to him. They were like inmates in an asylum, but they didn't know it because they were all suffering from the same pathetic mental illness. These fans were "struggling to come to grips with the grotesqueness of real life." While most listeners took what they could take from Dylan's music and moved on with their lives, obsessed fans continued "to draw and suck and crave far beyond the boundaries of good sense." They listened to Dylan sing and talk about how wrongheaded it is to lead a life of lifelessness, and then they went on with their conventional lives.

The self-flagellation went back and forth for a few issues, but

Bauldie got over his crisis of confidence quickly and the *Telegraph* continued on, evolving into a glossy publication filled with interviews, bits of biography, and its own brand of song criticism. Bauldie grew into a central figure in fan circles until his death at age forty-seven in a helicopter crash.

In 2000, Weberman was busted for money laundering, and while in the Metropolitan Detention Center in Brooklyn he returned to his old obsession. He used the time inside to work out new and complicated theories about Dylan's lyrics. He had never let go of the idea that there was a decipherable system to the lyrics, even the songs that sounded like streams of consciousness. "It borders on being a code," he explained. Weberman decided he could translate Dylan's words using a complex analytical system, a science that could "never be fully explained or demystified." He described his findings in a 536-page *Dylan to English Dictionary*, in which Weberman argued that in Dylan's language *Texas* might mean "Europe," *match* could be a code word for "Klansmen," *phone* sometimes stands for "radio"— "it could go on almost *ad infinitum*," he insisted.

Reading Weberman brought to mind the workshop of the paranoid schizophrenic scientist John Nash in *A Beautiful Mind*, the walls plastered with newspapers, words from disassociated articles circled and connected by a thousand red lines, a lunatic's web of meaning.

"Why are Dylan fans the worst?" an interviewer once asked music writer Greil Marcus. He didn't mean *all* Dylan fans. He meant obsessives like Weberman.

"I don't know the answer to that. There's no question you're right," Marcus said. "Hm. Not just the worst—they're the stupidest. I think it's because something in Dylan's writing leads people to believe that there is a secret behind every song. And if you unlock that secret then you'll understand the meaning of life. Like every song is this treasure chest, and nothing is what it seems."

Weberman knew other fans reviled him. He thought it was be-cause they didn't want to admit they were wrong. They didn't want to acknowledge that they had missed what he had found. Like his other conclusions, this one missed the mark. The reason he repulsed other obsessed fans was that they feared he was just a crazier version of them.

Over the years, Weberman theorized that in addition to being a junkie, Dylan had contracted HIV. Contradicting everything that had been written about the man, Weberman concluded that Dylan was a conservative, a racist, and a Holocaust denier. After his many decades of analysis, he had decided that the transcendent song Dylan wrote in the Village in the spring of 1962, "Blowin' in the Wind," was actu-ally a racist rant in code. Dylan's unspoken question was what to do about blacks demanding civil rights, and his answer was to "let 'em blow . . . in the wind," or, in other words, to lynch them. "Nobody's going to believe that in a million years," Weberman told me. "Yet it's true. That's it, man. That's where the guy is coming from."

Even he, A.J. Weberman, father of the Dylanologists, could barely believe what his long search had uncovered. "I wasted my fucking life on this shit."

THOSE WHO SEARCH

The man liked to talk. He would smile and tell weird, wonderful stories about people he met in Woodstock and Afghanistan, in the Dylan universe and just around the block in Greenwich Village. But Mitch Blank, one of the world's preeminent collectors of Dylan material, didn't get where he was by having loose lips. When he spoke, some great percentage of his mental energy went toward protecting his reputation as someone who could keep secrets—or, as he would put it, a man whose "hipness credentials are still in order and can be trusted in a ruthless society." When some sensitive matter came up, he fell into a language of thinly veiled hypotheticals and plausible deniability. He would not name names. He himself *might* have done this or *might* have heard that. He would use a lot of words to say something, all the while cultivating the air of a man who knew things he could never say without putting his carefully constructed state of affairs in jeopardy. "Understand," he acknowledged once, "that when I say anything, it isn't far from the truth." Mitch Blank was something of a legend among those who followed Dylan.

On a Saturday afternoon in his apartment, rain slapping against the windows, he hitched himself up on the arm of a couch and held forth. Guests were over. Nina Goss and Charlie Haeussler, the Hibbing pilgrims from Brooklyn, had arrived at his doorstep for the same reason everyone else did. They needed something, and he had it.

Mitch's place was on the top floor of a redbrick four-story walk-up in the Village, around the corner from the tavern Dylan Thomas and Bob Dylan frequented a half century ago. He'd bought it in the 1980s when real estate was cheaper. That's the only reason he could live in a zip code so ridiculously expensive that Jennifer Aniston had moved in. Like many visitors, Nina and Charlie were goggle-eyed. They could spend a week in this room and not be done digesting its contents. Something claimed every last inch. Binders strained shelves, boxes were stacked in piles on the floor, autographed artifacts hung on the walls. In a glass case behind them rested a harmonica holder Dylan used years ago, and the case sat atop piles of crates holding milk bottles from Max Yasgur's farm, authentic Woodstock artifacts that Mitch salvaged in a moment of great foresight, for they are worth something now. Hanging on the wall in the corner was a copy of *The Freewheelin' Bob Dylan* from 1963, the one with the singer walking arm in arm with his girlfriend up Jones Street, a few blocks south. It's signed by Dylan.

Nina and Charlie sat politely, hands in laps, resisting the urge to manhandle his fabulous artifacts. In a moment, as if to put them at ease, Mitch stood up. "Let's go walk around the apartment and see what's going on," he said. They hadn't asked for a tour. But people visit Mitch all the time, and everyone wanted the tour. One awed visitor marveled, "There's mojo in that apartment."

He padded in stockinged feet toward the kitchen. He had a bushy

Vandyke and wire-frame glasses. In the 1970s he had a massive nimbus of hair, but now his curls were orderly and gray. "Please excuse the bomb that's gone off in here," he warned his visitors. They walked past a full-size sign that someone stole from Highway 61 in honor of Dylan's most famous record. They passed a button that read BOB DYLAN FOR US PRESIDENT 2008, and a belt buckle from a long-ago Dylan tour. They passed by Superman statuettes, concert posters, pictures of his friends, assorted dulcimers, and shelves of cassette tapes. They passed multi-volume reference books, lined up like *Britannica*s, that detailed the particulars of Dylan's recording sessions. Perched above his bed were rows of baseballs that had been autographed by musicians and poets.

But those artifacts were only window dressing. Nina and Charlie were guests of the Blank Archives, the beating heart of which was music and paper. It was preserved on vinyl, cassette tape, DAT, CD, and DVD, and protected in plastic sleeves tucked inside labeled binders. Mitch had underground recordings, newspapers, magazines, concert programs, business cards, and copies of letters, draft lyrics, and manuscripts—thousands of pieces of tape and paper having to do with Dylan, the counterculture, the Village folk scene, and whatever else that had, at one time or another, captured Mitch's fancy.

He cherished the music above everything else in his apartment. Mitch was a member of a small brotherhood of collectors across the globe engaged in what he liked to think of as archaeology. "I like to find pieces of material that are not part of the known universe," he said. "I rescue material that's in danger of becoming obsolete and destroyed off the planet." The soldiers in this army were after the songs that got away. They were hunting for the equivalent of a lost Shakespeare manuscript, a sketchbook by Vincent van Gogh, or a forgotten Mozart symphony. Of course, they were also driven by a more immediate desire. They wanted to listen to the stuff, and they couldn't download it from iTunes.

Mitch put himself in the position to be the man to call if you had a valuable open reel so old and fragile that even trying to play it might cause it to disintegrate. Discreetly, he took the tapes to technicians who could transfer the music to digital formats before it was too late. He was also called in to collect rare tapes that were about to be thrown out by their owners or by next of kin, people who really didn't know what they had in their house, or who didn't care and just really wanted to be rid of the stuff.

He and a group of volunteers salvaged thousands of recordings made by Bob Fass, a legendary disc jockey at WBAI, the New York public radio station. He archived a batch of tapes owned by banjo player and radio host Billy Faier, and several hundred hours of open reels recorded for *Broadside*, the folk song publication. A friend, Jeff Friedman, agreed to listen to everything, because recordings were sometimes mislabeled or unlabeled or in the wrong boxes, and they didn't know where they might find a lost gem. If it required sifting through tons of material for just fifteen minutes of something rare and wonderful, it was worth it. Listening to one of the *Broadside* reels, Jeff heard Dylan and a woman play a couple of songs in the middle of a taped letter sent to Pete and Toshi Seeger. Some music they salvaged found its way into a university research library collection and onto archival releases.

Mitch had spent a lifetime building bridges with people in and around the music scene. Musicians would call and ask if he had a certain record, and as an aside, they'd ask what recordings he had of *them*. He struck up a rapport with Dylan's manager, Jeff Rosen, and helped with a series of Dylan archival projects, which won him the immortality that comes with having his name appear in small print on the CD sleeves. His credit line for helping with Martin Scorsese's authorized documentary *No Direction Home* was inspired by a line in "She Belongs to Me" on *Bringing It All Back Home*: hypnotist collector. As Mitch liked to say, employing another Dylan quote, he couldn't help it if he was lucky.

The harvest of Mitch's work was crammed into his tiny apartment.

It looked precarious. His mattress was a lifeboat on an ocean of trunks and suitcases. CDs sat piled in stacks on the floor, on his desk, on a big square coffee table. But given his day job—a photo researcher at Getty Images—he brought a professional's care to his collection. He had a system. He knew how to find whatever someone wanted.

He told people he was afflicted with the collector's disease. He insisted he didn't take it so seriously that it crowded out the rest of his life. He had a lot of friends, and they weren't all Dylan people. He came to the conclusion early on in life that he could justify having all of this stuff only if he shared it, or at least shared whatever he could without sacrificing those hipness credentials, and every weekend, his apartment was abuzz with friends and acquaintances and people sent by people, all of them looking for something. "I've obsessed for you," he liked to say. "That'll be the motto of my company: 'Let Me Obsess for You.'"

Nina and Charlie didn't want much. They had come because they were launching a new Dylan journal, and the first issue would examine a record from 1989 called *Oh Mercy*. On the cover of that album was a photo of a mural on a building at Fifty-third Street and Ninth Avenue, in Hell's Kitchen, and Mitch, as they knew he would, had a videotaped interview with the artist. He slid the tape into the machine, pushed play, and then went about his business. On the television, the painter talked about how he would die happy because, in a stroke of total serendipity, his art had been seen by the masses.

They lingered for a while watching some of his other videos. Then they made their way to the door. Mitch wished them luck with the journal. "Don't follow leaders," he said, quoting "Subterranean Homesick Blues" by way of good-bye. "You know the rest."

Sometimes Mitch thought that his friends were right. Sometimes he thought he needed to turn people down more often. He didn't mean Nina and Charlie. But some of these people! Mitch's friends knew him to be slightly neurotic, and he lived in a neighborhood famous for its eccentrics. But some of these people were bizarre even by Mitch's standards. It was like they woke up in the morning, ate breakfast cereal sprinkled with lead paint chips, then picked up the phone and dialed his number.

He told one story quite a lot. Now, Mitch liked to exaggerate. ("Everybody lies," he said.) But this one, he said, really happened. A man from the Netherlands was visiting. Showing him around the apartment, Mitch pointed out that he had the music stand from the piano at Big Pink, the famous Woodstock house where Dylan and the Band recorded in 1967. Mitch lived up there when the musicians moved away, and because he knew the right somebody, he managed to get the piano, an out-of-tune upright. After years on the road, he was left with only the music rack.

The man's eyes grew wide. If it's not too much, he asked, could he have just one screw from the piano?

Mitch shrugged. This acquaintance had an impressive collection of material, and who was Mitch to judge anyway? He got a screwdriver, removed the screw, and handed it over. What would the man do with it? Wear it on a necklace like a totem from some dark religious cult? Mitch didn't know, and he didn't care. Whatever made him happy.

After his guest left, Mitch said, he found another screw, went back to the bedroom with his screwdriver, and replaced it. Just in case it happened again.

2

There's one Dylan song in particular that Mitch cherishes. On "Bob Dylan's Dream," written in 1963 for *The Freewheelin' Bob Dylan*, the singer recounts falling asleep on a train and dreaming of his former life, when he laughed and sang and told stories with friends living carefree, uncomplicated lives. He would pay a small fortune "if our lives could be like that," Dylan sings, but he knows nothing can bring back those times and those people. The song always transports Mitch to a cabin in upstate New York and the warm feelings he had listening to Dylan bootlegs by a fireplace surrounded by some of his closest friends.

"Nostalgia is a mild form of depression," Mitch says, quoting an aphorism of yippie hero Abbie Hoffman's. Maybe Mitch had been vaguely dispirited since the world changed and he got off the road, since the promise of the 1960s faded and, to his way of thinking, the planet got jaded and greedy again. Maybe that was one reason he spent so much of his time delving into the music from the era that formed him. It brought back a time that seems magical to him today.

Growing up, Manhattan was right across the East River, a subway trip away, but Mitch usually couldn't spare the fifteen cents it cost to get there. He lived in Long Island City public housing. It was a tough neighborhood and he was a nerdy Jewish kid collecting stamps and baseball cards and devouring *Mad* magazines and *Classics Illustrated*; he had his eyeglasses broken by thugs on the street. He was a kid with a sensitive antenna. He swept up all of the scary electromagnetic transmissions in the air. The pall that descended after Kennedy's murder felt like communal post-traumatic stress disorder, and he internalized it. He still recalls the joy he felt seventy-nine days later when he watched the Beatles on Ed Sullivan. Just like that, it was all right to have fun again. Ten days later he turned fourteen. Already his life was outlined by dread realities and the joy of music.

At home, the record collection didn't go beyond show tunes and the odd obscene Yiddish comedy that was played only after the kids went to bed. An uncle who performed in off-Broadway theaters showed him a first glimpse of a more interesting world. A girl with a guitar played him songs from Joan Baez's first record; just talking about it, Mitch could still smell the cedar rushing out of the instrument case when she lifted the lid. Like others of his generation, he lay under the covers at night with his transistor radio and tuned in to the world. He discovered WBAI and *Radio Unnameable*, the pioneering free-form show that piped the counterculture into the ears of whoever was awake in the early hours. You could hear pranks, off-the-cuff live music performances, interviews, bizarre calls, and political speeches. Bob Fass was the host, and he signed on each show by saying, "Good morning, cabal."

Cabal: They were all secret plotters, meeting in the dead of the night, scheming about revolution and talking openly about marijuana. Long before anyone dreamed of flash mobs, Fass moved masses with his honeyed voice. He compelled his listeners to dance, sing, toke up, and hand out flowers at the airport (the Fly-In), or in Central Park's Sheep Meadow (a sort of East Coast Be-In). When frequent guest Abbie Hoffman and his cohorts came up with a name for their radicalized gang of pro-pot, anti–Vietnam War pranksters— the yippies—they were listening to *Radio Unnameable*. Dylan himself went on with Fass now and then. The program kept the Mitches of the world from going insane amid existential anxieties global (nuclear annihilation) and personal (the draft). The host sounded like some crazy uncle carrying on about things you were not supposed to hear, and the show ushered Mitch into a trippy era. "How did I know people were going to get together on Sheep Meadow to dance around a giant banana?" he asked. "Because I heard it on WBAI."

The way Mitch saw it, there was really only one college in New York for a kid like him in 1968. New Paltz, not far from Woodstock, was earning a reputation as a sort of Berkeley of the east, a mecca for hippies—"freaks," as they called themselves. There, alternative studies were ascendant: Students could take a primitive-literature course that concluded with the class tripping on mushrooms. (Or was that peyote?) The best way of standing out was to act normal. New Paltz was an enclave where the real world did not intrude very often.

The town is tucked between the Hudson River and the Shawan-gunks, a deeply wooded mountain ridge that draws hikers and climbers. In the 1960s, back-to-nature hippies camped out in the woods, where they stripped down, got high, and let days pass swim-ming naked. Mitch lived with a group of people who survived their college years on cheap vegetables, apples swiped from orchards, bags of brown rice, and a few bucks. They looked like dirt freaks because they *were*; it was no fashion statement. Mitch had the thought that they were all like broccoli on the leaf. "Everybody bloomed." The locals—by and large rednecks and farmers and stolid conservatives—didn't much like these kids.

But New Paltz also harbored an indigenous creative community and a thriving film, art, music, and literary scene. Students fell in love with the place and stayed put after they graduated. There were writers and painters and video artists living up in the woods. You could run into beat poets at P&G's, the bar at one end of the thor-oughfare. Down the street at the Homestead, another drinking spot, you'd find music around the clock, chess games in the back, a lot of hippie chicks. A former middleweight boxer with long hair and a broken nose worked the door; he was said to be running from the Mafia. Students treated downtown like a big outdoor living room. An impromptu "happening" might break out anywhere people gathered: A musician would start playing, or a couple of kids would stand up and perform a bit of improv.

Mitch contributed to the underground literary journals and comics. He wrote poetry, and once did a reading with Ray Bremser, a beat legend who would recite verse while lying on his back. Mitch was also inspired by Mikhail Horowitz, a wild genius of a writer who would do things like take a bath on the college quad and declare it performance art. Mitch put together a chapbook and sneaked into a school printing room to run off copies. The title, *Optimistic Lemming,* grew out of his view of a warped world. He sold the books door-to-door, one dollar apiece, at nearby colleges, hiding his desperation and trying to charm people. It took chutzpah. Sales peaked when his friend, a future *Playboy* model, went into a roomful of men and made the pitch.

Some genius at New Paltz, a future lawyer, figured out how to commandeer the student activity fee to pay for real bands, and Mitch and the rest of the concert committee brought in the Band, the Who, Joe Cocker, and the New York Dolls. Jefferson Airplane played a campus lawn known as the Tripping Fields while students ate mescaline Jell-O and danced in the mud. The college had just the man on staff to deal with bad trips—William Abruzzi, festival physician at Woodstock in 1969.

Mitch worked Woodstock, and some of the other music festivals that followed, including Watkins Glen. The day after Halloween in 1973, he stuck his thumb out. He had a teaching degree but no driver's license. (He never did get one.) It seemed insane for him to teach kids when he hadn't seen anything of the world yet. He set off to live life. New Paltz friends had scattered across the country. They were safe houses for Mitch, places where he could hunker down for a while until the itch to travel returned. He was in no rush to get to the other end of the road. "We had our own world," he said.

The plan at first was to travel to California, where friends were supporting themselves by, of all things, playing the horses. But hitching brought detours. He ended up at the Astrodome doing security at Millennium '73, the three-day festival led by an Indian guru who promised that one thousand years of peace would greet those who accepted his special knowledge. Later that month Mitch

shared Thanksgiving dinner with a group of people who believed
that the imminent arrival of Comet Kohoutek heralded doomsday
for the United States.

He visited a college friend in the desert outside Phoenix whose
postcollege life revolved around motorcycles and guns. He hitched
to Basalt, Colorado, in a snowstorm and ran into New Paltz friends
playing pool in a bar, prompting him to stop and hang out for a
while. Dylan and the Band played in Denver in 1974, and somebody called up one of Dylan's Woodstock acquaintances, who located free tickets for them. Mitch made a lot of road friends. They
were as close as brothers and sisters for however long the journey
lasted. When it was over, they never saw each other again.

He hung around for a while in San Francisco, where several
friends had a few houses in the Lower Haight, and New Paltz
alumni would come and go. They had a regular dinner they called
"communion," at which they would take off their shoes and eat
their rice and vegetables in silence. They were feeding their bodies
and their souls.

For a while he had a job working fairs and festivals, sleeping in
tents alongside itinerant midway curiosities, the bearded ladies and
"world's greatest face contortionists." His employer sold clothes,
blankets, bags, and puppets imported from Nepal, Pakistan, and
Afghanistan. (The Afghan socks were particularly big sellers.) That
grew into a job with a shop in Boulder, Colorado, which was how he
ended up in Kabul in the spring of 1978. Mitch was buying fabric
and meeting with tailors when suddenly he found a notice on the
door of his guest house. Politely it asked him to depart before May
4. It was clear something was going down. The streets were tense.
Within days, the progressive Afghan president would be killed in a
military coup, and blood would be shed all over the capital as his
supporters were purged.

Mitch's friends flew to Kathmandu, fourteen hundred miles away in Nepal. Mitch decided to take the scenic route. As usual, he wanted to see the country, meet some people, accumulate stories. He traveled through the Khyber Pass, across Pakistan, and into New Delhi, where he caught a slow ride on a painted bus to the ancient city at the edge of the Himalayas.

Not knowing exactly where his friends were, he loitered around a square in front of the royal palace. Every town has a street that draws freaks. Mitch figured this was as likely a place as any to spot one of his friends.

Days passed. He sat there waiting. He split a hotel room with a junkie. Finally, he spotted one of his friends, who led Mitch up to a house on the edge of the city.

There was a problem. On the bus trip from New Delhi, he started feeling pins and needles in his stomach. Whatever he ate passed straight through. Now in Nepal, he grew deathly ill. His friends were alarmed. Someone took him in the sidecar of a motorcycle to see a traditional Hindu doctor. But when alternative medicine didn't cure him, they decided he needed to get out.

His father was called, and a flight to Kabul was arranged so he could retrieve his belongings before returning to New York City.

He recuperated and moved to the Village. He turned thirty, and he got off the road. For one thing, hitchhiking had become more dangerous, and besides, you could only live a nomad's life for so long. A close friend was hit by a car and killed; another died in a plane crash. The deaths traumatized Mitch and his tight circle of friends. "Our sense of invulnerability was shattered," one of them said. They all began to settle down, Mitch included. He found a job with an archiving company. He got married and took out a mortgage. But something always felt off. "I've never felt like part of the real world," he told me one afternoon. "Right now, talking to you, I feel like a charlatan in the real world. Am I grown up? Am I settled? The mother ship could come down and offer me a better deal and I'm out of here."

He laughed after he said that. But I wasn't entirely sure he was joking.

3

The motorcycle wreck in 1966 created a vacuum. Dylan disappeared. Concerts were canceled. His long-awaited book was shelved indefinitely. Then, with psychedelia spreading across the country, he reappeared in 1967 with the quiet *John Wesley Harding*, filled with allegories and soaked in the biblical. The old liberals and newer rock fans who made up his fan base weren't sure what to make of 1969's *Nashville Skyline*, which was as country as its title. Their hip hero sounded like a fat and happy country rube during an interview with Jann Wenner in *Rolling Stone*. In 1970, he accepted an honorary degree from Princeton, which was strange, and released *Self Portrait*, which nearly everyone hated. On one track, Dylan harmonized with himself on a cover of Paul Simon's "The Boxer." Dylan stopped touring for nearly eight years, and to the conspiratorial, it was an intentional effort to muddy his reputation and claw back the privacy and freedom and creative space he had lost in his rise to fame. (Years later in his memoir, he would write that fans who smelled a plot were correct. *Self Portrait* was part of an effort to transmit "deviating signals" and make his image "something a bit more confusing." But it was the sort of confession that only made people wonder if he was still messing with their minds.)

In the middle of this, a glimmer of the old Dylan reappeared on unmarked vinyl sold in plain white gatefolds. Mitch was in line for a concert in the summer of 1969 when he saw somebody hawking this "new" Dylan LP. He coughed up a few bucks and walked away with *Great White Wonder*. He went over to a friend's place and put the needle down on the first commercial bootleg of the rock era. They heard songs from a tape Dylan made in Minneapolis during a triumphant return in December 1961, and alternate takes from later recording sessions. Among these were songs Dylan taped with the Band at Big Pink in the year following the wreck. The musicians had put down more than a hundred tracks of rootsy Americana, fourteen of which were distributed as publishers' demos for other artists to record. *Rolling Stone* caught wind, and in a 1968 cover story lobbied for the release of "The Missing Bob Dylan Album." It would take seven years for the basement tapes to be officially released, but in the meantime, seven tracks ended up on *Great White Wonder*. The bootleg album was a revelation for serious fans. Not only was there more music—demos, abandoned live albums, forgotten early con-certs, and "outtakes" from recording sessions—but if you were lucky and industrious, you might be able to actually hear it.

The hunt for secret Dylan recordings had begun years earlier. Among the first to begin turning over rocks were Sandy Gant, a computer programmer in New York, and A.J. Weberman, the man who would go on to create the Dylan Liberation Front. Gant, an aficionado of sax giant Charlie Parker, was steeped in the world of unofficial, unreleased jazz recordings. Once he discovered Dylan, it was only natural for him to start searching for lost tapes. Want ads were placed in the *Village Voice*. Friends shared what they had. Reviewers and writers who were friendly with Dylan quietly passed recordings along to the collectors. The biggest hurdle was that a lot of the material floating around were tapes of tapes of tapes, and sounded like it. Gant did what he could to find pristine copies, and he quickly built a reputation as the premier Dylan collector of the late

1960s and 1970s. He also searched for accurate information about the recordings, and he compiled one of the first unofficial discographies, in 1968, a green-bar computer printout he sold for a dollar or two through advertisements in music magazines. It was known as the Cog.

Great White Wonder drew hoards of fans into the hunt. At the same time, it complicated matters. Tape owners got skittish. They didn't want to share their material, fearing that bootleggers would get inferior copies of the tapes, chop them up, and sell them. Hours of great music went into lockdown. Dylan hated the unauthorized releases. "I mean, they have stuff you do in a phone booth," he protested. "Like, nobody's around. If you're just sitting and strumming in a motel, you don't think anybody's there, you know . . . it's like the phone is tapped . . . and then it appears on a bootleg record. With a cover that's got a picture of you that was taken from underneath your bed." Why did people think it was kosher to circulate songs leaked from the studio? "It's like taking a painting by Manet or Picasso," Dylan said in *Rolling Stone* in 2006, "goin' to his house and lookin' at a half-finished painting and grabbing it and selling it to people who are 'Picasso fans.'"

The way traders looked at it, they were "liberating" recordings. They were fans swapping tapes, not bootleggers selling them. The music wanted to be free. For a while, until the cease-and-desist letter arrived from Dylan's office, Weberman touted himself "Director of Dubbing Services" at his "Dylan Archive" on Bleecker Street in the Village. He would copy whatever you wanted from the Gant discography. All he asked for was enough to pay for blanks and postage. Some people didn't even ask for that much; they would fill entire boxes of blank tapes with music, free, for someone they'd only just met. It was a form of evangelism—spreading the good news to the faithful.

In 1974, Dylan returned to the road with the Band for his first tour since those contentious English shows in 1966. New tapers got the chance to run their recorders and capture material. Finally, they had leverage to trade for the most exceptional recordings from the 1960s, all the ones they had not been able to acquire with polite questions and pestering and guilt trips.

The more tapes they got, the more they obsessed over uncovering the rest. The aim was to be complete, to own everything, every concert, every studio outtake, every known tape floating around anywhere in the world. Some completists were not satisfied until they owned every taper's recording of a particular concert. Sometimes money was thrown around to buy a tape on the market, but a lot of music came to hand by simple networking. People wrote letters to fans in every city where Dylan toured. They worked their contacts at television stations and record companies to get tapes pulled from vaults. They hit up musicians who played with Dylan, who might have rehearsals or demos. One collector befriended a disc jockey who put him in touch with a Woodstock musician who had recordings, and he came away with two sought-after tapes, Dylan sessions with Johnny Cash in 1969 and George Harrison in 1970. These were gold at the time, and they helped him shake loose two cherished tapes a music writer had locked away in his vault.

A man in Toronto spent his twenties in pursuit. He would get leads from other Dylanheads or friends in the music industry—even from the guy who cut his hair, a rock-music aficionado whose gabbing with customers had an uncanny way of turning up tips about rare recordings. Word that someone had a tape of an as-yet-undocumented performance from 1975 had the collector knocking on doors at one A.M. in Rochester, New York.

Jeff Friedman, Mitch's compatriot, contacted one of Dylan's early managers and copied a 1961 tape she recorded at the Gaslight.

A friend of director Sam Peckinpah's son gave him outtakes from Dylan's music for the 1973 western *Pat Garrett and Billy the Kid*. Mitch connected with Dylan's bass player, Rob Stoner, and Jeff was able to convert a bunch of cassette-taped tour rehearsals to reel-to-reel. He put ads in papers in Mexico City and Guadalajara searching for missing shows. He asked writers for their interview tapes. He furnished one biographer with all the music he needed but pestered him to ask interviewees if *they* had any recordings. ("Jeff," the biographer protested, "you're killing me!") He's indefatigable. "I just pursue shit like crazy," he said. He's privately published a discography to keep things straight, for himself and others.

Occasionally, it took more than shoe leather and goodwill. Some tape hunters took liberties that would be frowned upon by the more ethically minded. One cajoled the owner of an ultra-rare tape into playing it for him over the phone and ran a tape recorder so he could have his own copy. Once, collectors got hold of a tape that had been delivered to the U.S. Copyright Office by Dylan's office to register a batch of songs; it was either copied in the office or swiped outright. To get a copy of Dylan's 1978 film, *Renaldo and Clara*, a band of traders arranged to screen it publicly. A theater was booked and tickets were sold. The movie was rented and shown, and then, in the brief period before they had to ship the film cans back, they took it to a mental health facility—somebody knew somebody—and ran off a video copy. Half the appeal of the unauthorized tapes was simply that they were unauthorized.

Collectors took pains to distinguish between the unreleased recordings that they traded and the commercial bootlegs that were available for purchase. Many of the serious traders condemned the sale of underground recordings, believing that the tapes were not theirs and they should not make money off them. The corollary was that as long as they were not profiting, they saw no problem with owning the unauthorized recordings and sharing them with others. They thought it gave them moral cover. But inevitably, tapes they traded ended up in the hands of the shadowy characters producing the commercial bootlegs.

Stopping the flood of these unsanctioned releases was impossible, and eventually Dylan's record company did the inevitable. It waded into the business itself by releasing sought-after session outtakes and legendary concerts. But the record company never went far enough for the completists. After the label released *The Bootleg Series: Volumes 1–3: (Rare & Unreleased) 1961–1991*, the real bootleggers countered with another twelve discs of unheard material. The studio release of *The Basement Tapes* from Big Pink had twenty-four songs, while the bootleg had 108. Columbia released one concert from 1966, the famous night in Manchester when a folk enthusiast yelled "Judas!" at the newly electrified Dylan. Not to be outdone, a bootlegger released every recording from that spring tour in a deluxe eight-disc box set. Even with the studio tapping the vaults for official releases, many more recordings still circulated only on the black market.

In the Internet age, anyone could hear it. Over the course of a week, a recently converted Dylan fan could download the sort of collection that took Mitch his entire life to build. In a flash, he could have everything—almost everything. Not every Holy Grail had surfaced. On one "secret" tape, Dylan sits at a piano and plays most of 1978's *Street-Legal* for several musicians at his rehearsal space in Santa Monica. Dylan writer Clinton Heylin described the recording in a book, and some people whispered that they had heard it, but copies did not circulate widely. Rank-and-file collectors desperately wanted the tape.

Still deeper below the surface were the tapes that were so underground that the men and women who had heard them had sworn to say nothing about them: Tapes That May Not Be Mentioned. A group of preeminent collectors sitting down for dinner would own recordings they could not even discuss with each other. One esti-mated that as many as twenty-five of these did not circulate. It was likely that no single person had everything. Even big-time collectors like Mitch were suspicious enough to worry about who was meeting behind their backs. Some lost sleep over the idea that a fellow collec-tor might own a tape that they didn't even know existed.

The skullduggery rankled those on the outer rings of the trading networks. This was one of the raisons d'être of *Freewheelin'*, a fan-zine begun by a group of Brits in 1985. To break the stranglehold on rare tapes, the group's twelve members agreed to share everything they owned with each other. Major-league collectors called it *Freeload-ers*, but the group was just reacting to the tightfistedness prevailing in England at the time. You might have something rare to trade, but the other party might decide it was only worth giving up *half* of his rare recording. Six tracks from your audio tape might get you a single song from a video. Trading partners might screw around with your copy so theirs retained its value. A minute might be chopped out of the middle. The video might be intentionally degraded. The original was saved for major-league players who had special material.

It was all so ridiculous. "I was really hacked off at all this rub-bish," said one of the twelve members, John Stokes. "I mean, what's the point?" It seemed crazy that people would acquire some rare tape and lock it away until somebody appeared with something equally scarce. Stokes just wanted to listen to the music before he died. Didn't that make more sense than just "putting it on your mantel-piece and staring at it and knowing that nobody else has it"?

Mitch had trouble understanding why some tapes were under lock and key. He wondered if the owners believed they had been ordained to decide what recordings should not be shared. It was as if Bob Dylan himself had appeared through the marijuana haze one night and whis-pered, *You shall not circulate!* Mitch thought some of them were on a power trip. "Some people think if you have a secret Dylan recording you have some mojo. What are you, nuts? That's not power."

But it was hard to make judgments. Mitch had his own secrets. When he helped someone rescue a fragile recording, the owner sometimes agreed to let him keep a copy. But that didn't give him the right to share the recording with others. He didn't talk about the secret tapes he had. It would only create problems for himself, or for the person who shared the tape with him. "People could be embarrassed," he said. "They could lose a job." Keeping secrets was simple: Just don't tell anyone, no matter how much you trust them.

He took other precautions. If someone shared a sensitive tape, he never labeled it properly. If someday he were to receive a recording of Dylan playing Paris on May 24, 1966, he instead might call it *Dean Martin, Chicago, 6/12/82*. The key to this encryption did not exist outside Mitch's brain. And should he forget what was what? "If you have sixteen kids," he would ask, "do you ever forget their names?"

The awed visitor was right. There *was* mojo in Mitch's little apartment. But there was always room for more magic. Recordings of other ancient performances still had not surfaced. The official vaults still held reels and reels of unreleased music Dylan recorded in studios over his lifetime. *All* of it hadn't leaked out yet. And old Dylan friends and acquaintances still had hidden tapes in their basements and attics and shoe boxes. Mitch knew for a fact: More music was locked up, waiting to be liberated.

4

Dylan was a scruffy kid with holes in his pants in the spring of 1960 when he played a little pizza joint in St. Paul called the Purple Onion. Technically speaking, he was a freshman at the University of

Minnesota in Minneapolis, but he was spending more time honing his music than studying.

One day a teenager hanging around the Twin Cities folk scene struck up a conversation with him. He asked her if she had a tape recorder. He said he had never heard what his voice sounded like on tape. The girl told the young singer that her father owned a reel-to-reel and promised to make arrangements to borrow it. She still lived at home, and asking her father—a St. Paul policeman—would have meant uncomfortable questions about what was going on. So she enlisted her older sister, Karen, to get the machine, bring Dylan over to her attic apartment, and record some songs after his next gig at the Purple Onion.

Everyone sat on the floor of Karen's apartment as he sang and played into a microphone that was slung over the side of a chair. She played each song back for him. It took half the night. At dawn, she dropped him in Dinkytown on the edge of campus. She kept the tape.

In 1978, when Dylan was back in St. Paul for a show, Karen called the paper to tell them about her chance meeting with Dylan. A journalist listened to the tape, reporting that it ran for about an hour and included twenty-seven songs "full of darkness and sorrowful tales." Dylan did "Roving Gambler" and "Delia" and "Blue Yodel No. 8" and "Go Down You Murderers."

This was the most prized of artifacts, a true landmark. It was believed to be the earliest recording of Dylan. In a few weeks, collectors began to write and call. Karen ignored an inquiry from California, another from New York. She parried with a man in Ohio who wanted to buy the tape, but feared it was a hoax. On the early tapes that circulated at the time, Dylan had a harsh voice, but on the St. Paul tape he sounded angelic. (The man wrote a piece in a fanzine questioning its authenticity, which some blame for scuttling a deal to buy it from Karen.)

Then a Dylan fan in St. Paul called and said he had a friend coming into town. Could they visit and hear the tape? His friend, Brian Stibal, ran a Dylan fan magazine, and he wanted to write about the recording. The man sounded friendly and earnest, and Karen liked the idea of sharing the tape with others who would appreciate it, so she invited them over.

Stibal had been well-known in Dylan fan circles since creating *Talkin' Bob Zimmerman's Blues* in 1975 as an undergraduate at Boston University. It was believed to be the first Dylan fanzine, and for a buck, subscribers got guest columns, tour itineraries, and "Recent Developments in Dylanology." At the time Stibal arrived in St. Paul to hear the tape, his interest in Dylan was fully aflame.

Karen and her husband had been thinking about the windfall their tape might bring if they were to sell it, and Karen's husband was suspicious of the two Dylan fans. He insisted they listen to the tape in the kitchen, where he noisily did the dishes. Karen turned the volume down low and played only snippets of the songs. Then the men went on their way. It would take many years before Karen realized that her husband's suspicions were well founded: The Dylan nuts had a hidden recorder.

Collectors couldn't believe how awful the resulting artifact sounded. The thing was notoriously bad. It came to be called the "armpit tape." (Stibal said his friend had actually hidden the recorder in a jacket pocket, but it was the more evocative nickname that stuck.) Anyway, the sound hardly mattered. This was a rarity, and it circulated for decades.

When she found out, Karen was incensed. "The only pleasure I got from the thing was playing it for somebody," she said, "and all they did was rip me off."

But the full tape, uncut and pristine, remained locked away for the next three decades. Karen had hoped to sell it for $10,000 or more. The most anybody offered was half that. As the years passed, a number of earlier Dylan tapes had surfaced, making hers less momentous. Apparently, Dylan's appeal to the girl in St. Paul had been a come-on line. Almost four years before, he'd gone into a record store with friends and recorded "Lawdy Miss Clawdy" and "Earth Angel," and he had made other tapes with musicians in Hibbing.

But collectors still considered it an important artifact, and in 2011 Mitch called Karen, now retired and living in St. Paul. He told her what he did. He earnestly explained why it was important to have the fragile tape preserved. It could be argued that it was the first recording of *Bob Dylan*, not the neophyte named Bob Zimmerman. Mitch told her he could help her, quietly, if she wanted.

Karen listened and stood her ground. The conversation didn't go anywhere. The night in St. Paul was a warm memory, but the tape had become a curse. She had made up her mind. She wasn't going to sell it to anyone. She was going to give it to the Minnesota Historical Society. It would be worth more to her as a deduction on her tax return anyway. If somebody wanted to hear it in all its glory, they'd have to trek to Minneapolis.

Mitch shrugged. He could wait.

WOMEN AND GOD

In 1994, a Dylan fan from outside Chicago named Michelle Engert stumbled onto a priceless opportunity. She got the chance to spend more than a month immersed in the most legendary of Dylan artifacts, a small red notebook in which the singer had written drafts of the tortured love songs that would appear on his acclaimed 1975 record, *Blood on the Tracks*.

Four years earlier, Michelle had graduated from high school—not a minute too soon—and rather than going to college like her friends, she moved to a place of her own. She just didn't feel like being told what to do anymore. In the summer of 1990, at seventeen, she found a calling of sorts: She started following the Dylan tour. It was during a break from the road that she met Joel Bernstein, a guitar tech for Dylan during the tours of the 1970s, but better known at the time as the archivist for Neil Young. Michelle walked up to him at one of Young's concerts in Chicago, and they got to talking. They stayed in contact, and a year and a half later he invited her to come to his home off Haight Street in San Francisco and work on the notebook.

Bernstein was helping a wealthy financier, George Hecksher, manage his large collection of Dylan manuscripts. Around the same time Michelle hit the road, Hecksher bought his first Dylan piece, handwritten lyrics to 1969's "Tonight I'll Be Staying Here with You." Within a few years he had acquired hundreds of pages—songs and poems and fragments. He quickly accumulated the largest cache of original Dylan documents in the world, barring the singer's own private papers. Hecksher bought lyrics to more than ninety songs, including "Blowin' in the Wind," "Like a Rolling Stone," and "Masters of War." He bought Dylan's early copy of *Bound for Glory* and his Woody Guthrie songbook. He bought an illustrated diary that Dylan kept during his comeback tour with the Band in 1974. And he bought the red notebook. He was not particular. He arrived on the scene and swept up everything he could find. Three dozen artifacts came from one antiquarian bookshop in Beverly Hills, Biblioctopus. When the dealer visited Hecksher's home later to see what the man had gathered, he was shocked. "This is the single greatest collection of *anything* I've ever seen in private hands," he said. "A thousand years from now, that collection will be revered as greater than any."

In the early 1990s, only a few people knew about the little *Blood on the Tracks* notebook. They heard a murky tale about how the artifact ended up out in the world: It was said to have been stolen from Dylan, and then bought and sold several times among collectors. Later, when word about it spread, a journalist likened the artifact to a missing Dead Sea Scroll, lamented its apparent disappearance, and begged for whoever had it to please forward him a copy. (Hecksher later donated the notebook, and many of his Dylan papers, to the Morgan Library in Manhattan; access was restricted until Dylan's death.)

From the way the notebook was creased, it looked as though Dylan carried it around in his back pocket. The words were barely legible. Phrases were crossed out, and words and fragments were jotted here and there, up and down the page at times, in ways that made it difficult to follow. The lyrics were not always identical to what he had sung on the record, and the differences were not easy to make out. The notebook also included songs that had never been released, or perhaps never even recorded.

Bernstein had the idea to decipher and transcribe it so they wouldn't have to struggle to read the thing. It was obvious Michelle was the person for the job. She could recite the lyrics to every song without a hiccup. "Those songs are absolutely inked in me. I know them all." Hecksher agreed to leave the notebook with her at Bernstein's, and she flew out to California. Though the financier promised to pay her for her time, she would have done it for nothing.

She couldn't believe her luck. *Blood on the Tracks* was a masterpiece, as nakedly personal a record as Dylan ever wrote. She settled in to work at Bernstein's house, which looked like a satellite office of Neil Young's archive. The notebook was fragile, the paper frayed along the spiral. She worked on it cautiously, washing her hands before starting, touching only the edges of pages, trying to keep it under plastic as she studied the words. She made a map of each page in longhand, then Bernstein typed her transcriptions into a computer.

Later, she would feel strange about the time she spent as an interloper in Dylan's private space. Michelle wondered whether people should be going into trash cans and hotel rooms and taking what Dylan left behind, and whether fans should legitimize that mischief by reading it, studying it, copying it, publishing it. Dylan delivered a record; wasn't that enough for fans? Poking around in the scrap heap felt disrespectful. But at the time, Michelle had no misgivings about it. She was too enthralled. She was plunging into the record's creation with pages the author had kept in his pocket during those painful days in the summer of 1974.

Dylan had married on November 22, 1965, in a private civil ceremony on Long Island. The wedding was a secret, just as the relationship had been. Sara Lownds, dark-haired and beautiful, was a former Bunny in the Playboy Club previously married to a fashion photographer. She was also smart, and apparently not awed by Dylan's fame. Steeped in Eastern spirituality, she became a grounding influence on a mercurial man. Dylan was hard on people who tried to get close to him. He had a vicious streak, a way of finding someone's sensitive underbelly and cruelly attacking it. "I worshipped Sara as a goddess who not only could calm the storm," said Al Aronowitz, a writer who was familiar with Dylan's squalls, "but who also could turn Bob into a human being."

Sara and Dylan had four children together and tried to settle down. Dylan hated how fame had cost him his privacy and his freedom. He hated how he was condemned to live an abnormal life. Whenever he went anywhere, the vibe instantly changed. Rooms fell silent; people got weird. He hated that people stalked him on the street. So he and Sara fled Woodstock and Manhattan in search of new hideouts. Dylan bought the farm in Minnesota and a hilltop property in Malibu where they began to build a copper-domed mansion for the family.

The domestic experiment lasted eight years. But the itinerant musician had not disappeared. Dylan fled the conventional life at nineteen, and he could not settle down at thirty-two. His family idyll began to fall apart. In early 1974, he returned to the big-time rock 'n' roll life for a month and a half, a noisy reunion tour with the Band that drew enthusiastic crowds. Soon, his marriage was splintering. He struck up with a woman from Columbia Records whom he met one night in Sausalito toward the end of the tour, and he spent the summer of 1974 at the farm with her. Ellen Bernstein was twenty-four, and, she said, flattered. She played housewife. She cooked, his kids played. He would disappear into a study upstairs early in the morning and write, appearing later in the day. He pulled out the notebook and played her the songs, which he seemed to have copied from scraps and various drafts. To Ellen, he seemed relaxed on the farm, where he had an art studio and the kids could ride ponies and his brother had his own house down the driveway. The property backed up against a river and a thick stand of trees, like the corner booth in a bar where you could see anybody coming at you for miles. His wife never came up in conversation.

But nineteen years later, as Michelle trained a magnifying glass on the pages of the red notepad, she found a window into Dylan's writing studio, where his life seemed far more complicated. There, he was consumed by the ruins of his romances past and present: his deteriorating marriage, the lost love from those early days in New York, the effervescent but obviously temporary affair with the woman in the house that very summer. Bitterness and melancholy and remorse filled the pages.

Eight of the songs on the record appeared in the notebook in various stages of construction, along with nine other compositions. Most striking were page after page of work on "Idiot Wind." The performance on the album is fuming and unforgiving, beyond intense. People are out to get him. Nobody he meets knows how to act around him; their thinking is twisted. And suddenly it seems his "sweet lady" doesn't know him either. She's an idiot like everybody else. She lies. She hurts him. He envisions the day she is dead. This is unalloyed rage.

But the early versions Michelle transcribed were something else entirely. These had moments of poignancy. There was room for regret. Deciphering the jumbled pages, she found the singer addressing a lover as if in a letter. He wonders whether he ever really knew her. It seemed now that she had been wearing a mask all this time: "I never saw your face." He figures it's hopeless, it's over, he's lost her for good. But he's reluctant to end it once and for all. He wants to call her but he hasn't. He imagines the annoyance of "trying to talk through wire." He knows he would need some "lame excuse," and anyway, "I knew what we were going to say, but I hadn't memorized my part of the speech." The verses underwent change after change on the page. One read, "We didn't talk for days and days, and when the rains came the words were gone." The drafts amazed Michelle: "This could have been a twenty-minute song."

At the end of the summer, Dylan headed to New York to record the songs. After the record company had run test pressings but before the record was released, Dylan went into a studio in Minneapolis and re-recorded parts of it with a band, including a song that would make his growing list of classics: "Tangled Up in Blue." When the album appeared in 1975, it was followed almost immediately by a bootleg with the songs recorded during the New York sessions. The fans who heard both debated which was better. Many of them thought the resigned, acoustic "Idiot Wind" from New York trumped the howl of protest from Minneapolis.

All in all, *Blood on the Tracks* overwhelmed Dylan's followers. They loved it with an intensity that scared Dylan a little. It seemed odd that his suffering could give others such pleasure. "A lot of people tell me they enjoy that album," he said in a 1975 interview with Mary Travers of Peter, Paul and Mary for a radio show she hosted. "It's hard for me to relate to that. I mean, you know, people enjoying that type of pain."

"Maybe the word *enjoy* is the wrong word," she replied. "You're *moved*. I was moved by the album."

This became a record his audience put on when it fit—when they were lovesick or pissed about a girlfriend or longing for a man they had lost. It got to be pathetic, music critic Lester Bangs decided. He recalled at first dismissing "Idiot Wind" as "ridiculously spiteful" and the record as an "absurdly pretentious mess." But he kept playing it. Sometimes he even thought it was amazing. Then he would realize he was just drunk. "I only really wanted to play this record whenever I had a fight with someone I was falling in love with," Bangs wrote. "We would reach some painful impasse of words or wills, she would go home and I would sit up all night with my misery and this album, playing it over and over, wallowing in Dylan's wretched reflection of my own confusion." By 1976, the year after its release, Bangs decided that *Blood on the Tracks* was "an emotional twilight zone," "an instrument of self-abuse," "a crying towel." It couldn't help him.

As it turned out, Dylan's marriage did not end the summer he wrote *Blood on the Tracks*. In 1975, he and his wife were together intermittently. In the spring he jetted off to France and she didn't go. According to his host, Dylan called her every day. In the meantime he drank and messed around with French women. He recorded another album, ending it with an ode to his muse; he even titled it "Sara." That fall, Dylan put together a circus of a tour, a ramshackle affair during which the musicians filmed an avant-garde movie, and Sara went along. But in 1976, their relationship took a turn for the worse, and in Fort Collins, Colorado, he sang a blistering "Idiot Wind" while she watched. In 1977, they were divorced. The following year, *Street-Legal* appeared. On the cover, a tan line replaced the wedding ring.

It was a cult favorite. The last song in particular affected fans as much as anything on *Blood on the Tracks*. "Where Are You Tonight? (Journey Through Dark Heat)" dealt with the same dramas Dylan had wrestled with on the farm in the summer of 1974. His love was gone, and this time it really was for good. He had made it through the dark days and he was still alive. He was a man. He would survive. So why couldn't he get her out of his head?

Some years later, in a bedroom in St. Cloud, Minnesota, a Dylan fan was suffering his first heartbreak. It had been a teenage romance. There had been others, but until now he'd always done the breaking up. She was older and had gone off to college, and he felt left behind and forgotten. Obliterated. So Lucas Stensland pushed the repeat button on his CD player, sat on the floor in his closet, slid the doors shut, and hid out while "Where Are You Tonight?" played over and over and over again.

The song captured his hurt and alienation so perfectly, with such honesty and beauty. Lucas felt a kinship with Dylan. He didn't know anybody who could give him more than pat advice when he just wanted somebody to understand the turmoil he felt. But the song understood. It was the cry of a man who had wrecked his life but now was getting himself back together. It made Lucas realize that the world wouldn't take care of him; he had to do it himself. The ending crushed him, like a great wave arriving at intervals of six minutes and fifteen seconds. "But without you it just doesn't seem right. Where are you tonight?"

Lucas thought that it could be the anthem for every broken person in the world.

2

Lucas's father told him there was no God. His son had to think he would know, because he taught the course on death and dying at St. Cloud State University. He kept a collection of coffins at the school. His son called them "dead suitcases" when he was very young; the baby coffin freaked him out quite a bit. Sometimes his father would hide inside a coffin as the starting time of the scheduled class came and went. The students would get impatient and ask each other whether they had the wrong day or wrong time or wrong classroom. And then, just as they began to walk out, he would rise, very slowly, from the coffin. He brought his profession home with him, too. He ran a nonprofit to protect relatives of the recently departed from being fleeced by funeral homes, so the family had two phone lines at home, a personal line and a nonprofit line. When the second phone rang, they all knew some stranger had died.

Lucas was a depressed high schooler, and he knows that it sounds silly, but when he'd think about killing himself—not for real, just in that adolescent way of thinking heavy thoughts to make himself feel important—he racked his brain to come up with one good reason not to do it. The reason wasn't God, of course. It wasn't because he looked forward to college or a job or life after he got out of St. Cloud. It was this simple: He was a Dylan fan, and he wanted to hear the next record.

As he turned thirty in 2006, he found himself working as an analyst at a New York City law firm by day and writing novels at night. He had a hangdog face and was prematurely bald, but he was smart and snarky and living the city life in America's hipster capital, Brooklyn. Sometimes he grew a mustache that seemed ironic. He started going to a Dylan fan meet-up with an eclectic bunch of fans, among them a former go-go dancer turned Messianic Jew, a writer/model, a musician, an English professor. One of them was Nina Goss, the Hibbing pilgrim who was then in the nascent stages of her own obsession. Lucas and Nina became fast friends. She demanded a level of seriousness from her Dylan acquaintances, and Lucas knew what he was talking about. It was not just dates and details, though he had those firmly in hand. If, say, Dylan's *Shot of Love* came up for discussion, he could tell you that it was released not in 1980 but 1981, and, by the way, it featured sidemen from both the Rolling Stones and the Beatles. But he also had insights about the songs and the man, and he took Dylan as seriously as Nina did. In no time, she became Lucas's closest Dylan friend. He helped her launch the Dylan journal. There was a time when they spoke or e-mailed every day.

Then, in 2010, Lucas's life unspooled. He had married his girlfriend the summer before, and by spring it was over. He had no sooner ended things than he left New York and moved back to his sleepy hometown of St. Cloud. A new relationship bloomed, then withered. He fell into a deep depression. He had been diagnosed with anxiety and obsessive-compulsive disorder years earlier; therapy and pharmaceuticals helped keep his brain in check. But back in his hometown, alone, he stopped taking the drugs and started medicating himself with heavy doses of alcohol. He couldn't sit still. He was frightened of what was happening to him. It was then, at this the lowest of lows, that Dylan's music stepped in to save him.

He had always carried lyrics around in his head like refrains. In therapy, he learned techniques for coping with problems. But Dylan songs helped in different ways. They illuminated how he was feeling. Lucas could play some song and find that it said exactly how he felt at that moment. Lucas would listen to Dylan with girlfriends. Songs would grow into *their* songs. With one girl it was a track Dylan recorded during his time with Sara, "Never Say Goodbye." ("You're beautiful beyond words, you're beautiful to me . . .") When the wounds were still open, Lucas would torture himself by listening to that song. That one and "Simple Twist of Fate," the *Blood on the Tracks* classic about a lover who disappears. The last happy night he had with this woman, she had given him a slip from a fortune cookie that read FATE WILL FIND A WAY.

Although he was living in St. Cloud, he was still telecommuting for the New York law firm. But he decided it would be too depressing to actually sleep in his place in his old hometown. So just about every day, he was driving back and forth to his brother's in Minneapolis, an hour south on Interstate 94.

On the road one night in a brand-new Volkswagen, he had a panic attack. He could barely breathe. When he lost it like this, he would think, *Oh, my God, I can't move my right arm,* and even though there was nothing physically wrong with his right arm, just thinking it would make it so. He knew he should pull over. Questions flitted through his mind. *What am I doing? Why am I in Minnesota? Why do I fucking own a Jetta?*

The car had a six-disc changer, and he started manically flipping through them. Merle Haggard, nooooo. Guy Clark, not now. Dylan—incredible. It was *Saved.*

When Dylan's marriage fell apart in 1977, he soon found a new obsession. In November 1978, toward the end of a year-long world tour, somebody tossed a silver cross onto the stage in San Diego, and Dylan picked it up. Two nights later he played Tucson, Arizona, and in his hotel room the singer felt a supernatural force. "Jesus put his hand on me. It was a physical thing. I felt it all over me. I felt my whole body tremble." He started wearing the cross onstage, and close listeners noticed a new twist when he sang "Tangled Up in Blue" from *Blood on the Tracks.* On the record, he goes home with a stripper and she reads to him from a book of Italian poetry. Toward the end of 1978, the stripper and the singer are reading from the Holy Bible.

Two of his bandmates were members of a California congregation, the Vineyard Fellowship, as was his new girlfriend, actress Mary Alice Artes. After the tour ended, she spoke to the pastor about Dylan, and he sent over two men to talk with Dylan. He started going to Bible classes, four mornings a week for three months in an office building in Reseda, California. The anarchist who had warned against taking orders from anybody had found a leader. In 1979, a new record appeared, *Slow Train Coming*, with a pickax on the cover shaped like a cross.

Saved was Dylan's next release. It was straight gospel. He had been touched and healed and delivered by Jesus' crucifixion. He had a covenant with God. The Messiah was his rock. No longer would Dylan be held back by bad habits and old temptations; he had a higher calling. Everyone did. "Shake the dust off your feet," he sang, "don't look back."

The closest Lucas Stensland ever got to religion was when he was a teen and he went to church to rebel against his parents. "I don't have a spiritual bone in my body," he says. But that night on the highway, *Saved* captivated him. Listening intently, he began to breathe again. And he had a revelation. It wasn't the same as Dylan's. He wasn't ready to follow Jesus. It was this: Bob Dylan went through a divorce and years of turmoil, and he survived it. He discovered something that had meaning for him, and so could Lucas. "It was like therapy. I took advice from him—a cue."

He was not going to make his happiness dependent on someone else. He was going to stand for himself. He would save himself.

He pulled himself together. He got back on his medication and moved into an apartment in a bustling section of downtown Minneapolis. He started writing haiku, a bit obsessively to be honest. He'd carry a notebook around with him and jot down poems by the dozen. He went to haiku meet-ups and met haiku people and got his verses published.

The pain of his divorce was still raw. There was another Dylan song, "Standing in the Doorway," from 1997, that would run in his head, picking at his feelings, demanding that he listen. He *had* to listen. He had no choice. Maybe that was how he would get it out of his system. The singer wanders through a night alone. It's summer. Everybody's laughing and it's bringing him down. He dances with a woman but thinks of his true love. When he sings at the end, "You left me standing in the doorway cryin'," Lucas could almost see Dylan at the microphone, his knees buckling from the agony of the line. This was no performance. Dylan was *feeling* it.

A year after Lucas's marriage fell apart, he wondered if leaving his wife so impulsively had been a mistake. Had he bolted instead of taking time to think it through? "Standing in the Doorway" seemed to be the cry of someone who had betrayed himself, and Lucas could relate. He found strange comfort in the singer's torment, just as he had as a teenager listening to "Where Are You Tonight?"

"I can't lie and say I'm not a lost person. Obviously I'm a lost person," he says. "I wish I could turn to God like he did."

3

In 1979 and 1980, Dylan concerts took on the air of tent-show revivals. The performances were not for the weak-hearted. These were end-times songs. Jesus was coming, soon, and he would separate the righteous from the wicked. This new message would not surprise anybody at the Vineyard Fellowship. They studied Hal Lindsey's *The Late Great Planet Earth*, the best-selling nonfiction book of the 1970s. Lindsey argued that the events of the day—Israel's rise, nuclear weapons, natural catastrophes—had been foretold in the Bible and presaged the apocalypse. But for the old fans watching Dylan's first Christian concerts in November 1979 at the Warfield Theater in San Francisco, the new message was bewildering. That first night, some of them were frustrated to the point of crying. A clutch of them surrounded the promoter in the lobby and berated him. *You've got to do something.* As Dylan and his backing singers left in a van, they were beset by concertgoers. One faction yelled, *Bob, why are you doing this?* Others hollered benedictions: *God bless you!*

Dylan's conversion tested the staying power of his fans. To the nonbelievers, skeptics, and intellectuals among Dylan's base—they were no small percentage of it—their hero was too smart to fall for evangelical Christianity. Jewish fans felt scorned. One thought it smacked of cult brainwashing. When it came out that his girlfriend had helped usher him into Christianity, the secular fans prayed that this conversion was just a phase.

Music writer Paul Williams saw a number of the Warfield shows, and he quickly dashed off a slim but open-minded volume called *Dylan—What Happened?* He counted himself among the disciples who appreciated Dylan's music by identifying "100% with most everything he says and feels." He hypothesized that Dylan wanted to unload his flock on someone else, somebody who could carry them. "If you don't want to be the messiah, and people keep treating you like one anyway, it makes sense to hook up with somebody who's willing to accept that karma," he wrote. " 'No, I ain't the messiah, but let me introduce you to my Friend . . . '" Williams understood the betrayal fans felt. Before, they all felt like they were on his side when he pointed fingers at those who didn't get it. They had all sung along to 1965's "Ballad of a Thin Man." ("Something is happening here, but you don't know what it is.") Now he was pointing at *them.*

Dylan started preaching from the stage, and in Tempe, Arizona, a month into the tour, he met a hostile crowd. People had been walking out at earlier shows. These fans were jeering and shouting. "Well," he said from the stage. "What a rude bunch tonight, huh?

You all know how to be real rude. You know about the spirit of the Antichrist? Does anybody here know about that? Well, it's clear the Antichrist is loose right now."

He tried to tell a story. The crowd interrupted with shouts of "Rock 'n' roll!" He stopped.

"You wanna rock 'n' roll," he responded, "you can go down and rock 'n' roll. You can go see Kiss and you rock 'n' roll all your way down to the *pit*."

He explained that there were two kinds of people in the world. "Don't matter how much money you got," he said, "there's only two kinds of people. There are saved people and there's lost people. Yeah. Now, remember that I told you that. You may never see me again. I may not be through here again. You may not see me. Sometime down the line you'll remember you heard it here: that Jesus is Lord and every knee shall bow to him."

One follower wrote, "Perhaps we're lucky he's only claimed he's *found* Jesus; it wouldn't be totally surprising if he claimed he *was* Jesus."

Six months into this, the tour rolled through the northeast. Peter Stone Brown—the Dylanhead raised by ultraliberal Jews in Philadelphia—caught the act in Hartford, Connecticut. Fifteen years earlier he'd been at the scene of that near-riotous electric show at Forest Hills. He'd left unbothered back then. This time, at the end of the show, he walked out seriously angry at the man onstage.

Looking back, he couldn't say he was surprised by Dylan's conversion. He had almost been expecting it. Asked what his songs were about during those ridiculous press conferences in 1966, he said, "They're all about the Second Coming." Everybody laughed. But the next year, after Dylan recovered from the motorcycle wreck, he released a record, *John Wesley Harding*, that was crammed with scripture. Its most famous cut was "All Along the Watchtower," an ominous dialogue on the cusp of Armageddon. "The hour is getting late," a thief tells a joker in that song. Like artists throughout history—painters, authors, singers—Dylan had long mined the Bible for phrases, stories, and images. "The Times They Are a-Changin'," from 1963, recalled the Great Flood with its rising waters: "You better start swimmin' . . ." He used the scriptures in subversive ways. A jive-talking Abraham appears on "Highway 61 Revisited." ("Man," Abe says to God, "you must be puttin' me on.") "Can You Please Crawl Out Your Window," a love-triangle song, has been interpreted as a hipster recapitulation of the Bible story of kings Saul and David.

After Dylan's conversion, Peter sat down and read the Bible start to finish. "I just figured, well, let's see what this is about," he said. "I started at the beginning and read the whole thing." He was not looking to be converted, and he wasn't. He treated it as a sort of academic exercise. What blew his mind was when he reached Leviticus, chapter twenty-six, in which God is speaking to Moses on Mount Sinai. Peter found several lines that unlocked for him the confounding *John Wesley Harding* song "I Pity the Poor Immigrant" from 1967—a full decade before the conversion. In the course of demanding obedience, God threatened his chosen people with utter destruction. Several curses mirrored those in Dylan's song: "I will make your heaven as iron"; "your strength shall be spent in vain"; "ye shall eat and not be satisfied." Whoever survived this holocaust would be scattered into enemy lands. In other words, they would be immigrants. Suddenly the song made sense. It was a lament for the wicked who turn their backs on God.

Peter didn't necessarily have a problem with Dylan finding Christ. As he pointed out, some of Dylan's great musical heroes—Little Richard, Elvis Presley, Jerry Lee Lewis—"had this Christ thing going on." Peter liked *Slow Train* enough that when he found a bunch of copies in the discount bins, he bought them for his friends. His *Jew-*

ish friends. He was not being ironic. "The singing on it is incredible!"

What did bother him in Connecticut was the right-wing political diatribe that Dylan spewed from the stage. Dylan started preaching about the Canaanites, and how God pronounced in the book of Genesis that Judgment Day would come for them someday, but "their iniquity is not yet full." Centuries later, the scripture says, God ordered his chosen people to slaughter the wicked Canaanites one and all. On the stage in Hartford, Dylan—erstwhile friend of beat poet Allen Ginsberg—linked the Canaanites with gays. "San Francisco is kind of a unique town these days," Dylan said. "I think it's either one third or two thirds of the population there are homosexuals. All right! I guess they're working up to a hundred percent, I don't know. Anyway . . . I guess the iniquity's not yet full. And I don't wanna be around when it is!"

Peter left Hartford appalled. "I was pissed at him for a really long time after that," he says. "I just couldn't believe the man who wrote 'Chimes of Freedom' was saying this total bullshit."

He didn't burn all his records. But when *Saved* came out, he gave it a bad review.

4

Dylan was taunting her.

Robin Titus, wearing her new leopard-skin hat, was in the front row with her husband, Lex LeSage. As usual. They always found a way to the stage, close enough to see his face and, if Robin was lucky, touch his boots. Sometimes they scored front-row seats. Failing that, they would sneak up. When there were general-admission concerts on consecutive nights, they would tear out of town after the first show so they could be at the front of the line for the next.

They'd been known to get in the line at four in the morning. Lex, the easygoing one of the pair, looked like Kenny Rogers. You could see Native American blood in Robin's face. Her eyes were small, and her hair streamed all the way down her back. Robin was all nerves, especially at the front of the line at a Dylan concert. Tension often crackled there, but Robin could hold her own. "I've gotta be first," she says. "Open the door, Robin's first."

If she wanted something, she pushed until she got it. Now, in the fall of 1995, Robin wanted Dylan to sign her copy of *Saved*, the album with the hand of God reaching down to touch the chosen ones. She tried on consecutive nights, and Dylan turned away, ignored her, flat-out refused. He asked for *her* autograph.

Finally, in San Antonio, Dylan told Robin he wouldn't sign it during the concert. She would have to come around back and meet him after the show.

That was all the opening she needed. She ran outside during the last encore with Lex and hustled to the backstage door. A phalanx of burly men guarded the path from the theater to the bus. When he walked outside she hailed him. "Bob," she said, in a scolding tone. "Are you ready to sign this?"

He told the guards to let her through, and he signed it, in giant letters, with lines above and below. As he did he asked a question: I want to know what this album means to you.

Robin tried to explain, but she knew he didn't have time to listen to it chapter and verse before he got onto the bus and headed to Austin. It was a very long story.

Her father's mother, a full-blooded member of the Sac and Fox tribe of Indians, grew up on a reservation in Oklahoma before moving with the family to Wichita, Kansas. Her mother, who was white, had seven children with a series of men. Robin's father left when she was three and died when she was nine. Before he passed away, he took Robin to an Indian Baptist church in Wichita, where lessons about Jesus were leavened with tribal traditions. Robin's mother was raised a Catholic, but it never took root in her daughter. How was it that you could commit some grievous sin and then get off the hook simply by confessing to a man in a box? As a teen she harangued her mother to leave Catholicism for a form of Christianity that went "all the way."

Robin had a son when she was sixteen. The boy's father split for another woman within a year. She moved out of her mother's house at eighteen and got a job assembling toy trucks and Popsicle trays and other random products at a plastics plant. When Robin met a new boyfriend, the partying started. Pills, pot, cocaine. "Whatever you got." She woke up and got high. Her mother used to tell people, *Don't talk to Robin until she comes back from the garage.* She would light up "big ol' fatties" on the way to work. She woke up hung over every day. If she woke up at all. She was calling in sick all the time. She was a mess.

But *Saved* had come out the year she turned seventeen, and she just about wore out the record. Her son was still in diapers when he learned to call out for his favorite song, "Solid Rock," on which Dylan sings about hanging on to the rock—Jesus—when the end comes. The kid knew all the words. Robin made him a sweatshirt with BOB DYLAN emblazoned on the front and a refrain from the song printed on the back: WON'T LET GO CAN'T LET GO. She wouldn't let him grow out of it. She just made bigger versions; he's wearing one in every single class picture.

Robin's early twenties were a tug-of-war between partying and *Saved*. It took a long time, but eventually, *Saved* won. She didn't go to therapy. Nobody did an intervention. She just did it. She quit the hard drugs (though not pot, not yet) and got herself right. She returned to the Christian life, and for this she thanked Dylan. Listening to his music over and over made the message sink in, she thought. On the Christian records, he may as well have been whispering it directly in her ear. "God is coming, Robin. Are you ready? Get ready!" Robin was certain that she would not have gotten clean without those songs.

She split with the boyfriend and rediscovered Lex, a childhood friend. It was 1987. She got a job at a hand truck manufacturer; he worked at Cessna, Wichita's top employer. He drove her to work every day. In fact, he drove her everywhere because for reasons she couldn't explain, getting behind the wheel freaked Robin out. Anyway, they were together so much that she never had to do it. They began going to Dylan shows in the Midwest and Great Plains.

Lex liked Dylan, but in the beginning the shows were just rock 'n' roll to him. He liked to travel around and see other fans and have a good time. But then in the summer of 1993, at an amphitheater outside Denver, something came over him. They didn't have seats up close, so they were plotting a rush to the front. It was Lex who led the charge this time. Robin couldn't believe it. "He heard it. It went to his heart."

It turned out to be a true metamorphosis. After the concert Lex tried to process what had just happened to him. He had a hard time putting the experience into words. It felt like a detonation. Suddenly he realized that there was a real truth that Dylan had been singing about all this time. He was warning them that the apocalypse was coming. Dylan had long sung about a higher power. He was preoccupied with the quest for salvation. He sermonized against the brokenness and injustice of the world. Signs of Armageddon were always there in the songs. The land is condemned, things are burning, the sky is split. The mountains are filled with lost sheep. There is thunder on the mountain. The chosen are preparing. Lex felt like he was seeing a prophet of sorts. Or maybe that wasn't right. Not a prophet—a preacher, of the old brimstone school.

Lex had been raised in the Catholic church, but he had drifted away from it long ago. Now, in the wake of his epiphany in Colorado, he did a number of things. He started to listen to the television preachers on Sunday mornings. He picked up the Bible and began reading, and not with the book of Genesis, mind you, but with Revelation. That did it. Crack the shell on Revelation and you could get straightened up right away. Robin and Lex decided they ought to school the kids—they each brought a son to the marriage—and so they went to a Pentecostal church in town. It only lasted a couple of years. Two aspects of it pushed them away. It started to grate on Lex that the preacher had an expensive home and a fancy car and took lavish vacations with his family. Then someone suggested to Robin that she was possessed because she couldn't speak in tongues.

They were through with organized religion. It seemed their convictions burned too hot. Her mother tried to get them to go to her new congregation, said they needed fellowship. But Robin had a different idea. "I got my church," she said, looking around her house. "It's right here."

The place was a shrine. On their walls, Dylan seemed simultaneously a member of their family and a sort of religious figure. Maybe he was an older brother done good; maybe he was a saint. Robin made homemade plaques she called "woods." She would glue photos and words to a board and slap a coat of varnish on top. She made one to give her hero. It had a portrait of Jesus in the middle surrounded by miniature crosses, small images of Dylan's Christian records, and excerpts of his gospel-era concert preaching. She handed it to him in Little Rock in 1995, a few days before that fateful night in San Antonio.

Her own Dylan woods hung all about their tidy house, alongside family photographs, crosses, images of Jesus, and Native American artifacts. Hanging from the ceiling above the couch in the living room were dream catchers, a graduation tassel, and what looked like homemade Dylan prayer cards. She had attached one of her tiny crosses to a photo of Dylan from the 1960s and laminated it. Another, attached to a white hanging cross, read DYLAN LOVES ROBIN T and had an invocation on the back: "I said a prayer for you today / And knew God must have heard." Everywhere Robin and Lex had Stars of David. Their favorite was formed out of the letters L-O-V-E, and it appeared in custom-made stained glass over their front door, and in tattoo ink on his shoulder and her neck. They adopted this symbol of Judaism because "Jesus was a Jew." But in Robin's favorite necklace, the centerpiece of the star was an emerald, Bob Dylan's birthstone.

Robin told her mother that she could get her spiritual fill any time she wanted. It was as simple as slipping a Dylan disc into her CD player. She and Lex listened to other musicians, but they were just so much rock 'n' roll. Bob was *church*. She wasn't calling him God, or Jesus, or even a prophet. She was just saying he was the best preacher she had ever heard. When she listened to *Saved*, she was wide awake. She felt it in her soul.

That night in San Antonio, there was no way she could tell Dylan all of this. There wasn't time. So she told him about her son rocking out to "Solid Rock" in his diapers. He just listened, and in a moment he was on the move.

Robin swore she was different from other women who went to show after show following Dylan. A lot of them wanted to sleep with him. She didn't. She was married to Lex, and she wouldn't be unfaithful. Not even for Dylan. God's honest truth. Her mother didn't raise dishonest girls. Still, she's the kind of woman who put her hands on people, and she was afraid of what she might do to her pastor if he gave her an opening. So she stood there with her arms crossed and her hands on her shoulders. She tried her best to control herself.

It was Dylan who grabbed her by the waist. He pulled her over, kissed her, and strode off.

She couldn't walk. She literally couldn't order her legs to move. Lex had to pick her up and carry her away. Dylan may as well have been a televangelist smacking Robin on the forehead and trumpeting a blessing—*Be healed!*—as she fell into Lex's arms. She was swept away.

5

The conversion and its aftermath heralded a new sort of parlor game: debating what Dylan believed.

A year after the San Francisco shows, he brought his nongospel repertoire back to the stage. In 1983, he released an album called *Infidels* that was welcomed as less overtly Christian, more open to interpretation, more Dylanesque. "Jokerman" sounded like a return to form, a meditation on the doubt that goes along with faith. There is a moment when he sings about a "manipulator of crowds" and it's unclear whether he's singing about Jesus or himself or both of them. It seemed to the fans who bought the record that his born-again fever had broken.

Dylan never renounced Christianity, but he did deny actually saying he'd been born again. ("That's just a media term.") While he didn't regret "telling people how to get their souls saved," the time had come for him to do something different. "Jesus himself only preached for three years," he told the *Los Angeles Times*. Jewish fans clung to any sign that he might be returning to his childhood faith. They noticed when Dylan appeared in Jerusalem wearing a yarmulke and a prayer shawl for his son's bar mitzvah, or sang for a Chabad-Lubavitch charity telethon, or sat in on a Passover seder.

Christian Dylan fans noted that in the midst of this, he was singing gospel up on stage. Throughout the 1980s and 1990s, he performed "In the Garden," which asks whether the soldiers who came for Jesus on Gethsemane knew he was the Son of God.

As the years passed, writers have taken to their keyboards to claim him for one faith or another. Seth Rogovoy wrote a book highlighting lines in Jewish scripture that appeared in Dylan's songs. In "Crash on the Levee" (1967), the Great Flood was recast as a prophetic warning in slang and blues jargon. Rogovoy saw it as hip midrash, Jewish scholars' interpretations of scriptural texts. The "bread-crumb sins" of "Gates of Eden" (1965) bring to mind the Jewish tradition of ridding themselves of transgressions by casting bread into water; so did "Jokerman" from *Infidels*. "Father of Night" (1970) reminded the writer of observant Jews reciting morning prayers wearing shawls and tefillin. On "Forever Young" (1973) he heard "a sophisticated code built into the song." It sounded a lot like the Kabbalah's *Sefirot*, "ten manifestations of godliness on earth."

On purely technical grounds, Rogovoy disputed the notion that Dylan really was born again. He could have been baptized and converted, but "once a Jew, always a Jew, is the rule," he wrote. He preferred to think of the Christian episode as an isolated dalliance lasting a short time, and he did not consider it inconsistent with what Dylan had written before or after. Many of the songs could work as Christian or Judaic. Yes, being saved by the blood of the lamb was a reference to Jesus dying on the cross, but it also worked as a nod to the Passover story. The way Rogovoy saw it, Dylan really may have identified personally with Jesus in 1979, but wasn't it more likely that he was just putting the New Testament drama to creative use?

Stephen Webb, an evangelical Christian turned Roman Catholic who teaches religion and philosophy at Wabash College in Crawfordsville, Indiana, didn't think so. As a child, Webb sang "Blowin' in the Wind" at church camp and thought it was an old hymn. (It's a testament to the song's ecumenical spirit, or Dylan's precocious genius in 1962, that many Jews had warm memories of singing the song at *their* camps growing up.) Webb was a high school senior and editor of an evangelical student newspaper when Dylan converted, and to him, *Slow Train Coming* was thrilling. "The word went through the evangelical community like wildfire," he says. Why did it matter so much? It wasn't just that the record was Christian. It also was filled with thorny questions and mature philosophical musings. The songs captured ideas Webb was wrestling with himself.

Like a lot of people, he lost track of Dylan in the late 1980s and early 1990s. Years later, when he came back to Dylan, he was shocked. The more he listened to *non*-gospel Dylan, the more he heard Christian themes pouring out of the speakers. Webb decided to write a book, *Dylan Redeemed*, in which he would pull apart the religious and political themes in the music. He argued that left-wing critics had gotten it wrong from the beginning: "The impossibility of locating Dylan along the spectrum of leftist politics has afflicted Dylanologists with a plague of anxiety," Webb wrote. They concluded that Dylan was wearing masks and changing identities because they were uncomfortable with the idea that he might not be the liberal they thought he was. "Even in the sixties," Webb argued, "Dylan was more of a religious than a political artist. He has often been called a philosopher and a poet, but I think he is best understood as a musical theologian."

It struck Webb that Dylan has never been in tune with his listeners, or his times. He sang not what people wanted to hear but what they needed to hear. His work pondered original sin and "the tragic inevitability of human failure." He did not share the view that man was essentially good. People were essentially broken, in need of salvation. If he had to bet, Webb would say Dylan is still a Christian.

He's not the only one who thinks that. "I would like one person to produce one shred of evidence that he has renounced his faith," says Clinton Heylin, author of the Dylan biography *Behind the Shades*. In 2009, Dylan released, of all things, a Christmas record, and an interviewer asked him about his rendition of "O Little Town of Bethlehem": "I don't want to put you on the spot, but you sure deliver that song like a true believer."

"Well, I *am* a true believer," Dylan replied.

"That's as unequivocal as it gets," Heylin says. "I don't even understand why the debate even happens. I understand people are uncomfortable with the idea."

The thought of anyone trying to classify Dylan's religious thinking makes men like Stephen Hazan Arnoff crazy. A Jewish scholar in New York who knows pop music as well as he knows the Talmud, Arnoff considers most commentary on this subject to be superficial and unsophisticated. Think about what the world really knows about this, he says. Dylan went through a divorce, was born again, maybe dabbled in fundamentalist Judaism, then went radio silent. He renounced nothing and he claimed nothing. "Most people who are serious about religion are as complicated as that," Arnoff says.

Dylan seems to have dabbled in every religious, mystical, and philosophical school known to man. He grew up steeped in Judaism. He read the Bible. He talked about the I Ching, the Chinese book of changes, and the Bhagavad Gita, the Hindu scripture. He lifted from ancient Egyptian beliefs and he flicked through the tarot.

Mysterious as ever, Dylan turned the questions about his faith back onto his audience. "People want to know where I'm at because they don't know where they're at," he told one interviewer. That was as succinct a description of his view of the artist-audience dynamic as he ever gave. Naïve writers kept asking him to clarify his religious beliefs, and he kept declining to give straight answers. In *Rolling*

Stone, five years after the gospel concerts shocked his audience in San Francisco, he said this: "I've always thought there's a superior power, that this is not the real world and that there's a world to come. That no soul has died, every soul is alive—either in holiness or in flames. And there's probably a lot of middle ground."

In later years, Dylan said he believed God put him on earth to write songs. He said he found the sacred not in churches, but in music. "Those old songs are my lexicon and my prayer book. All my beliefs come out of those old songs, literally, anything from 'Let Me Rest on That Peaceful Mountain' to 'Keep on the Sunny Side.' You can find all my philosophy in those old songs. I believe in a God of time and space, but if people ask me about that, my impulse is to point them back toward those songs. I believe in Hank Williams singing 'I Saw the Light,' I've seen the light too."

On *60 Minutes* in 2004, Dylan described what sounded like the flip side of Delta bluesman Robert Johnson's crossroads deal with the devil. He said he still toured because in order to get where he was, he made an agreement—a "bargain," he called it—with the "chief commander."

"On this earth?" interviewer Ed Bradley asked.

"In this earth," Dylan replied, "and in the world we can't see."

"HE CASTS A SPELL"

Seven years after *Saved*, Dylan was at low ebb. Deep into his forties, his life seemed as chaotic as ever. In the years after his marriage to Sara foundered, Dylan had fallen into relationships with women one after another after another, several of whom were backup singers hired during his gospel years. He married and divorced once, or possibly twice, according to biographers; his was "a polygamously peripatetic lifestyle," Heylin wrote in *Behind the Shades*. Dylan seemed to age in a matter of a few years. Where he appeared hale and strong in 1980, he looked haggard by 1985, his hair thinner, his face suddenly craggy, his vocal cords beginning to turn to gravel. It happened that quickly.

Dylan's standing as the most important artist of his generation was in grave danger. He had become, he later wrote, "a fictitious head of state from a place nobody knows." His conversion had provoked a revolt in his base. Some fans left and never returned. He shot awkward music videos at the dawn of the MTV Age. He did a parody of himself for charity on "We Are the World." With some two billion people in sixty countries watching on television, he played a set at Live Aid in Philadelphia that was so ramshackle his supporters could not bring themselves to defend it. He had become an embarrassment. The world had stopped listening.

He was thinking of giving up music altogether. "I was going on my name for a long time—name and reputation, which was about all I had," he would say later. "I had sort of fallen into an amnesia spell." No longer able to put fans in seats, Dylan was touring with bigger artists, and in 1987, dates were scheduled with the Grateful Dead.

At rehearsals, the band suggested playing some of his old songs, but he had lost touch with the words and couldn't recapture the emotions that created them. Annoyed, he went for a walk. He wasn't planning on going back to the rehearsal. After a few blocks, he heard jazz coming from a bar, and he walked inside to find an old man in a mohair suit singing ballads. He had a flash of realization. He felt as though the jazz cat was telling him, *You should do it this way.* He was reminded of a forgotten "formulaic approach to the vocal technique," and energized, he returned to the rehearsals and sailed through the summer concerts on autopilot.

In September, he set out for two months of shows with Tom Petty, beginning in Tel Aviv and Jerusalem, then wending through Europe. In October the concert caravan made its way north from Milan to Locarno, Switzerland, a quaint lakeside city hemmed in by mountains. The stage was set up in the cobblestoned Piazza Grande on the edge of the city's old district. Picturesque buildings lined the square, some painted in jaunty blues or yellows and roofed with red tile. Above shops and restaurants, flower boxes clung to the balconies. At the cafés and pizzerias, customers sat outside under striped awnings. In 1480, a Franciscan monk said the Virgin Mary appeared to him in the hills above town.

The night was foggy and windy as Dylan took the stage. He began to sing, and made a frightening discovery. His new approach to singing was falling apart, right there in front of the crowd. He panicked. His throat closed.

Then a thought flashed through his head, clear as a voice. It said, *I'm determined to stand whether God will deliver me or not.* "All of a sudden everything just exploded," he said later. "It exploded every which way."

He was born again, again.

"This gift was given back to me and I knew it," Dylan said. "The essence was back."

After he described this drama in interviews a decade later, fans rooted around for the tape and searched for this mystical moment, listening for a hitch in his voice, a change in intensity, some evidence of his life-altering transformation captured on their cassettes. They didn't find it, and most of them didn't expect they would. It had always been hard to take Dylan at his word. But however it happened, Dylan had come to the realization that his life's work was to be about one thing: performing music to crowds. That was what he wanted to do, and that was what he was going to do until he died, or until his audience stopped showing up. Like most epiphanies, it only seemed inevitable in hindsight.

The Never Ending Tour started in the summer of 1988. (A British rock music writer coined the catchy phrase during an interview with Dylan, but when he wrote the story, he quoted Dylan saying it.) Backed by a taut three-piece band, Dylan played both his own songs and the traditional music he had long loved. The first shows lasted barely more than an hour and were met with brutal reviews. He mumbled. Everything was sloppy. He was galloping through songs at breakneck pace. But he persisted. He knew the tour would not take off right away. He was breaking everything down, and rebuilding it from the ground up would take time.

Beyond the supposed groundbreaking new vocal technique— even aficionados would not notice much difference—Dylan decided that he needed something else: a new audience. As he looked out from the stage, his fans seemed like "cutouts from a shooting gallery." He could not conceive of them as living, breathing people moved by his music. They had grown up with his records, and he felt bogged down by them and their demands and expectations. They came with baggage, "mental psychic stuff." They couldn't think of him in a fresh way, so they would only be confounded by this new turn of his. He was sure of it.

"In many ways, this audience was past its prime and its reflexes were shot," he would write in *Chronicles*. "They came to stare and not participate. That was okay, but the kind of crowd that would have to find me would be the kind of crowd who didn't know what yesterday was."

2

Glen Dundas figured that the people who knew him in Thunder Bay, Ontario, his frigid home on the northwest shore of Lake Superior, would never believe half the stories he could tell about following Dylan around in the 1980s and 1990s. Their Glen Dundas was a quiet accountant whiling away his middle age. They didn't know that when he traveled the world to see Dylan shows by the hundreds, he illicitly recorded most of them. That he had established himself as a respected hub in a global tape-trading network. That he and his wife, Madge, had like-minded friends in Sweden,

Italy, England, Germany. That they had partied in their basement with Dylan's guitar player and his security chief when the tour came through Canada. That Paul Shaffer had played his wedding in New York City. The Never Ending Tour literally changed Glen's life. As far as he could tell, most of the people in Thunder Bay had no idea who Bob Dylan even was.

Glen's father worked in gold mines and grain elevators and drove a truck for the pulp and paper company. Glen never wanted that life. He dropped out of college—it wasn't for him—and while he was trying to figure out what to do, he got a temporary job at the paper mill. They had an assignment tailor-made for newcomers and other unfortunates: "broke hustler." The enormous mill machines sat idle on the weekends. On Monday mornings when they first coughed to life, they would not run smoothly and the paper would tear. The broke hustler clambered inside the burning machines and cleared the jams and stuffed the paper down giant holes. After everything was operating, he was tasked to fetch coffee for the other workers.

Glen hated that shift, and dreaded the hassling he would get as he took the pick-me-up orders. Above all else, he hated being told what to do. So one Monday morning around nine-thirty he said, *Fuck this*. He grabbed his lunch pail and went home without telling anyone. Thinking he had fallen into the hole, the foreman shut down the operation until he figured out where Glen was. Later, a guy he grew up with told Glen he was an idiot. He had blown his chance to ever work in the mill again. Glen was flabbergasted. What could he say to make the guy understand? He didn't *want* to work in the mill. That was the whole point.

No wonder he loved Dylan. It wasn't just the music. The hard-headed side of Glen was continually amazed by Dylan's attitude. "He's always done what he wants to do," he says. "He never thinks twice about doing it. It's awesome, really." Glen went on to become an accountant, and over time he became a company man with a corner office. When he was pushed out, he couldn't say he was shocked. Looking back, it seemed inevitable. At a golf outing with some of his old colleagues not long after he left the company, one former coworker put it right: "Glen just doesn't fit."

Glen had been a Dylan fan for years, but had only made it to a single show. In 1986, his first marriage over and newly out of work, Glen heard Dylan was coming through the Midwest. This time he was going. He was dating Madge at the time, and she was game. Glen sold fifty bootlegs to a collector for two tickets to the Chicago concert—eleventh row—and enough cash to see two additional shows. He and Madge headed south, and into a new life.

One of the first people they met on the road was a man named Christian Behrens, who was in the middle of a month and a half following the tour with a recording machine. Glen was amazed: He had never heard of anybody doing that. That year, Behrens covered twenty-one thousand miles to see thirty-two concerts, driven by the sense that if he didn't record them, nobody would—not even the musician himself. Dylan prohibited taping and photography, so it took some nerve and some guile. At the time, capturing the music in sufficiently high quality required smuggling in a heavy deck. The one Behrens lugged around was designed for journalists, not spies.

To Glen there was a romance to the cause. Besides, he was a collector: If he had his own recordings he would be able to make trades. In 1988, at the dawn of the Never Ending Tour, he went into a Minneapolis camera shop and put down $500 for a Sony Walkman cassette recorder and a set of mics. The show was a few days later. Congenitally a worrier, he was in full fret as he wired up at the hotel, hiding the machine in his pants and the mics in his hair. Security wasn't likely to pick him out for further screening. He was short, balding, unobtrusive. He usually wore black shirts, black jeans, and black basketball sneakers, which made him look like a roadie. If anybody was going to be stopped it was his friend Ken, who planned to videotape the concert. He had cinched a camera around his wife's waist so it hung between her legs, hidden by a long dress. They got everything situated, walked over to the venue, and made it in unscathed.

Every taper got preshow jitters. Some of them actually had nightmares about getting caught. They would compare notes with other tapers. They all had the same dreams. But more often than not, they came home with their illicit recordings. Sometimes security didn't even care. Mitch's tape-hunting friend Jeff Friedman started taping in 1974, and he would sweat every last detail. He flew to San Francisco and documented the first gospel shows at the Warfield in 1979. His gear was the size of a couple of laptops stacked together. His microphone was a foot and a half tall. He stashed everything at the bottom of a rucksack beneath piles of clothing. When the security men looked—if they looked—they just made sure he wasn't selling unofficial Dylan T-shirts and let him pass.

Short of mass strip searches, security could do little to combat the smugglers. The tapers had too many tricks. The ripping you heard in the bathrooms before a show was the sound of men pulling off gear taped to their legs and backs. They would disassemble their video cameras and give the parts to friends to smuggle inside. They would sneak gear inside a loaf of bread. One hid his lens inside a coffee thermos with a false bottom just an inch or two from the top. When he poured a little coffee in, it looked like a full pot. One guy stuffed all his gear inside a pillow and strapped it to his girlfriend so she looked like she was with child. At a major festival, where people posted flags to help friends find their spot, a taper posted his mic atop a giant pole hidden behind an arrow. In 1986, Behrens got to Berkeley to find particularly tight security. He came up with an unconventional plan. In the afternoon, he hopped on board a soda truck making a delivery inside the venue. He put his recorder in a plastic bag, hid the bag behind a plant, and slipped back outside. Returning through the gate later with his ticket, he was horrified to discover a guard stationed beside his plant. What to do, what to do? He walked up, concocted a story about some trouble in some other part of the theater, and when the guard went to deal with the matter, the taper grabbed the bag and got his tape. There were a thousand and one ways to get the stuff inside. Beating security became part of the buzz of the concert. One fan took to taunting security at the turnstiles. *Don't you see? You have no chance. We're smarter than you.*

The tapers approached the concerts as they would a job. They scouted the venues closely, sometimes a day ahead of time. They were not on the road to drink and dance and blow off steam. If they wanted a decent tape, they couldn't make any noise at all. They couldn't talk to their friends. They couldn't run to the bathroom. If they clapped, they did it quietly, preferably silently. They didn't stand where they had the best view of the stage, like most fans, but where they could capture the best sound. Some of them would get as close to the speakers as possible to drown out gabbers. Others searched for a sweet spot farther back and centered between the speakers.

If you saw them in the postconcert hotel party rooms, they were likely to be in a corner talking not about Dylan but about technical taping questions. Sometimes they would bring their recording of that night's show to play on the stereo. The generous ones made instant copies. A guy from St. Louis had a computer in the back of his van, and he'd burn discs for friends so they could listen en route to the next show.

Glen tapped into a network of men—the tapers were almost exclusively men—around the world. They tried to cover every show. He upgraded his cheap mics to Sennheisers, the gold standard of the era, and did his part. It gave Glen cachet. He wasn't just buying or collecting the underground music everyone wanted; he was capturing it himself. The tapers believed they were doing important work. They were documenting music that otherwise would have floated off into the ether, never to be heard again. Maybe it was illegal in a technical sense. Maybe Dylan hated it, and hated them for doing it. But as far as Heylin, the biographer, was concerned, these men were "custodians of popular music."

A year after his first nerve-wracking experience as a taper, Glen flew over to Europe for a run of concerts. One night in the Hague, he scrambled for a spot up close. He ended up standing next to the speakers among three of the biggest names in taping circles. What was notable about the show was that Dylan performed an electric version of the traditional folk song "Trail of the Buffalo," a real surprise. Collectors still consider it a favorite moment of the Never Ending Tour.

Glen would remember that night for another reason: It was the night he knew he had joined the brotherhood. He was a taper, and proud of it.

3

Dylan played a four-night stand at New York's Beacon Theater in 1989, and the crazies flew in from all over. Glen had met some of them at Dylan fan conventions in Chicago and Manchester, England. In the UK, the conventioneers listened to talks and tribute bands, while the Midwestern crowd spent most of the time in taping rooms. People brought audio cassettes and videotapes, and the dubbing went on twenty-four hours a day. Glen met a lot of people at these affairs, and one was a musician named Steve Keene who was capable of sounding a lot like Dylan. (He later released albums with Dylan bandmates.) He had recently won the big impersonator contest at a bar in the Village. He lived in New York, so in 1989 the traveling crowd relied on him to come through with tickets.

He went to the Beacon the night before and waited in the line, which by four-thirty in the morning stretched down the block. Somehow Keene got enough tickets for everybody on his list. Glen and Madge had never been to the city before, and they stayed in a hotel that first night. But Keene let them crash at his place on Eighty-fifth Street the rest of the week, and soon they knew enough New York City Dylan people that they hardly ever had to pay for a room again. A lot of longtime friendships began in 1989 at the Dublin House, an Irish bar on Seventy-ninth Street where a few dozen serious Dylan fans retired for postshow libations. The tour had been getting terrible reviews, but Glen and Madge didn't care because they were in Manhattan, with their kind of people, people who got it.

Onstage, Dylan looked pissed off, Glen thought. Like he wanted to be anywhere else. He tossed harmonicas across the stage. But the shows had fans buzzing. Dylan had just put out *Oh Mercy*, his best record in years, and he played a number of the songs live for the first time. A version of "Queen Jane Approximately" was a wonder to behold. On the last night, Glen and Madge ended up at the very front, and when Dylan shocked the crowd by singing "Precious Memories," he was so close to them he might as well have been playing their living room back in Thunder Bay. He wore a gold lamé suit that night, and during the last song he wailed on the harmonica, jumped off the stage, shook hands, and walked off through the crowd, never to return.

Glen and Madge started going to shows by the dozens. They carpooled and they crammed into hotel rooms. Someone came up with the brilliant idea of using lounge chairs from the pool as beds instead of sleeping on the floor. They got a decent night's sleep but woke up with lines across their faces. They were semiprofessional fans fitting their lives around Dylan; they knew it was not normal behavior.

Glen and Madge sometimes traveled with Bev Martin, a school-teacher from Madison, Wisconsin. Bev thought the tour felt like the 1960s, when there was a sense of us versus them, the freaks versus the straights. It reminded her of the era when you could roll into a certain kind of city, a college town—Taos, Española, Ann Arbor—and find the record store or café and hook into the counterculture. On the road, they met doctors and drug dealers, left-wingers and conservatives, old hippies and teenagers. If this gypsy band had anything in common, it was that—like Glen back in Thunder Bay—they didn't fit. "We were all a little weird," one of them said.

They learned not to say much back home about these jaunts. People gave them strange looks when they did. Besides, more than a few of them were calling in sick from work or inventing ailing relatives so they could disappear for a few days. "People would not understand," Bev said. "They would think you're crazy."

Dylan was playing to almost nobody in America's nowheresvilles: La Crosse, Sioux Falls, Fargo, Bismarck. It looked like it was being done on the cheap. Though the venues were small, they did not sell out. Once, Dylan implored the audience to come and fill the empty seats up close. "It was like a secret tour," Bev said. Once, she walked into a record store near a venue where Dylan was playing and an employee asked, "Is he still alive?"

The performances themselves felt chaotic and raw. You didn't know what you might get from night to night. He would pull out obscure songs with lyrics that were not so easy to remember, songs that would not have made a top-one-hundred list of possible one-offs. Sometimes it was as if the band didn't even know what it was going to play. To Heylin, the tour was a perfect metaphor for Dylan's career: sprawling and messy, the highs jostling for attention with the many lows. For all the brilliant work that Dylan had produced, "there is nobody I can think of in his league who has produced work as *bad* as Bob Dylan," Heylin would say. But they all kept going, year after year after year, searching for the jewels.

In January 1990, Dylan played on short notice at a little club in downtown New Haven, Connecticut. One of the regular travelers who heard about it, Roy Cougle, had impacted wisdom teeth and was advised not to fly, so he hitched out of Chicago and made it as far as Cleveland before a snowstorm stopped him. He took a bus to New York and met up with a friend, who got them to Connecticut.

Jeff Friedman, the taper and tape hunter, made it up for the show, but he got nabbed by security on the way in. He had his taping gear in the small of his back, and when they pulled his shirt up the wires came out. He was marched over to the box office and told to put the gear back in his car. He said he couldn't; he had taken the train up. He offered to give up his batteries. Security accepted that deal, but, naturally, Jeff had brought extra batteries. He always brought extra batteries.

For some reason he'd also brought extra cassettes that night, and he ended up needing them. Toad's Place held only seven hundred people and the show had been billed as a tour "warm-up." Not long after Dylan came on stage, wearing a black leather vest over a red T-shirt, the audience began to realize it would be a special night. Jeff felt like he'd arrived in heaven and walked into a random club to find the world's greatest bar band playing. Dylan was in high spirits and fully engaged, not rushing, not angry, not listless. He played unexpected covers like "Walk a Mile in My Shoes," and rarities from his deep catalog like "I Dreamed I Saw St. Augustine" and "Tight Connection to My Heart (Has Anyone Seen My Love)."

Then, unbelievably, he started taking requests. "What you wanna hear?" he asked the crowd. "Ballad song, or up-tempo song?"

Cougle yelled song titles all night, and deep into the fourth set he screamed out for "Joey."

Dylan laughed it off: " 'Joey'? 'Joey'? Ha! Ha! Oh, no. It's gonna take me all night." The song, from 1975, was an ode to a New York City mobster, "Crazy Joey" Gallo. Rock critic Lester Bangs had called the song "one of the most mindlessly amoral pieces of repellently romanticist bullshit ever recorded." Gallo was a "psychopath," not a man worth celebrating.

"'Joey'!" Dylan said again. "You sing it! We'd be willing to play it for you if you sing it." But the cheering crowd got behind the request and finally he relented. "All right, let's try this. 'Joey,' okay. Yeah, here's a song about a, sort of a, kind of a . . . hero of sorts. God knows there's so few heroes left."

Dylan played four sets, four hours of music, fifty songs in all, including a joyous butchery of Springsteen's pop hit "Dancing in the Dark." (He didn't know it; he made up a batch of nonsense verses on the fly.) Before he walked off the stage, Dylan gave Cougle a limp-fish handshake. The crowd broke up at two-thirty in the morning.

A year later, Dylan staggered through Europe. In Glasgow, he dropped his guitar and wandered offstage midsong. He looked drunk. He sounded uninterested. As the tour moved on through Europe, the shows did not improve. "Every night he would get up on stage and *murder* masterpiece after masterpiece," Heylin recalled. In Brussels, Dylan sang off-mic most of the night. From what the audience could hear, he was slurring. In London, fans could not believe how bad the show was; the regulars retired to the bar and drank like they were at a wake. In Stuttgart later that year, Dylan opened with a version of "New Morning" so unintelligible that it sparked an argument between two knowledgeable fans about what song he had played.

But by the end of the year, he had turned it around again, and in 1992, Heylin flew from England to California simply because Dylan had started playing "Idiot Wind," the classic from *Blood on the Tracks*, for the first time in sixteen years. Heylin needed to hear it live, and who knew if Dylan might just as suddenly yank it off the set list forever?

As time went on, the music came to be less important; the regulars kept going because they wanted to see what would happen on the road before and after every show. They shadowed the crew, who, like the serious fans, arrived early and left late; inevitably they got to know each other. They would bullshit with the people who made sure the shows went off every night: Dylan's muscle, the merchandise guy, the soundmen, the bus driver, the tour manager. Sometimes—by coincidence or by design—fans stayed at the same hotels as the band and ended up at the bar having drinks with the guitar player or the drummer. "I'm sure they just wondered what the fuck we were doing with our lives," Roy Cougle said. "*Don't you have jobs?*" He and another regular traveling companion, Keith Gubitz, got roadies to give them old laminated passes; even expired badges got them backstage. (A shirt that read SECURITY also worked for Roy.) Some fans started wearing a glow-in-the-dark dog on a string around their necks. Soon everybody had them, the crew, the roadies, even guys in the band. Gubitz said that on occasion, wearing a glowdog would actually get you inside. It got to the point where the band and crew took notice when the whacked-out superfans weren't there.

Soon enough they all felt like part of the tour family. When the show came through Thunder Bay in 1992, Glen drove from bar to bar searching for the crew. He found guitarist Bucky Baxter, and next thing he knew, Baxter was down in his basement doing his laundry and listening to old tapes. Dylan's security chief, Jim Callaghan, had trouble getting back over the border, so he hung around in Thunder Bay partying with Glen while he waited.

It helped to know the help. A while later, venue security in Chicago caught Glen and took the expensive battery for his taping machine. When Glen went to claim it after the show, he was told Callaghan had it. Glen figured he would get some ribbing but he wasn't prepared for what Dylan's security man did the following night in the lobby. He lumbered over and made a great show of ripping into the Canadian. Callaghan was a big man, built like a stevedore, and he towered over Glen. He turned to the others and told them to watch out for this concert scofflaw. *You ever see this guy taping, you come and tell me!*

Then he opened the door of the theater and dragged Glen inside like a perp. But after Glen stopped stuttering, he realized it was a show. Callaghan gave him the battery back, smiled, and left him with a clear view of the sound check.

The regulars would see Dylan all the time. He might be riding his bicycle in the middle of the afternoon, sometimes in the pouring rain, sometimes fifteen minutes before he went on stage. He'd be seen in trunks swimming laps at the pool or doing doughnuts in the parking lot on a motorcycle. If you were out at three in the morning you might see him taking a walk in the street. Some thought Dylan reversed his days. He performed a little while after waking up, then stayed up all night. The fans learned that he didn't stay in the best hotels; that he preferred lodging where he could open the windows because he didn't like air-conditioning; that he boxed on the road to stay in shape. He got a sweet tour bus and spent a lot of time on it. At the end of a show he'd hop aboard and head to the next city while the crowd drifted out. The smart fans knew to keep their distance or risk getting grief from tour managers. "We always tried to respect the bubble around Bob," Cougle said. "I don't think any of us tried to bum-rush Bob and ask him the meaning of life."

But, inevitably, they ran into him. There were a hundred stories of brief encounters, and despite his gruff reputation, many of them were pleasant enough, or not disagreeable, anyway.

One year in New York, fans discovered that Dylan was hanging around in a tour bus behind the venue. He came outside wearing a cowboy hat and sucking on a cigar, and to their immense surprise, he began talking to them. Dylan asked them what they wanted to hear him play and people shouted requests. He laughed when he learned that one of the fans, an attractive woman, had red lacy underwear embroidered with the name BOB. She was going to throw them onto the stage—a lark, she swore. She was there with her husband.

Somebody joked that Bob ought to wear them. But randy as ever, Dylan said he wanted to see them on the woman.

Whoa, her husband said.

Then a legendarily obnoxious New Jersey woman came up and started asking stupid questions, like whether Dylan was breast-fed as a boy.

Just like that, he was gone.

Sometimes Dylan would agree to sign autographs. Sometimes he would shut down. Sometimes nobody said anything.

Once, a fan was at a hotel waiting for the elevator to the lobby when the doors opened and he came face-to-face with Dylan. The fan happened to be wearing a shirt advertising the organization behind the *Telegraph*, the big British fanzine. The front was emblazoned with a photograph of Dylan's face and the words WANTED MAN.

Dylan looked at the fan, looked at the shirt, looked away. Downstairs, the doors opened, and idol and fan parted wordlessly.

4

One morning in June 1990, Glen and Madge got breakfast and checked out of a hotel in Fargo, North Dakota. They had seen Dylan play a twenty-song set at the Civic Center the night before, and they had a three-hour drive west for Dylan's Friday-night show in Bismarck. As they drove out of the Red River Valley toward the plains on I-94, they spotted a figure on the side of the road. It was a woman hitchhiking alone in the summer heat. She looked so vulnerable. Realizing it was a member of the tribe, they pulled over for her. That was the way it was on the road. They all needed the same basic things: tickets, a ride to the next town, a bed and a shower, some food. They might never have socialized with some of these fans if they lived in the same town. But out on the road, they took care of each other. When Glen stepped out of the car to offer the woman a ride, he saw her writing down his license plate number, a precaution by an experienced and wary traveler.

Glen and Madge had seen her up front at the shows, sometimes talking to herself, tooting on her harmonica while Dylan performed, flipping coins at Dylan's feet, putting up an umbrella, playing cards onstage. She told people her name was Sara Dylan—like Dylan's first wife—and that she was his twin sister. Dylan didn't know her because they were separated soon after their birth in France. He was adopted by Minnesotans; a couple in Texas raised her. If it bothered her that she couldn't explain why he was thirteen years older, she didn't say so. Fans thought she was unbalanced. On the other hand, they met lots of strange people on the road with Dylan.

She wore her hair in a bun and favored long dresses and gloves. Waiting around at the shows, she seemed aloof. But on the way to Bismarck with Glen and Madge she chattered away. She told them she'd lived in Duluth for a time, and how, to help make ends meet, she sometimes lifted Bibles from hotel rooms and sold them to used-book stores. It never seemed that she had much money. She hitchhiked from show to show. She used to tell the front desk at the band hotels that she was Dylan's sister and try to get a room on their tab. She could be quite convincing. The year before in New York, she managed to reserve eighteen rooms on the record company's account.

She traveled all over the world following the tour. It was her life. In 1986, she made it to Canada, where Dylan was playing an aging rock star in *Hearts of Fire*. A documentary filmmaker visiting the set to interview Dylan found himself staying in the room next to hers. "I had a drink with her and she tells me she's your sister," Christopher Sykes said when he met Dylan.

"Well, there are people who follow me around, you know," Dylan replied. "They have passports and they have driver's licenses and they all have Dylan as their name. What can I do about that? I mean, I can't do anything about that." Sykes found Sara frightening. "Is that something that bothers you ever," he asked Dylan, "the idea that because you are very famous, someone who thinks they love you might want to kill you?"

"Well, that's always the case, isn't it? Isn't that the way it always happens?" the singer answered. "Aren't you usually killed by the person who loves you the most?"

Keith Gubitz was one of Sara's traveling companions, and he didn't think she meant Dylan any harm. She could have sought him out every day on the road. Instead she went to the venue early, before the tour bus arrived, and hoped that when Dylan got off *he* would summon *her*. He never did, Keith said.

But in 1990, she ran into him in the street in DeKalb, Illinois, and Dylan asked her what she wanted from him. Free tickets? Was that it?

What she really wanted was for Dylan to love and accept her, Keith said. But in the moment of truth, she apparently didn't tell him this. Did she want a ticket to the show? Sure. After that, she always had one waiting for her at the box office, as far as Keith could tell.

Not everyone was so easily mollified. Moving away from New York had not made it harder for fans to find Dylan. His Malibu house and Santa Monica rehearsal space, Rundown Studios, were easy enough to locate, and in 1981, one of the obsessed stalked out there. Her name was Carmel Hubbell, and her story was that she and Dylan had had an affair in 1978 when the tour went through Kalamazoo, Michigan. She went west to pursue the relationship.

At the time, Dylan and his people were on high alert: In December 1980, John Lennon was gunned down at the door of his Upper West Side building by a mentally ill fan who had approached him for an autograph.

That summer, Hubbell stormed Rundown Studios issuing threats and had to be forcibly removed. Later, staff found threatening notes on their windshields. Hubbell walked onto Dylan's property in Malibu nineteen times in less than a month, leaving behind notes to her "sweetheart," a test tube full of nuts, and the key to her motel room. The letters got scarier as the days passed and she could not get through to Dylan. "Ms X = Ms Manson," one read. Finally, Hubbell called one of Dylan's backing singers and told her that her life was in danger. Dylan's lawyers took Hubbell to court to end the harassment. By 1983, the singer was telling an interviewer that he had "walls up all over the place," suggesting both human gatekeepers and concrete barriers. His office kept a list of potential threats; it had hundreds of names on it.

Bev Martin, the Madison schoolteacher, couldn't help but think Dylan was partly responsible for some of the unwanted attention. Onstage, he would flirt with women. He would walk up and play his guitar *to* them, stare into their eyes for an entire song, put a hand out and reach for them. Whether this was a stage act or a play for postshow action—both, probably, depending on the object of his attention—it hypnotized women. "He casts a spell," one of them mused. Even psychologically balanced women were drawn to his magnetism. For others already predisposed to delusions, it stoked their fantasies. "All it takes is one time. He makes contact and they're hooked for life," Bev said. They fall in love, and hope Dylan will, too. "They think every song he writes he writes to them."

So there was the woman from West Hollywood who wrote lengthy letters to Dylan and mailed them to his office in New York. She seemed to survive on apples and peanut butter and rice cakes and slept in her car. There was the woman who followed the bus to Malibu and was slapped with a cease-and-desist order. There was the woman who said she helped Dylan write songs on one of his records. ("It's about mulberries," she revealed.) There was the woman from Italy who tracked the tour around the globe and stood outside venues holding a sign for tickets. She lived a gypsy life, bumming rides and lodging from whoever would help. She told people that Dylan had supernatural powers and was speaking directly to her from the stage, that the concerts were elaborate rituals designed so Dylan could communicate with her, and the rest of us were irrelevant, mere set pieces.

These women were almost always up at the front of the stage, dancing, swaying, some of them accompanying the music with theatrical interpretations. At a few concerts, security asked them to stay back and give someone else a chance. Dylan didn't want them there, they were told.

Women came and women went. Often they disappeared as mysteriously as they had materialized, and so it was with "Sara Dylan." One day she was there, and the next day she was gone. In 1992, she followed the tour to Australia. She made it to the next stop in Maui but missed the concert two nights later in Waikiki. She wrote Keith saying she would meet him April 27 when the tour went to Seattle for a nineteen-date West Coast leg. She didn't show up. Keith looked for her at shows for the next month, figuring she had changed her plans without telling anyone. But he never saw her.

Keith was one of the few on the road who knew her given name, Renee Shapiro, and her hometown, Pharr, Texas. He went home and looked up the family. They told him that their daughter disappeared from time to time. Several years later, Keith called again, and when her mother picked up she broke into tears.

In 2012, everyone's worst fears were confirmed. A detective had called. Some of Shapiro's belongings had been discovered inside a black zipped bag locked in a safety deposit box in Reno, Nevada. The owner was accused of killing four women in northern California, and police suspected him in other murders, including Shapiro's. Investigators found Shapiro's passport, her driver's license, her business cards, and a slip of paper that suggested she was on her way to her next Dylan show—but never made it.

The note, written by the suspected killer, read, "May 4 1992 Monday pm." Dylan played San Francisco that night.

5

In one way, Keith Gubitz could relate to Sara. He too hoped that his hero would stop someday and notice him. The first time he saw a Dylan show, he was frustrated. His seats were in the far reaches of the arena. The man would never see him up there, he thought. So he pulled a lighter, flicked the switch, and hoped it might catch Dylan's eye. "I just wanted him to know that I existed and that I loved what he did," he said. "But it goes deeper than that. I don't know why, but if Bob is sad, or his music is sad, I feel sad, and I feel sad for him. When he's singing and he's hurting, it hurts me, too."

More than a few people believed their long-distance relationship with Dylan was something special. The way they identified with him felt exclusive and intimate. They understood Dylan and his music in ways others did not. They were cautious when talking about this. They knew they were veering into hazardous waters.

Keith made great sacrifices to get up close. He waited forever in lines for tickets, and then again to get onto the floor. He pushed for position. He sneaked into empty seats. If he still couldn't get up front, he waited for the stage rush. Keith said that for a while, near the end of every concert, the road crew would encourage regulars to dash up to the stage and dance. After Keith made his first run, no Dylan concert was complete without it.

He didn't do it just to see better. He needed to be counted as present. He wanted to be seen.

But even if he saw you, who could say it meant anything? Andrew Muir, of Cambridge, England, taught public speaking, and the trick he shared with nervous people was this: Gaze over the heads of your audience. They will believe you're looking directly into their eyes. Was it not far more likely that Dylan was focusing on the middle distance, staring at the lights, lost in the music? Muir heard people say that Dylan was looking at them—them alone—and he wanted to slap them. "It's madness!" he said. "It's just not true."

Still, he couldn't say it never happened. A legendary fan named Lambchop ended up at the front every time Dylan went to England. Lambchop was a character. He tried to support himself by playing the horses—his passport listed his job as professional gambler—and he smoked pot every day. "You could get a high from the wallpaper at his place," a friend said. Lambchop wore a huge white hat, which he would wave at Dylan. Between songs he would shout, "Thanks for coming, Bob!" When the crowd screamed for songs, he would bellow, "You play what you want, fuck 'em, Bob!" If people sat down, he'd cry out, "They don't fucking deserve it!"

So Dylan noticed Lambchop. He could hardly have missed him. One night in Utrecht, Lambchop and Dylan had a brief conversation, front row to stage. The singer asked the fan why he'd missed some shows in the United States, and Lambchop said he hadn't been invited.

"How about giving the Chopper a hand!" Dylan told the crowd. "He's seen me play more times than me!"

Caroline Schwarz and Kait Runevitch knew that Dylan noticed them from the stage, and they didn't care what anybody said. They believed what they believed. "All kinds of people experience this," Kait said years later. "You can't deny it's happening."

The two of them met on the road. Caroline started seeing shows regularly after losing her job. Kait was between school and real life. Traveling to concerts by the dozens, they did what it took to get up front. Caroline admitted throwing an elbow or two. Snarky fans dubbed them the Glitter Girls because they favored cowboy hats and sparkly body makeup, boogied up front, and were not afraid to flaunt their cleavage.

One night at a show in Joliet, Illinois, they got up close, and near the end of his set, Dylan sang "Honest with Me." A man is telling his woman that he loves her but she needs to be straight with him. He sang, "You don't understand it, my feeling for you—*aw, you don't*," and looked directly at her and Kait "with serious intent and fire," Caroline wrote in her tour journal. A year later in Chicago, Caroline was at a show with another friend when Dylan eased into "Every Grain of Sand" and locked onto her again. "Bob sings my favorite line of this song full of favorite lines right fucking at me and it is almost too intense," she reported in her journal. "I know now for sure, if I had any doubt, that he knows I'm here. And he's looking at me and I've been singing it along softly and he gives me that squint, that level gaze, and he's shaking his head softly with a smile and so am I. Yup, here we are again. Mmmmm. Something." Two nights later, he pivoted and zeroed in on her during "Cold Irons Bound" as he sang the words, "I'm gonna remember forever all the joy we've shared."

Caroline swooned at "this blatant admission of affection" from her hero. She had never been happier in her life. She couldn't lie and say it hadn't dawned on her that if they went to show after show, maybe they would get to meet the man. One July evening in St. Paul, they were in their usual spot up front when Dylan's stage manager appeared to fetch them. They walked backstage, legs shaking, and there was the legend standing between two trucks.

Dylan wore motorcycle boots and what looked like a bowling shirt. He was smoking American Spirits. He told them he loved seeing them out there. He remarked about Kait's green eyes, saying that he'd been looking for a woman with green eyes all his life. He asked what they did, and when Kait said she worked at an art gallery, he asked for a card. She scrawled her number on a piece of paper. He pocketed it.

Then he got down to business. He wanted them to do something for him: start a fan club. Caroline and Kait were perplexed. Was he serious? Though there had never been an official club, there were a lot of fan communities. Wanted Man in England. The Cambridge Bob Dylan Society. The Dylan Pool, an online forum that ran a contest to guess which songs the singer would play onstage. The Usenet group rec.music.dylan and its offspring, the Exchange Dylan Lyrics Internet Service, or EDLIS, whose members met up at many concerts. Expecting Rain, a clearinghouse for Dylan news run by a man near the Arctic Circle in Norway.

Dylan told Caroline and Kait they needed to spread the word. He performed for people like them—people who understood the songs and why he still traveled the globe singing them. The media got it wrong.

Sure thing, they told him. Whatever you want.

Back out front, they giggled throughout the show. When they got home they built a website and launched the Bob Dylan Fan Club.

Dylan never called.

6

Michelle Engert, transcriber of the *Blood on the Tracks* notebook and tour regular in the early 1990s, couldn't think of anything she wanted less than to meet Dylan. During her four years on the road, she went out of her way to *not* make contact with him. One night in

Germany after a concert, Michelle's friends stopped at a gas station in the middle of the night on the trip between towns. She walked through the sliding doors of the convenience store to buy some bottled water. She looked up and found herself face-to-face with Dylan. Startled, she turned around and went right back to the car. She didn't even say hello to be polite. He was known to be mercurial and moody even with his bandmates and friends. Sometimes he could be the best friend in the world, people said; other times he could be rude or silent. What if they met and Dylan treated Michelle cruelly? She would never be able to enjoy the music again.

Michelle stumbled into the orbit of the tour regulars when she was only eighteen. She had moved out of her parents' home and gotten a job at a hair salon, but she had a major case of wanderlust. A friend introduced her to Keith Gubitz and Ray Cougle, who took her out west to see Dylan in Texas, New Mexico, and Arizona. She met Bev Martin and eventually fell in with Glen and Madge and their band of tourgoers. She was absorbed into the tribe, even though she was decades younger.

She had an uncanny knack for getting a spot front and center. She might slip in a side door unnoticed before the venue opened. Or at a general admission show she'd bat her eyelashes at a guy up at the front and tell him how she'd driven all the way in from Chicago and she'd only seen Dylan a few times and could she scoot in here? They always said yes. She was young and attractive, with long black hair and alabaster skin. She would chat up strangers at the front of the line until there was no question she would be going in with them instead of heading to the back. She once went so far as to set up a row of chairs for herself and her pals between the stage and the actual front row, and somehow no one stopped her. She also became close to people in Dylan's circle, the crew and the musicians and the security. In a jam she'd beg them for help. She always got in, by hook or by crook.

In 1993, word spread that Dylan was going to play two nights at the tiny Supper Club in Manhattan, an acoustic performance that would be professionally filmed. All of the regulars sprang into action to get passes. They were free, but scarce: two per person. Fans started lining up the day before the tickets were available. But not everybody could get there in time—Glen and Madge had to arrange flights—so one of them started hiring people from a homeless shelter across the street. They paid guys $200 to wait around in line all night. Everyone scored tickets.

Michelle got inside early with help from her friend, the sound engineer, and she watched the rehearsals crouched down under the mixing board. When the doors opened she had a head start, and she helped the rest of the regulars as they dashed for the tables up front.

It was at the Supper Club that she and Dylan shared a moment. She would never forget it; it was hard to say whether he would even remember it. The band started in on "One More Cup of Coffee," a song Dylan recorded in 1975. He could not recall the first line, so he turned to his bass player, Tony Garnier, who shrugged.

"Your breath is sweet!" Michelle called out.

Dylan looked over, smiled, and sang the song. After what Michelle thought was the last song of the night, she grabbed the set list off the stage, only to have Dylan return, and as she went to put the list back he called her over. "Okay," he said, "now I want you to tell me the first line of 'I Shall Be Released.'" She was overjoyed. It was the sweetest acknowledgment. She was twenty-two, and she wondered if the very best moment of her life had already happened.

Once, after several years of traveling, Michelle had a conversation with Dylan's guitar player at the time, Bucky Baxter, over breakfast at a German hotel.

"When are you going to get your own life?" he asked her. "When are you going to go and do something? Because you can't do this forever."

The idea stuck in her brain and weakened her resolve to stay with the tour. Then somewhere in Florida she finally decided that Baxter was right. She needed more from life than she could get being a full-time concertgoer. She got off the road and enrolled in college.

Dylan's songs had taught her something about love and politics, and about the power struggles in the world. They made her think about things from the underdog's point of view. The songs pulled her into American history. Dylan listened to Guthrie, so she did, too, and you can't listen to Guthrie without learning something about the Great Depression and the suffering of the dust bowl. "Bob brought me there," she said. "Because he cared about it, I wanted to know what it was about. You either connect or you don't, and I did."

When it came time to choose a topic for her undergraduate thesis, Michelle decided to go to the Mexican border and interview *maquiladora* laborers, who worked long hours for low wages to manufacture products for foreign markets. She couldn't stomach the idea that the things she bought in Chicago were cheap because they were made by people working at cut rates. She decided to go to law school, and when she graduated she wanted to sue the corporations on behalf of these and other impoverished workers. She realized soon enough that she wouldn't be able to do that right out of the classroom, but she found something else that made her feel like she was serving society: public defender.

Michelle left the highway with street smarts. She learned how to be independent and fearless. She learned how to deal with people who were savvier than she was.

Nobody would have believed it in a million years, but she was sure of it: Dylan had made her a better lawyer.

7

In Glen's basement, an entire wall is given over to Dylan CDs. He collects a recording of every show, though he has less interest in listening to them these days; baseball, fantasy and the real thing, is his obsession. Over the years, when people shared recordings with Glen, he would jot down who taped the show and which songs Dylan played. That grew into *Tangled Up in Tapes*, a discography of underground recordings that earned him a measure of fame in the Dylan fan universe. Once, a woman came up to him on the road, and when he told her his name she said, "*The* Glen Dundas?" He couldn't lie: He got a small charge from that. He might never have survived life in his little frozen Canadian town if not for all those nights following Dylan.

One year, a *Los Angeles Times* music critic met Glen at a show, and Glen gave a copy of *Tangled* to the man, who then handed it to Dylan when they sat down for an interview. Dylan flipped through Glen's book for a moment and handed it back. "I've already been all those places and done all those things," he told the reporter. "Now, if you ever find a book out there that's going to tell me where I'm *going*, I might be interested."

A quarter century after he started, he was still touring, and most of the world had no idea. Fifty years after he left Minnesota, people could still go and see him play. Those who studied Dylan's music had a hard time wrapping their arms around the unpredictable mass of live performances. He said he had no choice. He made it sound like he'd become addicted. He said he wouldn't retire until he couldn't do it anymore. "It's as natural to me as breathing. I do it because I'm driven to do it, and I either hate it or love it," he told one journalist in 1997. "I'm mortified to be on the stage. But then again, it's the only place where I'm happy. It's the only place you can be who you want to be."

As time went on, some of the road regulars began to pass away. The survivors would write tributes and go to funerals. A lot of serious fans had long ago stopped going on the road to follow the tour as they once had—Glen and Madge included—and they could only shake their heads in wonder that Dylan, in his seventies, was still taking his act from city to city. Like clockwork, a new year arrived and new tour dates were announced. Beijing and Hong Kong. Brooklyn and Philadelphia. São Paolo and Buenos Aires. It really had become never ending, until it began to feel as if Dylan's road show would somehow outlast them all.

DOWN THE RABBIT HOLE

In September 2001, Dylan released an album with so many personalities that, a decade later, people were still trying to figure out who was who. *"Love and Theft"* choogled and swung. It sashayed. It burst into barroom rowdiness. There were bad jokes. There was Shakespearean burlesque and enough swagger for an army. "It speaks in a noble language," Dylan said cryptically as he sent the record out into the world. "It speaks of the issues or the ideals of an age in some nation, and hopefully, it would also speak across the ages." In case anyone thought about taking it too seriously, he also declared it a new greatest-hits record. "Without the hits; not yet anyway."

It was the second new release of what will come to be regarded, presumably, as Late Dylan. When the era dawned with the release of *Time Out of Mind* in 1997, he had gone seven years without releasing an album of originals. It was the longest gap of his career, so long that some people wondered if he had given up songwriting forever—Dylan included. "I really thought I was through making records," he recalled later. One reason was that he couldn't write the kind of songs he wanted. He would sketch out a few verses, then lose the thread and abandon the song. "Creativity is not like a freight train going down the tracks," he told one interviewer. "It's something that has to be caressed and treated with a great deal of respect. You've got to program your brain not to think too much." During this pause, Dylan immersed himself in the sort of traditional music he had loved since his days in Minneapolis and Greenwich Village. He had long been an aficionado of the hissy, antique recordings of early American artists: Charley Patton, Robert Johnson, Blind Willie McTell, the Carter Family, the Memphis Jug Band, Dock Boggs, Clarence Ashley, all those mysterious figures from generations past. Those songs were the roots of the music he grew up hearing, and they became the foundation of his own music. When the Never Ending Tour began in 1988, he sprinkled his sets with British, Scottish, and Irish folk ballads, rural blues, spirituals, and country standards. In 1992 and 1993, he set up in his garage studio in Malibu and, alone with an acoustic guitar and harmonicas, recorded two albums of traditional music, songs like "Frankie & Albert," "Delia," and "Ragged & Dirty." Late Dylan flowered from this rich soil. He rediscovered his urge to write.

But Dylan needed more than mere inspiration from the antediluvian songs; he needed the words themselves. His originals on *Time Out of Mind* were scattered with antecedents. "Tryin' to Get to Heaven" drew from familiar folk songs ("Hang Me, Oh Hang Me," "Goin' Down the Road Feeling Bad") as well as a handful of songs that could be found by flipping through Alan Lomax's *The Folk Songs of North America*. The title came from "The Old Ark's A-Moverin'" (page 475), and distinctive phrases from "John the Revelator" (480), "Miss Mary Jane" (498), and "Buck-Eye Rabbit" (504).

Four years on, *"Love and Theft"* went even further. The album was the logical conclusion of a musical career spent repurposing—a true mother lode of quotation. The title apparently came from academia, a book about blackface minstrelsy by an English professor at the University of Virginia. Just as the minstrels twisted black culture out of shape, so Dylan was now doing with what he was recycling. More studious fans, who didn't listen to new Dylan songs so much as dissect them, noticed a line from bluesman Robert Johnson, a bit of "Cotton-Eyed Joe," a snippet of Woody Guthrie, and a quote from W.C. Fields. ("It ain't a fit night out for man nor beast.") Somebody spotted Virgil. Admirers of F. Scott Fitzgerald caught dialogue cribbed from *The Great Gatsby*: " 'You can't repeat the past.' 'Can't repeat the past?' he cried incredulously. 'Why of course you can!'" Like the quotation marks around the record's title, his pilfering of that exchange between Fitzgerald's Nick Carraway and Jay Gatsby was a neatly nested in-joke. What with the antiquated musical styles and the borrowed words, everything about *"Love and Theft"* had to do with the past making claims on the present.

But two years after the record's release, Dylan's audience learned that his use of other material on *"Love and Theft"* was more wideranging and peculiar than it had first appeared. That summer, an English schoolteacher from Dylan's native Minnesota was poking around in a bookstore in Fukuoka, a teeming harbor city in southern Japan. He picked up an oral history of Asian mobsters, *Confessions of a Yakuza*, by Junichi Saga. It told the stories of the country's elaborately tattooed gangsters, men who live by their own code. (If they do something dishonorable, for one thing, they cannot just issue an abject apology; they must cut off a pinky.) On the book's first page, a mobster proclaims, "My old man would sit there like a feudal lord."

Reading this, the teacher, Chris Johnson, felt a rush of recognition. The words may as well have been highlighted, he said later. Johnson had listened dozens of times to the *"Love and Theft"* song "Floater (Too Much to Ask)," which is not unlike having an incoherent conversation with a crazy man you meet sitting on a bench in front of a general store, a man who insists on sharing an unexpurgated picture of the cumulus drifting through his mind. He wishes he could be with his second cousin, now and forever. He is "listening for footsteps" but he doesn't hear anything. Don't screw with him or he'll kill you right dead, understand? "My old man," he grumbles, "he's like some feudal *lawd*."

One match could be coincidence, but Johnson was intrigued, and he brought the book home. By the time he reached the last page, he had discovered more than a dozen likenesses, on "Floater" and other songs. His surprising find merited a story in the *Wall Street Journal*, with the newspaper raising the specter of wrongdoing by noting the recent exposure of plagiarism by historians Stephen Ambrose and Doris Kearns Goodwin. But Saga felt flattered that Dylan had read his words, and his publisher only wanted a blurb from the musician for the next printing. Sales of the book jumped.

The discovery raised so many questions. It was one thing for Dylan to reuse ancient melodies, folk lyrics, and blues riffs. But taking random lines from an unknown book published halfway around the globe—that seemed like appropriation of a different magnitude. Were there other such thefts? Was Dylan trying to get away with them, or did he expect fans and scholars to catch on? Above all: Why?

In Albuquerque, New Mexico, a music fan named Scott Warmuth read about the yakuza discovery, and he was astounded. Over the next decade, he would spend a lot of free time trying to answer the vexing questions about Dylan's borrowings. A rabbit hole seemed to open that summer in 2003 and swallow Scott up. On *"Love and Theft,"* Dylan recycled lines from so many different places that one writer guessed every word of it would eventually be traced back to another source. But it was not just that record. The more Scott dug into the writing of Late Dylan—post-1997 songs, the 2003 movie *Masked and Anonymous,* the 2004 memoir *Chronicles*—the more he thought the game went even deeper than anyone had realized.

2

In October 1961, Dylan visited the Folklore Center, a small storefront in Greenwich Village that was the hub of the folk music revival in the city. The man who ran the shop, Izzy Young, was arranging for Dylan to play the Carnegie Chapter Hall, and needing a proper program to give attendees the night of the show, he asked the young singer to come in for a short interview. Dylan, twenty that spring, was about to sign a deal with Columbia Records, and they got to talking about what he would play when he went in for his first professional recording session. His early repertoire was mostly borrowed blues and folk and old spirituals; the handful of "originals" he'd written at the time were straight from the Guthrie mold. He told Young he had about twenty songs ready to put down on tape. "Some stuff I've written. Some stuff I've discovered and some stuff I stole," he said. "That's about it."

Fifty years on, when he was an old man with six hundred songs to his credit, he could have said much the same, and it would have been just as true.

One of his first originals was "Song to Woody," a tribute to Guthrie built on the chassis of one of his hero's songs, "1913 Massacre." His next three records borrowed traditional lyrics and melodies for songs that would be instant classics, like "Blowin' in the Wind," "Girl from the North Country," and "Masters of War." It was no secret. Any musician in the Village folk scene knew the old songs that Dylan used as templates. That was how it was done. These songs had been passed on through the ages. They were there, free, for the taking. That was the folk tradition. Guthrie had told Dylan his secret: Just take some song and start messing around with it, and soon enough you'll have your own. Many times Dylan didn't even do that much. He let the original melody and some of the words show through like old layers of paint on a weathered house.

Soon, Dylan was incorporating other material. Michael Gray, whose *Song and Dance Man III: The Art of Bob Dylan* examined Dylan's songwriting in granular detail, conducted an exhaustive analysis of the musician's use of pre–World War II blues lyrics. Studying a concordance of commercial blues records from 1920–42, Gray found that 1960s Dylan, so hip with his sunglasses, so mysteriously avant-garde, had been performing with "the cloak of the blues around him." His roots were antique, rural, Southern. The signs were all there for anyone paying attention. In that photo on the cover of 1965's *Bringing It All Back Home*, the piles of records sitting around Dylan included Robert Johnson's *King of the Delta Blues Singers*. He named his next LP after the thoroughfare connecting the fountainhead of the blues to the north: Highway 61 runs from the Mississippi Delta through Clarksdale and Memphis and clear up through Dylan's birthplace, Duluth, Minnesota. That *Revisited* should've been a clue about what was at work.

When Gray looked over the blues concordance after listening to Dylan records hundreds of times, he had the strangest experience. "To put it wrong way first, I kept coming across bits of Bob Dylan," he said. "I came to realize Dylan was a closet blues freak." Dylan took ancient blues lines and sneaked them into songs, sometimes word for word, sometimes with a twist. Gray found the line "Sugar for sugar, salt for salt . . . it's gonna be your own damned fault," from Dylan's "Crash on the Levee" (1967), on a song that Rabbit Brown had recorded in 1927 and included on a popular folk music anthology. It had first sounded to Gray like drug slang, or "Dylan-esque playful weirdness." Dylan used "mama" to mean "lover" (not "mother") like the blues singers did. "Somebody got lucky, but it was an accident," a positively Dylanesque verse from "Pledging My Time" on *Blonde on Blonde*, echoed something Skip James, Robert Johnson, and Blind Willie McTell sang more than thirty years prior. The harmonica opening is like Jimmy Reed circa 1957. The melody is the same as the Mississippi Sheiks' "Sitting on Top of the World" and Johnson's "Come On in My Kitchen." Dylan "takes from the blues because he loves it," Gray wrote presciently in a book published a year *before "Love and Theft"* went on sale, "and then makes of it something his own."

Dylan wasn't doing anything blues and folk singers hadn't always done. Songs were handed down and passed around, mutating as they went, half remembered, patched together with spare parts. Stock phrases migrated from one song to another. Sometimes the new lyrics made sense; sometimes they became non sequiturs.

Gray studied literary criticism in college, and in his book he also plumbed Dylan's borrowings from poetry and fiction. The exquisite line in Dylan's "Tomorrow Is a Long Time" about wanting to lay with his lover once again came from a poem written five hundred years earlier. "Subterranean Homesick Blues" didn't just have the same ironic spirit as Robert Browning, but also some of the same line endings. It struck Gray that a century before Dylan rhymed "sandals," "scandals," and "handles," the English poet had done so.

It said something about Dylan's mash-up methods that the song also mimicked Chuck Berry's "Too Much Monkey Business."

"I like to think of it as deepening a resonance," Gray said. He saw Dylan taking things from the entire back catalog of human culture, and regenerating them. He was finding the innate poetry of a line and releasing it. "You want him to be this lone genius who came from another planet. He never pretended to be. He's created something out of something else. You can't make something from nothing."

Dylan didn't say much about this publicly, even on the occasions when he was asked. He did say once that when he read poems, like Shakespeare's sonnets, he heard guitar accompaniment. "I always keep thinking, *What kind of song would this be?*" The reports of his appropriations circulated in fanzines and dense, small-press studies. They were too picayune for mainstream publications. In 1985, Dylan came out with *Empire Burlesque*, a record beloved by no one, given its gloopy sound, but subjected to the fans' fine-toothed combs nonetheless. They found extensive borrowings from classic films like *Key Largo* and *The Hustler*. John Bauldie, editor of the *Telegraph* fanzine, got a chance to quiz Dylan about it at a London press conference in 1986. He asked Dylan whether he had seen *The Maltese Falcon* before writing the songs. "It was full of lines that sounded as though you could have written them," he said.

The singer played dumb. "I might have seen it. Were there lines from the movie in there?"

"Lots of them," Bauldie answered.

"Were there really?"

"Yeah. Is it one of your favorite films, that?"

"I don't remember. Which lines were they?"

"Do you want a list?"

But before Bauldie could go through it chapter and verse, others jumped in with their own questions, and Dylan escaped unscathed.

3

Scott Warmuth had listened to a little Dylan over the years, but *"Love and Theft"* made him sit up and pay attention. That fall, as the world convulsed following 9/11, Scott had his own crisis. Doctors had found a mass in his chest, and he suffered through weeks of worry before learning it was a benign tumor. Then he had major surgery and an excruciatingly painful recovery. He couldn't play guitar, holding a book was uncomfortable, and he didn't watch television, so he just listened to a lot of music. *"Love and Theft"* was at the top of his playlist for months. It was "very strong medicine." There was a line on "Mississippi," the second track, about how the narrator needs a distraction. Man, how Scott could relate to that. He couldn't tell you how many times he played it as he lay in his bed. "I couldn't go anywhere physically, so I would travel to that world," he said. "I lived there."

A decade later, the album was still in regular rotation at Scott's house, and he was still teasing out its fifty-seven minutes of secrets.

It seemed that all his life Scott had been unwittingly training for this peculiar job. He grew up in suburban Long Island. When Scott was young, his father worked at a vinyl pressing plant, and one of the perks of the job was that he could bring home LPs. They had everything the Doors recorded, and a pile of Judy Collins, the blues and folk music of the day, Moog synthesizer music, 1960s bubblegum records, space-age pop, Engelbert Humperdinck. At ten, Scott would go to the library, where he had learned how to thread microfilm, and dig into the musical backstories of his favorite records. He didn't simply listen to *The Beatles' Second Album*. He researched the men who wrote the songs. That was how he discovered Chuck Berry and Little Richard. He tracked down their records, too, and then, an archaeologist chiseling through sedimentary layers, followed those singers' roots back to music they loved and movies they watched. His library card was always maxed out, with most of the books coming from the 700s: music, photography, art, drawing. He was fascinated by special effects in science fiction and horror films.

If it takes ten thousand hours to become an expert in something, Scott was destined to become a radio disc jockey. When he was old enough to get a cash allowance but too young to drive, he would walk four or five miles to the record shop in the next town. His vinyl filled the shelving that ran the length of a wall in his bedroom. (He now has four thousand records.) He seemed to know everything about every artist, as if he'd memorized the liner notes. "He was the original musical polymath in our neighborhood," says Tom Gogola, who grew up around the block. Scott wore John Lennon glasses and his dark hair freakishly long. Tom called him "the W." Scott was the guy who introduced Tom to the obscure and the eccentric. The more bizarre, the better. If not for this friendship, Tom might never have learned about, say, the big-breasted sexploitation flicks of Russ Meyer (*Faster, Pussycat! Kill! Kill!*) or Stiff Little Fingers, the Belfast punk band. Tom remembers Scott going through one musical phase after another. He had an Elvis period, a big Ramones era, even a B-52s episode.

In high school, Scott was known for being widely read, scarily smart, and wickedly funny, if a little aloof. The guys he ran with called themselves the Friends of the Friendless. He and Tom were enthusiastic teenage tricksters. They found *Frank* Kafka in the phone book and called him up to ask about *The Metamorphosis*. ("I just don't get it!") Scott would dial up the toll-free evangelical phone lines and pretend that he was in need of their help; his house filled up with their free literature and tapes. For a while, Scott's gang ran a routine at the local 7-Elevens. One of them would buy a Hostess cherry fruit pie, Scott would come in screaming gibberish like a lu-

natic and smash it to pieces on the counter, and as the buyer chased
him outside, Tom would eat the chunks—*Mmmm, that's good!*—and
stare at the cashier. They gave it up after one 7-Eleven manager came
after them wielding an ax handle spiked with nails.

Scott had been playing guitar since age eight. Early on, he got
together with friends and they recorded themselves playing whatever
they could. (He has a tape of them playing the head-banging riff
from Black Sabbath's "Iron Man" for half an hour.) In high school
and college he played in a number of bands: the Vogways, Blind
from Wild Turkey, Psychedelicatessen. He was briefly in a hardcore
punk band called Six and Violence.

But on air was where he found his home. His first radio show was
on the high school station. For years he volunteered at WUSB, the
noncommercial community radio station on the campus of Stony
Brook University, where he went to college. After he graduated, he
worked his way up to music director and hosted programs, including the Drive-In Show on Friday afternoons. Slipping into a cheesy
persona ("Why don't you get smart and call your old buddy Scott,
632-6901—that's the number for *fun!*"), he would play vintage advertisements and old movie trailers between garage bands and surfer
rock. He got married and moved to Albuquerque, where his first
gig was spinning records and performing at a 1950s restaurant and
car museum named YesterDave's. It looked like the set of the dance
scene in *Pulp Fiction*. Over the years he worked half the stations in
town. He did Big Oldies 98.5 and 100.3 the Peak and Sunny 95.1.
For a while, he could be heard on three different stations at the same
time. He loved the work. He studied music with a fan's passion and
a scholar's painstaking attention to detail. He could play you thirty
songs that Elvis Presley admired. He could name every singer who
recorded, say, "Tequila," or "These Boots Are Made for Walkin'."
Once, he produced a two-and-a-half-hour radio special on "Surfin'

Bird" by the Trashmen. Most people would consider it a novelty tune; Scott decided to research its origins, place it in a cultural context, and tell the definitive story.

One of the acts he loved was the Cramps, a "psychobilly" band founded in the 1970s by Lux Interior and his wife, Poison Ivy. Lux was known for stage antics that would make you think twice about getting too close. He might appear in low-rise black leather pants, mascara, and a crucifix—a cross-dressing goth. "It was kind of scary being in the front row," wrote Henry Rollins, frontman for the hardcore punk band Black Flag. "Lux would find something to swing from—if there were ceiling tiles, they'd all be on the floor by the end of the thing. Lux would somehow find his way out of his pants and be down to a pair of bikini briefs twitching all over the floor." The Cramps incorporated 1950s kitsch, horror, surfer music, rockabilly, punk. Lux sang lines like "Vampire lesbos are after me!" They once played a mental hospital in Napa.

Most people didn't take them very seriously, but Scott was fascinated with how the Cramps fabricated their songs from bits of pop culture—music and art and obscure films. Their rollicking song "Naked Girl Falling Down the Stairs" is a comic homage to Marcel Duchamp's modernist painting. ("Lux is really into Duchamp," his wife said. "I think if Duchamp hadn't died in Lux's lifetime, I'd think that Lux was reincarnated as Duchamp.") He found another line, "swirling through the vortex," in a how-to guide for astral projection—out-of-body experiences. Scott liked the way the Cramps took what they saw and then twisted it. "I liked that it had roots," he said. "It was thrilling to me. I wanted to know more. So I dove into it."

If anybody was primed to take what Chris Johnson found in that bookstore in Japan and turn it into his life's work, it was Scott, whose encyclopedic brain seemed to hold whatever he dug up in his research. As it happened, the primary tool in this effort would be his computer. Dylan had expected to keep the band of Dylanologists busy for a long time after his death. He said it would take a hundred years for people to figure him out. But he probably didn't foresee the scope of the Internet, and in particular Google Books. When the company started digitally scanning books of major libraries and making the pages available and searchable, the work of sourcing Dylan's lyrics became exponentially easier for the diggers.

Over time, Scott and others began unpacking *"Love and Theft."* The record amazed Scott. It showed hard work and focus and craft. The way Dylan juxtaposed the surreptitious quotes was intricate, and often funny. It rewarded repeat listens and careful study. "He takes all these lines from all these places," Scott said, "and they all come off as Dylanesque." In the opening track, "Tweedle Dee & Tweedle Dum," Dylan sings about various sets of twins, duos, and brothers, and the thefts harken back to earlier works on the theme. The characters in the title are best known as the copycats from Lewis Carroll. The Land of Nod is where Biblical Cain was exiled after killing his brother. "Your presence is obnoxious to me" comes from a minstrel sketch involving a woman who rents the same apartment to two men and they don't know it, since one works all night and one works all day. "Stab you where you stand" is a line in the Edgar Allan Poe short story "William Wilson," about a man and his doppelgänger. In a 1932 movie about circus freaks, one of the Siamese twins says, "Her master's voice is calling." The distinctive guitar riff comes from a 1961 rockabilly song called "Uncle John's Bongos" by Johnnie & Jack, who were brothers-in-law.

Scott made another, more surprising connection. The lyrics have a certain New Orleans flavor. Dylan sings of "a street car named Desire" and quotes that Mardi Gras cry "Throw me somethin', mister!" But Scott contended that the song is also seasoned with hidden references from a more pedestrian source, a travel guide to New Orleans. A throwaway phrase in a restaurant review finds a home on *"Love and Theft"* (and became something more grisly in the transference): Brains cooking in a pot are "dripping in garlic and olive oil." To those who thought it sounded like a coincidence, Scott pointed out that Dylan lifted several other phrases from the travel guide, including the clunky phrase "a multi-thousand-dollar gown."

Later, he discovered on "Tweedle Dee" bits of obscure recordings by the New Lost City Ramblers, an influential Village folk-revival band dedicated to old-time music. As these references piled up, Scott started thinking more about Dylan's musical template, "Uncle John's Bongos." He didn't think it was a coincidental choice. One of the founders of the Ramblers was John Cohen, who had been celebrated on the Grateful Dead's anthem "Uncle John's Band." The writer, Robert Hunter, sprinkled that song with nods to the band's recordings—just as Dylan had done here. (It's also worth noting that Hunter and Dylan have written some songs together over the years.) Scott figured that by tucking the hidden references into "Tweedle Dee," Dylan wanted to underscore how important the Ramblers were to him, and to folk music. His argument is bolstered by *Chronicles*, in which Dylan praises the band extravagantly. "All their songs vibrated with some dizzy, portentous truth."

None of Scott's detective work happened in a linear way; unraveling the threads took years. A decade after the release of *"Love and Theft,"* he and the others weren't done yet. And while they worked, Dylan continued to issue new recordings that were ripe for study.

In 2005, he released a song on a movie soundtrack called "Tell Ol' Bill." It's gloomy and cryptic: the tortured inner monologue of a man navigating a bleak landscape alone. "Secret thoughts are hard to bear," he sings. The specter of a lost love seems to hang over everything. Dylan's melody hews faithfully to "I Never Loved but One" by the Carter Family. Both songs' narrators wish for "one smiling face" to comfort them. "All my body glows with flame," Dylan sings, a curious line that appeared in the poem "The Geranium" by Richard Brinsley Sheridan (1751–1816). The poet put the phrase in the mouth of a woman convulsed in amorous rapture, for the flower is not just a flower. Dylan drew from two other poems of tragically lost love. The phrase "lying restless in heavy bed" was sixteenth-century Elizabethan poet Edmund Spenser's; the "thunder-blasted trees" were Poe's—like his narrator, they will bloom "no more." Dylan also seemed to be recycling the opening of an old folk song called "Old Bill" about a man who leaves his home in the morning and returns in "de hurry-up wagon"—a hearse—with "his toe-nails a-draggin'" following an encounter with a .38. "Oh, no, dat cain' be so," his wife cries out. Finding these allusions felt like opening up doors into new rooms where the same scene played out ad infinitum.

A diligent digger could find other echoes. Were those Virgil's "iron clouds," the ones that portend doom in his epic poem? And was that a snippet from *Don Quixote*? And was that French general Joseph Joffre speaking before the first Battle of Marne in 1914? The songs of Late Dylan are filled with rabbit holes like those, obscurities that could be allusions or could be the products of hyperactive Internet searches and overactive imaginations.

In 2006, annotators were given a new record to contend with, *Modern Times*. Studying the songs, Scott made a significant discovery: Dylan was reusing poetry by a forgotten Civil War–era Charleston native named Henry Timrod. "A round of precious hours," goes a poem published in 1857. "Oh! here, where in that summer noon I basked, / And strove, with logic frailer than the flowers." A century and a half later, Dylan sang, "More frailer than the flowers, these precious hours." Warmuth posted the find online, and within a week he had tracked down a dozen more phrases from Timrod in six songs. (He even found Timrod on "Tweedle Dee & Tweedle Dum.")

A story about the borrowings from Timrod made the *New York Times*, and that prompted Edward Cook, a Dylan fan and Dead Sea Scrolls scholar at Catholic University in Washington, D.C., to poke around in *Chronicles*.

The memoir started out as liner notes for reissues of three old records, and in the process it turned into something closer to autobiography. "I got completely carried away in the process of . . . I guess call it, 'novelistic writing,'" Dylan said. He didn't love the work; as all authors know, when you're writing a book you're not living your life. As he worked on it, he told music journalists that he was struggling. "My retrievable memory, it goes blank on incidents and things that have happened." So he was gathering stories about his life from others and using them, even if he knew them to be untrue. "I'll take some of the stuff that people *think* is true and I'll build a story around that." But when the book came out in 2004, Dylan said he had surprised himself. His memory had come back to him. "I found I could visualize what people looked like and what they were wearing and even how particular rooms were furnished." The memoir "set the record straight," Dylan told one journalist. He assured another that "when you write a book like this, you gotta tell the truth, and it can't be misinterpreted."

Even on the surface, *Chronicles* was an idiosyncratic book. Dylan told the story of arriving in New York and making it big; of dealing with fame in the late 1960s and early 1970s; of losing his way and struggling to record 1989's *Oh Mercy*. When it appeared, critics hailed the book for its candor. But Dylan had skipped over what biographers considered the stations of the cross: *Highway 61 Revisited*, Newport in 1965, the motorcycle accident, his marriage(s), the turmoil that led him to write *Blood on the Tracks*. The stories he chose to tell didn't ring true to people who had followed Dylan's life and career closely. Of course, anyone who expected the master fabulist to play it straight this time had not been paying attention all these years. Still, even considering the elastic rules of the memoir genre, *Chronicles* was notably unreliable.

But it wasn't until 2006 that anyone realized something else: Not all the words were his.

Given the Timrod discoveries in *Modern Times*, Cook decided to check out a few oddly distinctive phrases from a section about a couple who put Dylan up during his early days in the Village. The words had jumped out at Cook earlier when he tried to figure out whether the pair, Ray Gooch and Chloe Kiel, were real or not. (Probably not, he concluded.) When Cook searched the phrases online, he turned up jazz musician Mezz Mezzrow's 1946 book, *Really the Blues*, which was about a "white kid who fell in love with black culture." The book is full of jive, and Mezzrow describes a woman as "a Maltese kitten" and "a solid viper"—a pot smoker. Those were the exact words Dylan used to describe Chloe; he also threw in another bit of Mezzrow jive talk from later in the book, "cool as pie."

Cook didn't do anything with this information at first. For a week, he didn't tell *anybody*. He just enjoyed the sensation. He had a secret with Dylan. "It would be the only time I would have a Bob Dylan moment," he said. Cook also wanted to see what else was there. He reread *Chronicles* with a more critical eye and things started to jump out at him, things that looked suspicious. He found a line from Proust, and a phrase lifted from *Adventures of Huckleberry Finn*. When you find one or two thefts like that, he said, "you suspect *everything*."

Finally, Cook posted his discoveries on his blog with some critical words. He considered it "pretty close to real plagiarism." Borrowing material for songs was standard in the folk music world. But he had a problem with Dylan appropriating others' words in his book. "He's being lazy," he says. "You kind of want someone to earn it if they're going to get praise as a great writer. It ticks me off."

His piece was the beginning of a reappraisal of *Chronicles* by students of Dylan. The post started circulating among fans, and soon made its way to Scott.

He read it and sighed.

"Great," he told himself. "Now I've got the next couple of years booked."

4

Scott once sent me a little riddle, a bite-size taste of what he had been up against. "On page five of *Chronicles: Volume One* our chronic argonaut uses material from a classic work of science fiction in a most interesting way. It is in the first paragraph, see if you can find it." On the page, Dylan was describing John Hammond, the great-grandson of a Vanderbilt who as a talent scout and record producer had played an instrumental role in the careers of Billie Holiday, Count Basie, Charlie Christian, Aretha Franklin, and many others, including Dylan. Hammond "had been raised in the upper world, in comfort and ease—but he wasn't satisfied and he had followed his own heart's love, music . . ."

Latching onto that sci-fi phrase, "the upper world," I got to work. I pulled out "The Chronic Argonauts," an H.G. Wells short story from 1888, and read it straight through with Dylan in mind. Would he have appreciated this idea of a man lost in time, as Dylan had so often seemed? But there was no mention of "the upper world" there. Next I tapped "H.G. Wells" and "the upper world" into Google and discovered a section of *The Time Machine*. In the book, a man travels to the year 802,701, where he discovers humanity split into two races, the Eloi, a weak, indolent, unintelligent upper-world people, and the Morlocks, an apelike people who live underground and feed on the Eloi. Lamenting how the upper-world Eloi had devolved into ignorant frailty over generations, the time traveler "grieved to think how brief the dream of the human intellect had been. It had committed suicide. It had set itself steadfastly toward comfort and ease."

To Scott's thinking, this was Dylan's peculiar and hidden way of expressing contempt for an empty upper-class world, and his respect for a man who could have lived a pointless life of inherited wealth and privilege but instead made something of himself. It took me a couple of hours to unravel—there were other dead ends—and without Scott's hint I would never have thought to look.

Scott came to think Dylan had sprinkled hidden subtexts on nearly every one of the memoir's 293 pages. He compared notes via e-mail with Cook, who continued to dig up references, and soon Scott's working copy of *Chronicles* was filled with marginalia: Jack London on page 173, Henry Miller on page 174, Thomas Wolfe on page 175. They found Dylan recycling from magazines, novels popular and obscure, even the Internet.

One discovery came when Scott poked around in a section of the memoir about *Oh Mercy* that was set in New Orleans, where the album was recorded. It only seemed natural to check the same travel guide he had linked to "Tweedle Dee." His instincts were right. The guide described "pigeons looking for handouts" and a Cajun band's "chinka-chinka beat." Ten years later, Dylan used the same words in *Chronicles*.

A while later, Scott found that Dylan mined the March 31, 1961, issue of *Time* while writing about the era when his career took off. Dylan helped himself to descriptions of life in Hanoi and observations about nuclear-bomb "worriers." One article in the issue about the "Age of Anxiety" noted the prevailing wisdom that anyone could do or become anything, that "housewives can become glamour girls," that "the slow-witted can become intellectuals," and that "the indecisive can become leaders of men." Dylan swiped the line and then appended a gag: "If you were an indecisive person, you could become a leader and wear lederhosen."

In writing about the topical songs that 1960s folksingers wrote based on stories in the newspapers of the day, Dylan listed head-lines from a 1936 John Dos Passos novel, a work that itself used cut-up writing techniques. Dylan secretly paired Mark Twain with *The Return of Dr. Fu Manchu*, a 1916 novel by British novelist Sax Rohmer. Shelley verse was in one paragraph, Hemingway in the next.

Dylan's appropriations were not random. They were deliberate. When Scott delved into them, he found cleverness, wordplay, jokes, and subtexts. To portray the bearded, gruff folksinger Dave Van Ronk, a Greenwich Village denizen, Dylan chose the description of a wolf-dog in a Jack London story and melded it with a line about New Yorkers from a city travel guide. Scott found dozens of bor-rowings from London, and that was telling in and of itself: London had been accused of plagiarism in his time. By weaving these hidden quotations into *Chronicles*, Scott argued, Dylan was acknowledging that he is a product of his influences, that his voice is "an amalgam of the voices of so many others."

In 2010, Scott's friend Tom Gogola helped him get a piece in the *New Haven Review*, and his ideas began circulating widely in Dylan circles. His blog became a must-read for fans. "*Chronicles: Volume One* is loaded with things to be decoded," Scott wrote. "I think of it as *The Da Vinci Code* of rock 'n' roll." But he didn't believe Dylan had written the book in bad faith; he had just hidden another book between the lines. Scott thought Dylan was an artist toying with his audience. He loved it. He presented every find with the joy of a person solving a brain teaser.

A few guys longed for the old days, before everything was a search-engine click away. Peter Stone Brown followed Scott's work closely and he found the discoveries interesting. But he had misgivings about Scott's approach. "With each new Googled discovery," he wrote, "he seems more and more like a cat waiting behind a door ready to pounce on the next moving object." Peter would appreciate it more if Scott were reading widely and happened to stumble on the antecedents of Dylan's lyrics in the process. That was how Peter found the subter-ranean scriptural roots of "I Pity the Poor Immigrant." He read the Bible. Fans caught Dylan's musical borrowings because they knew those old folk songs; they owned the records.

Scott acknowledged that search engines made it possible for any-body to track down this stuff, not just scholars well versed in the classics or poetry or some other arcane field of study. But even so, it took time and effort, as the H.G. Wells example demonstrated. It was trickier than people might have imagined. "If it was so easy," Scott said, "there'd be fifty blogs like mine."

Some people doubted his conclusions. How did Scott know the matches weren't coincidental? Many apparent borrowings seemed like commonplace phrases. Was it not possible that Dylan had a photo-graphic memory for the things he had read? Couldn't he have a brain that worked differently from ours, one that sponged up choice bits of language, which he then unwittingly spat back out? Doubtful, Scott answered. Neither coincidence nor an overactive memory would ex-plain how seven phrases appeared on pages 203–04 of *Chronicles* that resembled the 1998 book *Confederates in the Attic* by best-selling au-thor Tony Horwitz: "an overhanging porch with support beams that had long ago rotted away"; "oiled ringlets"; "in the trees, a solitary bird warbling"; "moss covered logs"; a bumper sticker that reads "WORLD'S

GREATEST GRANDPA"; "hog parts hanging from hooks on walls—hog jowls, hog ears"; and "make you wanna squeal." (Horwitz was flattered. He only wished Dylan had cribbed lines for a song.)

This was not an exact science. I spent some time poking around on page 153, where Dylan described his epiphany in Locarno, Switzerland. He wrote that as he had struggled to sing that night, he managed to conjure up "some different type of mechanism to jump-start the other techniques that weren't working." Curious to see what I would find using Scott's approach, I searched "mechanism," "jump-start," and "techniques." Up popped page 27 of *The Complete Idiot's Guide to Singing*. File under: It couldn't be. (Could it?) Scott had a long list of phrases that could have been borrowed but more likely were not.

Some people seemed upset that anybody went searching at all. As if to even look for this stuff was tantamount to questioning the legend. Scott began to feel like he was moving too fast for people, even those who already accepted the idea that Dylan was doing some borrowing. Scott would make a claim, and they would say, *Now you've gone off the deep end*. He shrugged off the doubters. He had spent his life listening to and playing American popular music. He thought maybe he had developed "a freakish ability" to see what other people couldn't.

"I don't think that I'm inventive enough to dream up these impossible claims," he said.

Eventually people would come around.

5

The drip-drip-drip of discoveries divided Dylan's community of followers. People took sides. Over here, Dylan was lambasted as a thief of intellectual property, a copyright violator, and a plagiarist. Over there, he was doing what artists had done for all time. He was celebrated as a creator of "modernist collages." He was blurring the lines "between past and present . . . high art and low, scholarly and popular, exotic and familiar," Princeton historian Sean Wilentz wrote in *Bob Dylan in America*. "Dylan created a new magic zone where it was 1933 and 1863 and 2006 all at once, where the full complexity of human nature might still be glimpsed." He was a conjurer communicating with literary, musical, and cinematic ghosts.

No Dylan fan wrote more eloquently about his disappointment in Dylan than a librarian and poet in England named Roy Kelly. He came of age in the 1960s, so he experienced the albums contemporaneously, unlike someone who had to piece them together later. His manner was friendly if fussy. He'd written all his life, producing lush short stories, formal English poetry, and lengthy pieces with literary ambition for two of the Dylan fanzines, John Bauldie's *Telegraph* and its successor, the *Bridge*. He once wrote a piece about "Ron Bobfan," a fictional conglomeration of Kelly and Bauldie, sprinkled with bits of every other fan he had known. Looking back on the wonder and genius of Dylan circa 1966, Ron is filled with self-conscious nostalgia and melancholy, a longing for the time when his hero was so original and fresh, when listening to him was so . . . uncomplicated.

When *Chronicles* appeared, Kelly gave it a glowing review in the *Bridge*. Dylan, this man who onstage seems to be "deliberately absenting himself" from interaction with his audience, suddenly slung an arm around readers' shoulders and laid out his story. Kelly was deeply unsettled to find out that the words were not all Dylan's. "What did we praise him for then?" he says now. He felt misled, foolish, and let down—*personally* let down. Why not acknowledge his sources in some way? Why pass it off as his own? It prompted him to question not just the memoir but the music and the man. Was he entirely inauthentic? "All songs by Bob Dylan," the liner notes read. Kelly had believed that. He couldn't feel quite the same way about a cut-and-paste man. "It just bothers me," he says. "And I can't be unbothered now."

This squeamishness about artistic appropriation makes Jonathan Lethem practically foam at the mouth. Lethem, the best-selling author of *The Fortress of Solitude* and seven other novels, grew up in a bohemian, communal, countercultural household in a racially mixed neighborhood in Brooklyn. "The first time I realized that there were still people alive who thought rock 'n' roll sounded like noise, I laughed. I was like, *Really? You can still think that?* I thought this stuff was canonical for a thousand years." He lived in a bubble: He spent the 1970s wrapping his head around the idea that the hippies had *not* won. His parents were political activists who marched against the war. Lethem came from a place so left-wing that he couldn't even visualize a Republican. "Everybody knew Nixon was a vampire, right?" He thinks of people who get hung up on Dylan's writing technique in the same way. Are there really people who believe the words just poured out of his heart, totally original, unsullied by influences? Do they really think his songs open a window on his soul?

Lethem's mother had a "streak of yippie in her." She dropped out of Queens College in 1962 and ran away to the Greenwich Village folk scene. She hung around with Dave Van Ronk, knew Tuli Kupferberg, dated Phil Ochs, met Dylan once. After "Like a Rolling Stone" came out, the story in the Lethem household was that one of their Siamese cats inspired the line about riding on the chrome horse with the diplomat. The Lethems bred them, and his mother had given one to Ochs, who carried it around on his shoulder. "I don't know whether to believe it," Lethem says. "It was what I was told growing up."

The point is that his parents were invested in Dylan, and the myth was intimate. This was a catechism: Bob Dylan was the artist of their generation. "He was like total received information for me, part and parcel of coming of age in my family." He had to reject Dylan for a time and find his way back to him. At fifteen, Lethem claimed *Slow Train* Dylan as his own. The Christian era didn't bother him because, like rock music haters and Republicans, he considered fundamentalist born-agains figments of the imagination. *Slow Train* was like the science fiction Lethem devoured.

In 2007, *Harper's* published an essay by Lethem about creative borrowing that was itself cobbled together almost entirely from other sources; he outlined what came from where at the end of the article. Quotation is essential to creativity, Lethem argued. "The kernel, the soul—let us go further and say the substance, the bulk, the actual and valuable material of all human utterances—is plagiarism."

"*Original* is a fascinating word," Lethem told me. "People throw it around all the time. 'Oh, that was so original.' They mean they don't know where it came from." What he means is that everything comes from somewhere else. The most original writers—Updike, Hemingway, Beckett—all of them started by imitating those who came before. Lethem was incredulous that this was even a matter of discussion in the Dylan world. People who felt let down had been invested in a misunderstanding. Talking about it sent him into fits.

"Who *cares*?" he says. "If you don't want to know, don't know! Just enjoy what you're given. The thing that affected you is still exactly as it is. The sources are also still exactly as they were. If you want to read *Confessions of a Yakuza*, Dylan has not fucked it up for you. It's right there. Go read that. Now both things exist. Why would that *not* be better? *Chronicles* is still exactly what it is. It still does what it does. It's spellbinding. Dylan could have phoned in a book. This is Dylan making something for us. How can you complain? I just don't get it."

Everybody steals, Dylan's defenders cry. T.S. Eliot's *The Waste Land* was filled with allusive borrowings. William Burroughs sliced up sentences from newspapers and books and inserted the words in his own work. "All writing is in fact cut-ups," Burroughs said. "A collage of words read heard overheard." The Dadas suggested cutting up an article from a newspaper, putting the slips in a bag, shaking it, then pulling out the words and copying them down in order to form a new poem. French New Wave filmmaker Jean-Luc Godard was unapologetic about quoting material without acknowledgment. "Everything is a remix," argues Kirby Ferguson in a series of Web videos showing how Steve Jobs swiped ideas from his competitors when he built the Macintosh computer, and how George Lucas copied classic films to make *Star Wars*. It's an idea for our time. We live in an age of sampling.

Surely, Dylan knew that his appropriations would not go unnoticed, argued poet and scholar Stephen Scobie. "Dylan knows that all his work is subject to intense scrutiny; he must surely have expected that his 'sources' would sooner or later be revealed. There is no intent to deceive: rather, there is an invitation to join the game." It was hard not to read some sections of *Chronicles* as thinly veiled answers to his detractors. Dylan writes about playing *King of the Delta Blues Singers* for an unimpressed Van Ronk. "He kept pointing out that this song comes from another song and that one song was an exact replica of a different song," Dylan wrote. "He didn't think Johnson was very original. I knew what he meant, but I thought just the opposite. I thought Johnson was as original as could be."

In 2003, he described for a music writer how he meditated: by playing songs in his head. He may do it while he's driving, or sitting around, even having a conversation. "People will think they are talking to me and I'm talking back, but I'm not. I'm listening to the song in my head," he said. "At a certain point, some of the words will change and I'll start writing a song."

Other hints leaked out about how Dylan worked. Joni Mitchell recalled him telling her sometime in the second half of his career that he was having trouble writing. She told him that couldn't be, and cited some recent song he had written.

"Oh," Dylan told her, "the box wrote it."

"What do you mean, *the box*?"

"I write down things from movies and things I've heard people say," Dylan said, "and I throw them in the box."

"I don't care where you get your bits and pieces," she replied. "You still put them all together."

Larry Charles saw Dylan's box in action. In 2001, the TV writer, director, and producer was summoned to discuss doing a television series with the singer. Dylan and Charles instead ended up cowriting a movie, *Masked and Anonymous*, in which Dylan starred alongside John Goodman, Jeff Bridges, Jessica Lange, and Penelope Cruz. When he walked into the first meeting, Charles said he found a box on the table. Dylan dumped it, and out came scraps of paper, some of it hotel stationery. Every piece had a phrase or name or aphorism scrawled on it. These were Dylan's building blocks.

In 2012, Dylan finally dropped the pretenses with a remarkable answer to a question from *Rolling Stone*. At seventy-one, it turned out, he had not mellowed. He was as blunt and bitter as ever. He called his borrowings "quotation," and noted that it was a tradition in folk and jazz. His critics, he complained, were holding him to a different standard.

"And as far as Henry Timrod is concerned," Dylan said, "have you even heard of him? Who's been reading him lately? And who's pushed him to the forefront? Who's been making you read him? And ask his descendants what they think of the hoopla. And if you think it's so easy to quote him and it can help your work, do it yourself and see how far you can get. Wussies and pussies complain about that stuff. It's an old thing—it's part of the tradition. It goes way back.

"These are the same people that tried to pin the name Judas on me. Judas, the most hated name in human history! If you think you've been called a bad name, try to work your way out from under that. Yeah, and for what? For playing an electric guitar? As if that is in some kind of way equitable to betraying our Lord and delivering him up to be crucified. All those evil motherfuckers can rot in hell."

The interviewer, Mikal Gilmore, was taken aback. "Seriously?"

"It's called songwriting," Dylan continued. "It has to do with melody and rhythm, and then after that, anything goes. You make everything yours. We all do it."

6

Scott stayed out of the exhausting debates about whether Dylan was a plagiarist or not, and instead zeroed in on how specific borrowings worked. Much of *Chronicles* and many songs had been annotated, but the hard work of understanding Late Dylan really had only just begun.

People started to wonder how Scott had learned so much about the borrowings that Dylan hid in his writing. Some guessed that he was supremely well read. One asked if he was using some special software. Another theorized that Scott had access to Dylan's private papers. "I am very curious about Mr. Warmuth's methods," one follower of the blog wrote on an online forum. "I've often half-wondered if he isn't somehow linked to Dylan's people, like Dylan is trying to get the word out about it himself. After having read most of Mr. Warmuth's works, I'm pretty convinced." It amused Scott that people had built him into an enigmatic figure like Dylan himself. But maybe it was to be expected.

Scott's research took him into surprising fields, and he brought readers of his increasingly popular blog along for the ride. He studied circus sideshows, puzzle solving, cryptography, and magic. He searched for inspiration in *The Code Book: The Science of Secrecy from Ancient Egypt to Quantum Cryptography*. He read books about cheating at cards. He studied the ways Vladimir Nabokov used ciphers and hidden allusions. All the while he searched for ways past Dylan's defenses. Trying to figure out how Dylan might have hidden things, he contacted magicians and talked to pitchmen; maybe it would be helpful to learn a few of their tricks. He searched out people who performed in medicine shows. As it turned out, more than a few of them were Dylan fans.

Every September the New Mexico state fair set up shop at the expo grounds at the foot of the Sandia Mountains in Albuquerque. Scott loved the carnies and pitchmen, who seemed to represent the seedier reality lurking behind the fair's friendly, gaudy veneer. He liked to sit and watch the man who gave the elaborate pitch for expensive stainless-steel pots and pans, and the guy who sold trick toy worms for five bucks each. The midway had a snake woman. "Stop. Wait," a disembodied voice said from above the tent. "How could this ever come to be? The strangest illusion of all time—the head of a lovely girl, and the body of an ugly snake." One year, Scott struck up a conversation with the keeper of the World's Smallest Horse, a man named Ray. The tiny beast had lived with Ray for three years. He liked television and was pretty well housebroken, unless you didn't get the door open right away. Scott and Ray got to talking about the carny life, and Ray slipped into a jive that may as well have been a foreign tongue. For most of his forty-three-year career, he had worked rigged games called "flat joints," and as he told Scott about this, he slipped into memorized and barely intelligible patter. If you didn't understand it, that was exactly the point. Ray's idea was to relieve you of your wallet. Scott got to know all kinds of circus slang. Carnival "talkers" used chatter ("bally") to drum up audiences at sideshow tents. "Turning the tip" was when a talker converted lollygaggers into paying customers. And "G.T.F.M." was a carny slogan: Get The Fucking Money.

Scott's hypothesis was a work in progress, unfolding blog post by blog post, but the more he thought about Late Dylan, the more he saw the ethos of the carnival life. He called his blog Goon Talk, which is carny slang for carny slang. Understand this world, Scott thought, and maybe he could understand what Dylan was doing when he offered up something original and it turned out to be pastiche. Maybe the man who took from high culture and low and melded them into art was not so far removed from the pitchmen and con men at the circus.

Scott began to think of Dylan as a charlatan of sorts. He didn't mean that the singer was a fraud. Instead he thought of Dylan as a fabulous illusionist. He wasn't what he appeared to be. "Magicians do what con men do," Scott wrote, "except that the audience knows an illusion is being created." The singer had been fascinated by the freak show all his life. He told early interviewers that he had joined the circus as a child. His 1965 song "Ballad of a Thin Man" sends clueless Mr. Jones through a sideshow, where he is accosted by a sword swallower, a geek, and a one-eyed midget. The 1975–76 Rolling Thunder Revue mimicked a carnival: a caravan of performers would show up in some town with little announcement, make a spectacle, then disappear. Years later, on a TV ad for *"Love and Theft,"* Dylan played cards with master magician and actor Ricky Jay. For ten years, Dylan opened his concerts with an introduction taken almost verbatim from a gushing *Buffalo News* story in 2002. "Ladies and gentlemen," the patter went, "*please* welcome the poet laureate of rock 'n' roll, the voice of the promise of the sixties counterculture, the guy who forced folk into bed with rock, who donned makeup in the seventies and disappeared into a haze of substance abuse, who emerged to 'find Jesus,' who was written off as a has-been by the end of the eighties, and who suddenly shifted gears, releasing some of the strongest music of his career beginning in the late nineties."

"That's bally!" Scott says. *Step right up, folks, and feast your eyes on this!* It was the nonsense shtick outside a sideshow exhibit.

In the movie he made with Larry Charles, *Masked and Anonymous*, Dylan played a failed musical messiah. Reviewing the movie, the *New York Times* marveled about the mythology Dylan had built up around himself since arriving in the city in 1961. "His lifelong foraging in the overgrown pastures of American popular culture has taught him that the true prophet is often indistinguishable from the snake-oil salesman, and his gaunt, weathered frame contains both personas."

Dylan ruminated about prophets and false prophets three decades earlier in liner notes to 1967's *John Wesley Harding*, the record he released after the motorcycle wreck that amplified his mystique. Dylan lampooned three wise men who search for the key to the songs. "The key is Frank!" the men decide, and they visit an apparently ordinary man named Frank. Mr. Dylan has come out with a new record, they tell Frank, and they have been led to believe that he is the key. "Could you please open it up for us?" they ask.

"And just how far would you like to go in?"

"Not too far but just far enough so's we can say we've been there," one replies.

Frank puts on a great show for them, tearing off his shirt and punching his fist through a window, and the kings leave happy.

Read Scott's findings about *Chronicles* long enough and you get an unsettling feeling in the pit of your stomach. You feel like the police detective in the last scene of *The Usual Suspects*. On the trail of Keyser Söze, he spends the entire film questioning a man played by Kevin Spacey who says he worked for the legendary killer. At the end of the film, the detective figures out—just a moment too late—that the man in his office all day *was* Söze, and the mastermind had been concocting an elaborate cover story using words and names and images he found on the office walls.

"I know that he wanted to understand me more as we went along," Dylan wrote in *Chronicles* about Daniel Lanois, who produced *Oh Mercy* and *Time Out of Mind*, "but you can't do that, not unless you like to do puzzles." This was a little elbow nudge for the attuned reader. Like an illusionist, he was commenting on what he was doing while he was doing it. "It was always right in front of you, blended together," he wrote elsewhere in the memoir, "but you'd have to pull it apart to make any sense of it." Dylan also tipped his hand in interviews when the book was released. "*Chronicles* just means—I'm not sure what it means, but it would seem to be some kind of thing where you can make right use of the past," Dylan said. The tell was so subtle that you'd read right over it if you weren't clued in to the ruse.

If anything exemplified that this memoir was a game for Dylan, it came in a description of a guitar technique Dylan said he learned from blues singer Lonnie Johnson. Musicians who read *Chronicles* puzzled over this "highly controlled system of playing." It didn't seem to make sense. Then Scott figured out why: It had been cobbled together from parts of *The 48 Laws of Power* by Robert Greene. The book was a Machiavellian tome for the twenty-first century, and some of the advice could have come straight from Dylan's career.

Law 3: "Conceal Your Intentions."

Law 17: "Cultivate an Air of Unpredictability."

Law 25: "Re-create Yourself."

The phrases Dylan used came from a section of *48 Laws* called "The Science of Charlatanism, or How to Create a Cult in Five Easy Steps." It didn't matter exactly what he took from the chapter. The hidden suggestion that he was reading it—and so closely!—was too rich. "Always in a rush to believe in something, we will manufacture saints and faiths out of nothing," the chapter read. "Do not let this gullibility go to waste: Make yourself the object of worship. Make people form a cult around you." Greene wrote that the skilled charlatan should communicate ambiguously. "To emphasize your gathering's quasi-religious nature, talk and act like a prophet. You are not a dictator, after all; you are a priest, a guru, a sage, a shaman."

Finding something as devious and clever as that was what kept Scott at his desk picking through Dylan's midden field. He couldn't understand those who minimized the pursuit, as if appropriation was just Dylan's writing "style" and there was little point in figuring out what came from where, and how it changed the meaning of the words. Scott was particularly infuriated with Wilentz, the Princeton professor, author, and "historian-in-residence" at Dylan's official website. In *Bob Dylan in America*, Wilentz dismissed the diggers as "censorious sleuths" and minimized Dylan's appropriations. "Discovering a few phrases lifted from Mark Twain and Jack London in a book so engaging, fluid, and generous as *Chronicles* would not have been sufficient grounds for daring to knock a national treasure." To Scott, it was as if Wilentz were a policeman waving people past a five-car pileup. *Nothing to see here, folks, move along!* "It cuts the conversation short," Scott says.

Scott was no A.J. Weberman, as some critics claimed. He wasn't looking for an answer key or a master code. He wasn't trying to expose Dylan as a phony. He wasn't on some unholy mission to tear him down. He was having the time of his life working out an elaborately constructed puzzle linking his twin loves, music and books.

What he learned made Dylan's work richer. Songs suddenly spoke to the past. The memoir became a hall of mirrors. He was delving into worlds he never knew existed. What, exactly, was wrong with that?

"If you like someone's work," he once wrote on his blog, "the important thing is to be exposed to everything that person has been exposed to."

P.S., he added: Dylan said that first.

7

"IT'S WORTHLESS"

At the British Telecom building in the center of London on a Sunday afternoon, fire alarms were going off.

Alone in the office, Andrew Muir was coming unhinged. "I don't know what to do," he told his wife on the phone over the ear-splitting noise. "I'm in big, big trouble!" Andy's job—employee computer training at the phone company—occupied maybe three hours a day. He knew he should have been using the extra time to advance his career, but instead he spent it writing and editing a Bob Dylan fan magazine. He ordinarily produced the zine, titled *Homer, the slut*, on a bulky copier set up in the corner of his living room. But after he had published a few issues, the Virgin record store ordered up 750 copies, more than double what Andy had been sending out to subscribers. He would need to run off thirty-five thousand sheets, double-sided. If he had been thinking sensibly, he would have hired a professional printer to do the work. Instead Andy used his day off and half a dozen British Telecom copy machines.

He had been at it since eight in the morning, walking from one copier to the next, collating pages, adding paper, keeping things in order. Then something tripped the alarm. He was completely confused. He didn't smell smoke. He didn't see anything ablaze. Had making thousands of copies somehow generated enough heat to mimic a fire? Andy was too panicked to find out. It was 1992, and the Irish Republican Army had been setting off bombs in the city. He feared that police would storm the premises. He had a more distressing thought as he sprinted around, grabbing pages and putting the office back in order: Would his bosses discover that he had been printing a fanzine on the company dime? He dashed out, alarms still wailing, before anyone showed up. On Monday, nobody said a word.

But he had gotten the message. Clearly, this thing with Dylan was getting out of hand.

Andy was born in Cowdenbeath, Scotland, a coal mining town across the Firth of Forth from Edinburgh. He had the addict's gene in a country where drinking was a national weakness. Scottish folk music, Glasgow's Rangers Football Club, David Bowie, Philip K. Dick, nineteenth-century Russian literature, Shakespeare, science fiction—all of them had held Andy in their sway at one time or another. If he enjoyed a book, he would track down everything else by that author. So it was a matter of genetics exacerbated by an accident of birth. He became an alcoholic.

Andy had discovered Dylan in high school about the same time he found Sartre and Dostoyevsky, and he raved about *Blood on the Tracks* to anybody who would listen. Some years later, at a party in Helsinki, he met the most extraordinary woman.

"So," she said, "you're the Dylanologist, are you?"

It was well after midnight, and Andy asked the question he put to every potential love interest. What was her favorite Dylan album?

"*Blonde on Blonde* or *Blood on the Tracks*," the woman replied, "but I'd hate to pick one and have the other one be second." Andy was ready to propose right there. They were married two years later.

The first time Andy quit drinking, in his early thirties, he used the resulting burst of energy to start *Homer*. The fanzine's name came from the alcoholic in *Tarantula*, Dylan's difficult book of poetry. "got too drunk last nite. musta drunk too much," Dylan's Homer writes a friend. "woke up this morning with my mind on freedom & my head feeling like the inside of a prune." Soon it seemed that twenty hours a day wasn't enough for Andy to do all of the Dylan-related work he wanted. He also ran an information line that subscribers could call for news. He called it the Warmline, because another fan-ziner had a hotline already. Dylan tapes filled his flat. He got every show within a week of the performance; a week later he got them in better quality. At one point he hollowed out his couch so he could store his tapes inside it. (It later collapsed.) "I was completely crazy," he said later. "It was my entire life. Every minute of every day was Dylan." Not that he didn't take his problem seriously, but he once joked that he didn't know what was worse, waking up an alcoholic or waking up as the editor of a Dylan fanzine.

Andy felt strangely compelled to write about Dylan, and in that he was not so different from many compatriots in the United Kingdom. Michael Gray's critical analysis of Dylan's work, the heavily footnoted *Song and Dance Man III: The Art of Bob Dylan*, ran 918 pages. Not one for half measures, Gray then published a 756-page encyclopedia. Clinton Heylin became Dylan's most prolific biographer. Christopher Ricks—elected Oxford Professor of Poetry in 2004 and knighted in 2009—wrote as appreciatively of Bob Dylan as he had of Tennyson and Milton, and thereby lent legitimacy to the amateur intellectuals going on and on about the man's singular genius.

Even by the fastidious standards of the Dylan world, the Brits were known for a fussy, almost academic approach. They were the first to pull out pads and pens at concerts and Dylan talks. For twenty-eight years, a Brit named Ian Woodward logged and numbered bits of Dylan intel that crossed his desk from newspapers or other fans or his contacts in the music industry. The logs grew into a newsletter, the *Wicked Messenger*, named after the character in the 1967 Dylan song whose mind "multiplied the smallest matter." At the beginning, it circulated chain-letter style. Later, it became part of the *Telegraph* and then *ISIS*.

Sometimes it seemed that every fan in Britain had launched a fanzine. The editors all knew each other, met at conventions, and gossiped on Internet forums. The community had a hierarchy. Rivalries arose, some unkind words were said. "We are an audience of people who *hate* each other," Andy Muir told me. The men who ran the zines were essentially competitors. They all ran news stories, bits of trivia, interviews with ancillary Dylan associates, Dylan scholarship—anything Dylan-related they could find. For fans, the publications were a guilty pleasure. They should have come in plain brown wrappers.

Andy wrote and wrote and wrote about Dylan, first in *Homer*, and then, after it folded, in a succession of other journals: *Dignity, ISIS, On the Tracks, Freewheelin'.* He launched another fanzine, *Judas!* He wrote for Nina Goss's *Montague Street* journal. Remarkably, he also found time to write about Shakespeare and football. (He had trouble sleeping when he wasn't drinking.) He spent a lot of time documenting Dylan's sprawling tour; any show he didn't see in person he dissected on tape. But above all Andy became known in Britain's fan fraternity for his unpretentious, clear-eyed criticism, written with wit and the obsessive's grasp of detail.

Pondering "Maggie's Farm," Dylan's 1965 yelp against working for the man, he noticed how often the people who "grin" in Dylan songs tend to be doing it malevolently. This time, it was Maggie's grinning brother who asks if he's "havin' a good time?" while the narrator is being tortured. "In my gloomier moods," he wrote, "I feel that any society will, by its very nature, inevitably turn into a 'Maggie's Farm' that continually tries to entrap and torment the individual spirit of humankind." Andy sounded upbeat, and he could be quick with a joke, but he was a misanthrope through and through. The way he saw it, humans had been in a precipitous decline since we stopped hunting and gathering. "I hate people," he told me once. "I'm an angry bastard. There's two of me. You're only seeing one side of me."

In another dispatch, Andy wrote about sexual imagery in Dylan's 1966 song "Temporary Like Achilles." The window, hallway, and doors—in one case a "velvet door"—that appear in the song were metaphors for "sexual apertures," as Andy put it, much as "horseracing, baking, household parts and items, trains and above all cars" were all stand-ins for what was really on blues singers' minds: sex. If you didn't think "raise your window high" was suggestive, ask yourself, why didn't they just use the door? Predictably, readers were horrified.

He studied 1989's *Oh Mercy* and decided that Dylan was singing about both modern times and biblical times. Jesus' age was "superimposed" over our age. A decade after the born-again era, Dylan was still talking about corruption and ultimate judgment and the End of Days. "The last radio is playing," he sings, and it's the soundtrack to the Second Coming. "It is often difficult to tell in many of these songs if the singer's voice is meant to be portraying Christ himself or Dylan as Everyman on the Christian journey," Andy wrote.

There was a fine line between erudite criticism and insane interpretation, however, and the zines flirted with it in every issue. The credentialed and the crackpot got even billing. Readers had to be careful. They had to be open to chaos, because there was little settled law in Dylan studies. Mockery awaited anyone who took the songs too seriously or tried too hard to figure out which of Dylan's women were in which song, or searched for the unified Bob Dylan field theory. The specter of A.J. Weberman loomed over any effort to analyze. Tidy, all-encompassing hypotheses fell apart over time. Any fool could find whatever he wanted inside the vast Dylan songbook: drugs, Jesus, Joan Baez. Dylan was once told his lyrics were like the Bible because everything you needed to know was in there somewhere. He started to reply, then he stopped. "Well," he said. He let a long sarcastic pause linger. "That goes without saying."

Andy had a soft spot for one of the more fearless armchair correspondents, John Stokes, the man behind the fanzine launched, in part at least, to free up underground tapes from tightfisted collectors. *Freewheelin'* was strictly limited to just twelve subscribers: To get an issue you had to wait for a current member to drop out. The chosen ones shared recordings and contributed an article every month. Stokes, an accountant in Cambridge, insisted the limit was logistical. They all had to print out a dozen copies of their articles and send them to Stokes, who bound and shipped the zine. So it was not set up for mass distribution. But outsiders couldn't help thinking the Freewheelers liked the apostolic symbolism of their exclusive clique.

By design, there could be no editing, so no one could stop Stokes from circulating wildly unconventional ideas. He theorized that in "Series of Dreams," a song recorded during the *Oh Mercy* sessions and released on the first official *Bootleg Series*, the narrator was having slumbering visions of sexual impotence. Stokes suggested that the umbrella in the song was phallic, and the fact that it was "folded" meant that it didn't work. (Other writers thought Dylan was ruminating about inspiration, or the lack thereof; Gray called Stokes's article "perfectly dreadful.") Stokes later embarked on a two-year, twenty-three-part series on "Visions of Johanna," the beloved song from *Blonde on Blonde*, one of those classics that leaves listeners picking up words and turning them this way and that, just to see if they change in the light. On the surface, "Visions" is easily understood. A man is trapped in a relationship with a woman who's just "all right," but he longs for something more significant, and he can't stop thinking about fantastic, phantasmagoric Johanna. Stokes listened to "Visions of Johanna" and he saw Joan of Arc. *She* had visions. She signed her name "Jehanne." When Dylan sang that "the ghost of 'lectricity howls in the bones of her face," Stokes couldn't help thinking about the saint being burned alive as a heretic in 1431. Stokes went on for sixty-five thousand words, making his case. But he realized he sounded "quite mad," and in part twenty-two, he confessed to having second thoughts about his conclusions.

More notoriously, Stokes seemed to suggest that Dylan's *Time Out of Mind* foretold Princess Diana's fatal car accident in Paris, which occurred months after Dylan recorded the album. He identified a number of ties. On the song "Can't Wait," Stokes swore he heard car horns in the bits of organ at 2:12, 3:20, and 4:55. At the time of her death, Diana's sons were in the Scottish Highlands. Could it be mere coincidence that Dylan sang about his heart being in the Highlands? That these songs were written long before Di's accident made him wonder whether "someone who has been described as a prophet sensed something in the air and, no doubt unwittingly—as all good prophets do—put it into words."

A few years later, Stokes said his article was misunderstood. He vacillated on the crucial point: He wouldn't say that Dylan had been called by God to speak his truth. Still, who could say? Asked what reaction he got to his articles, Stokes replied, "Ridicule."

But Andy liked Stokes. He read every piece. "He's an artist in his own right," he said. His wild musings made Andy laugh and laugh. He couldn't say they were all crazy, and anyway, sometimes Andy himself felt insane spending so much time thinking about this man.

Of all the obsessives who followed Dylan, the interpreters and amateur critics did the most damage to the fans' reputations. The singer reserved his most blunt and direct hatred for them. In 2001, upon the release of *"Love and Theft,"* Dylan complained anew about these supposed know-nothings. He said his songs had been miscon-strued and bent out of all recognizable shape. "I don't even know if *I* would understand them if I believed everything that has been written about them by imbeciles who wouldn't know the first thing about writing songs." He handed down a withering judgment of the Dylan fan world. "These so-called connoisseurs of Bob Dylan music . . . I don't feel they know a thing, or have any inkling of who I am and what I'm about. I know they think they do, and yet it's ludicrous, it's humorous, and sad. That such people have spent so much of their time thinking about who? Me? Get a life, please. It's not something any one person should do about another. You're not serving your own life well. You're wasting your life."

In the weeks after that broadside, many fans said that Dylan was right, but he surely wasn't talking about *them* in particular. So many said it that Andy decided to create a checklist to help Dylan's followers determine whether "old grumpy chops" (his words) con-sidered them a "so-called connoisseur":

Have you seen a lot of concerts?

Fought your way up to the front?

Bought or listened to bootlegs?

Written about Dylan?

Then face facts: He was talking about you. "He's every right to say what he does," Andy wrote. "Every artist says it. Basically, you

see, they don't understand us. They've got this fantastic gift for looking at the world and coming up with something creative, and we
puzzle about how they do it. And of course to them it's not a puzzle.
It just comes."

Dylan had been going on about this for decades. Every time he
encouraged people to try to figure out the songs, he would turn
around and bash them.

He would say, "It's up to you to figure out who's who. A lot of
times it's you talking to you." If he sings in the first person, "I" could
be Dylan himself, or it could be the God who created him, Dylan
said. Or it could be another person. "When I say 'I' right now, I
don't know who I'm talking about." Then he would reverse course
and protest the intellectualization of his work. "They are songs
meant to be sung. I don't know if they are meant to be discussed
around the coffee table."

In one interview he'd say, "People can learn everything about
me through my songs—if they know where to look." In another
he would complain about biographical readings of his albums.
His repertoire was so "wide-ranging" that "you'd have to be a mad-
man" to use it to learn anything concrete about his life. He complained about people who saw his deteriorating marriage reflected
in *Blood on the Tracks*. On "You're a Big Girl Now," the singer
has just had a conversation with his lover and is dealing with the
painful realization that he's lost her forever. "Well," Dylan said
about that song, "I read that this was supposed to be about my
wife. I wish somebody would ask me first before they go ahead
and print stuff like that. I mean it couldn't be about anybody else
but my wife, right? Stupid and misleading jerks sometimes these
interpreters are."

People should just give up already, Dylan said. "What I've done,
what I'm doing, nobody else does or has done. When I'm dead and

gone maybe people will realize that, and then figure it out. I don't think anything I've done has been evenly mildly hinted at. There's all these interpreters around, but they're not interpreting anything except their own ideas. Nobody's come close."

2

One day in 1993, Dylan materialized on Camden High Street in London. Usually, Dylan wandered around in hoodies and sunglasses, sometimes in the middle of the night, but on this July day he went to a busy boulevard and was dressed to be noticed: He wore a black coat, leather gloves, and a top hat, and he swung a crook-handle umbrella. He spoke to passersby, signed autographs, threw an arm around a pedestrian for a photograph. He sat for tea at an outdoor table. There was a reason for all of this unlikely behavior: Cameras were following him around for a music video.

Word spread, and someone called Andy, who jumped into a cab and found Dylan sitting in a restaurant called Fluke's Cradle. Andy sat down at a nearby table, his heart racing. He felt ridiculous. He walked over to the bar and ordered a drink. He had two copies of *Homer* with him, and though he swore he'd never pester Dylan if he saw him in public, he wanted his hero to sign them. Dylan's security man, Jim Callaghan, knew Andy from the road, and after a few minutes he gave him the word: Now or never.

Andy approached, and the table went silent.

"Excuse me, Mr. Dylan," Andy said.

Dylan looked at him. "Yeah?"

Andy went to mush. ("I am dead," he would write later. "I want the ground to swallow me up and never let me out again.") He managed to hand his magazine over and Dylan signed it and Andy thanked him. Walking back to the front of the restaurant, Andy placed himself in a chair that everyone would have to pass—single file—on the way out, and placed his other copy of *Homer* on the table. Just as Andy planned, Dylan stopped, picked it up, and started flipping through the pages. He made a remark about the Warmline, listed on the inside cover, and laughed. He read a few more pages. When he started to go, Andy told him to keep it, and graciously, Dylan did. He gave his fan a squeeze on the shoulder and walked to a waiting car. As it pulled away, Andy caught a glimpse of Dylan still reading his fanzine.

He was dumbfounded. How could it have gone so well? Everybody knew the stories of Dylan's truculence. Andy was prepared for *I hate you*, or words to that effect. "Every fan he has met," Andy says, "he has hated."

The meeting added fuel to Andy's obsession. He continued following the tour relentlessly and wrote a book analyzing the concerts year by year. He took a new post at British Telecom that involved travel all over Europe, and he found that the firm had offices virtually everywhere Dylan played. He planned business trips around the tour. At perhaps the apex of his mania, he flew halfway around the world for the sole purpose of hearing that Holy Grail recording, the one on which Dylan plays *Street-Legal* at a piano in his rehearsal space.

Then something happened. Andy's passion cooled and reversed direction. His feelings for Dylan spiraled from love to doubt to deep disillusionment. "I was adrift on a raft of negativity."

The reversal took some time. Four years after Andy's momentous encounter, Dylan was hospitalized with severe chest pains and diagnosed with histoplasmosis, a fungal infection that can cause inflammation of the lining around the heart. He spent a week in the hospital, but he recovered and soon resumed touring. As it happened, *Time Out of Mind* was released soon after. Though he had written and recorded it before the ailment, its dark musings sounded like Dylan had written it on hospital stationery.

The health scare and the new record seemed to reignite media interest, as if writers, in preparing obituaries, realized Dylan had reached the age at which he ought to be treated as a living legend. At the same time, Dylan's office had been working to introduce the singer to the next generation and remind the world of the Bob Dylan myth. A Martin Scorsese documentary cast Dylan as an archetypal American character. A scrapbook re-created his 1960s glory. Pristine recordings of fabled concerts were officially released, bringing the Dylan of 1964, 1966, and 1975 back to life.

At the dawn of the new century, he suddenly seemed to be everywhere. The iconoclast who complained "everybody's singing about ketchup or headache medicine or something" went a bit corporate himself. He showed up in a TV ad driving a Cadillac Escalade through a desolate landscape. ("What's life without the occasional detour?" he asked.) He licensed a song to Pepsi for a Super Bowl ad with Will.i.am, and stalked a supermodel in Venice for Victoria's Secret. Official Dylan watches ($1,500) and hand-signed Hohner harmonicas in ebony boxes ($5,000) went on sale. He hosted a one-hundred-episode radio show on XM. He started producing paintings, exhibiting them in galleries, and selling the signed prints for thousands of dollars.

Despite the increased exposure, the world did not get closer to seeing the man behind the mask. Dylan's manager conducted the interviews that Scorsese used; the director never even met with the singer in the course of making his film. *60 Minutes* got a sit-down with Dylan, but not the customary chance to follow the star around with its cameras as he went about his life. He had always been both ambitious and paranoid; now he'd figured out how to be omnipres-

ent and invisible at once. Confidants who knew whether there was
a new woman in Dylan's life, for instance, weren't telling the world
about it.

Amid all of this manufactured hubbub, Dylan kept making
music. After 2001's *"Love and Theft,"* he released two albums cut
from the same mold, *Modern Times* (2006) and *Together Through
Life* (2009). Both of them tapped history, old folk and blues, literature and theater. Both were produced by "Jack Frost," Dylan's alter
ego. He was done with guys in the control room getting in the way.

For Andy, it felt like the air was slowly escaping from the balloon.
He fell for *"Love and Theft,"* hard, but he thought *Modern Times* was
marred by its "unfounded portentousness." Was Dylan just faking
it? He hated to be critical, but when Cook and Warmuth revealed
the borrowing in *Chronicles*, Andy couldn't shake the feeling that
Dylan was cheating, and possibly breaking the law. With *Together
Through Life*, Andy was officially off the bandwagon. The new songs
"sounded so generic and so blandly banal that I felt I was just suffering my way through listening to them, when really I should have
been doing something else."

There had always been a current of negativity running through
Andy's fan network. He and his fellow Dylan nuts would sit down
over beers and argue about which albums were the worst, not which
were the best. But suddenly, in the second half of the 2000s, he was
becoming repulsed by his musical hero.

Dylan's voice was broken. His advancing age, decades of smoking, the twenty-five hundred shows since 1988—all of it had taken
a toll. Dylan had never had broad range; now he had almost no
tone onstage. It was straight bark. It would have been okay, Andy
thought, had it not prompted Dylan to deploy a battery of new
mannerisms: "upsinging," or garnishing the end of every line with a
high note; reciting songs staccato-style; relying on "throat-clearing

to cover up forgotten words and lines, a long growl to indicate that 'there used to be something I wanted to say here but now this noise will suffice.'"

Dylan used to seem so authentic. He made Andy believe in him completely. He made audiences think he was singing from the heart, that this was not just another gig. Andy was savvy enough to understand that Dylan had been putting on a brilliant stage act all along. He had always been faking it. But now the vocal cords were so damaged that the production fell apart. It was like watching a play in which the acting and stagecraft weren't good enough to let the audience lose itself in the illusion. All he saw now was a careless, hollow performer.

Andy had discovered Dylan as a teen, and he always felt as if Dylan was a big brother. His disillusionment felt like the end of a relationship, a flesh-and-blood one. It seemed like the closest thing to a divorce he had ever experienced. "I was lost," Andy wrote. It seemed permanent.

When he wrote about his defection in the *ISIS* fanzine, he found himself on the defensive from the faithful. He could understand the ill will. "We invest so much in our Dylan experience that it takes on almost religious overtones," he wrote. "Those who still believe turn on the apostate as an evil heretic who should be silenced by whatever means necessary, the more painful the better."

But he was not alone. All over England you could find passionate fans who were upset with Dylan. On a Friday night at the Ship & Mitre, a bar in downtown Liverpool, Christopher Hockenhull, the city's resident Dylan authority, started in on the singer before he'd finished his first pint of ale. "I don't like this voice," he said. "It's gotten worse and worse and worse. And the standard of the shows. For the first time in my life, Dylan is predictable. Can you find any other time in the last thirty-odd years when you could use the word *predictable* about Dylan? And the band is no better than a band I could take you to see in any pub. What's this keyboard about? It's *dreadful.*" He took a swallow of his beer and continued. "You've got to be objective. It's horrible organ. It's like a *child* up there with the organ you buy for a child."

Hockenhull, like Andy Muir, had the credentials to complain. He was a card-carrying Dylan man for decades: founder of a fanzine, *Fourth Time Around*; a collector serious enough to have rarities land in his lap; inhabitant of an office crammed with books and bootlegs and fanzines. He still loved Dylan's music. He still performed the songs when he played at a bar near his home. But he was bewildered by what the man was doing these days.

A measure of Dylan's appeal had always been that he was not a massively popular mainstream star. He was literary, eccentric, an acquired taste, a cult figure. He sold a lot of records, but he was no Michael Jackson. It used to be that not doing ads was part of Dylan's authenticity. He was above all that. Now it seemed that Dylan was becoming a brand. "The whole thing has become basically a Bob Dylan PLC," Hockenhull griped at the bar. "Would you have ever thought you would have seen a Bob Dylan cigarette lighter and mouse mats, all that crap? It's just so corporate. Well-oiled."

Michael Gray, the *Song and Dance Man* author, said that when a Dylan tape came into the house in years past, he would listen right away. Now a friend would send him a tape and he might listen to a track or two, if that. Sadly, fixing a broken doorknob might be more interesting. This was a man who had written millions of words about Dylan, who traveled the world speaking about him, who (for a fee) hosted fans to his house in a tiny village in the south of France to talk Dylan. He acknowledged the extraordinary greatness of Dylan's music. "I have long accepted that when you enter the Dylan world," he once wrote, "you sign up for life." But the last time that he sensed he was in the presence of greatness was in 2000. He didn't want to sound like some old man recalling the great days gone by. But decades ago, an entire show could blow the fans away. Then people would only rave about three or four songs. When it got to the point that fans were singling out a lone phrase as evidence that Dylan still had it, Gray found himself wondering, *What about the other ninety minutes of sludge?*

In 2002, Gray went to a show in Stockholm. He filed in with the regulars who followed Dylan around in what looked, to Gray's eyes, like a stupor; "These people depress me," he wrote. He could only wonder how it felt for Dylan: "night after blurred night, seeing these defeated faces starting up at him in inexplicable glazed agitation?"

As for the show, he hated it. "Most of the time it seems to me that the real Bob Dylan is largely missing and he's busier faking it than trying his best," he wrote. "Where once he was so alive, communicating so much quick creative intelligence so alertly and uniquely, now he snatches at showbiz cliché he once recoiled from." When he had been at his best onstage, Dylan "lived in the dangerous moment." In Stockholm he played it safe. "We expect much less now," Gray wrote, "and get it."

One night in the spring of 2009, Dylan played London's Roundhouse, a converted train-repair shed dating to 1846. It was located up the street from the Fluke's Cradle on Camden High Street, where Andy had nearly fainted getting Dylan to sign an issue of *Homer* sixteen years earlier. The Roundhouse gig proved to be a sought-after ticket. The venue held only three thousand people, and with Dylan releasing a new record two days later, fans were hoping he would play a few songs they hadn't heard before.

But when Andy got there, he had the sense that everybody was spoiling for a fight. Dylan had made it clear in the past that he didn't like seeing the same faces up front. On occasion, people who had waited in line all day were ordered *back* by security. Sometimes individuals were informed that Mr. Dylan did not want to see them at the rail. They were cleared out and replaced with hand-chosen concertgoers. One night the back of the line got into the venue first. This sort of thing happened a lot around 2000 and 2001. One regular took to calling it the *Fuck You, Everybody!* Tour. In Switzerland, a fan up front said Dylan leaned down and said he didn't *ever* want to see him at the rail again. The man swore that he had done nothing to trigger Dylan's temper. "I usually play to the people in the back," Dylan said around that time. "I disregard the people in the front." The superfans would be there every night no matter what he did. He wanted to reach people who had never seen him before.

Waiting for the Roundhouse show to begin, Andy could see Dylan standing just offstage. He didn't look happy about what he was seeing. "He was standing with the most depressed look on his face, really, really down, as if he'd rather be anywhere else in the world but here." It could have been nothing. Dylan could have been preparing himself mentally to go on stage. Maybe it was just a trick of the lights. But Andy couldn't shake the feeling that the man was in a dark mood.

The lights went down, and it was Andy's turn to be sour. After a few songs, he decided he had heard enough. He walked out and headed home. He had better things to do. He checked the time on the way out. He'd lasted thirty-two minutes. "It was awful, it was just rubbish," he said later. "Plinky-plonky piano. Singing every song the same. He was just faking it. His voice is gone and he's using tricks to replace emotion."

Andy had made arrangements to see Dylan a week later in Edinburgh. He scored tickets in the front row and booked a flight. But a few days after the Roundhouse concert, he was still trying to reconcile his years of passion for Dylan with his bitter feelings about the show. It was psychologically traumatic. He felt guilty about leaving with his old hero up there onstage. "Thirty-four years of unalloyed love for the man, and I walked out on him."

When the time came to leave for Scotland, Andy stayed home.

3

Michael Gray and Clinton Heylin, the world's most prolific Dylan writers, didn't get along. When the men crossed paths, they were loath to share even pleasantries, and by all accounts they held each other in mutual disrespect. It was probably unavoidable. Their personalities did not mesh. Gray was reserved, Heylin brash. They were men of ego, and they didn't put up with fools without good reason.

But on the question of the merits of Dylan's recent work, they were in general harmony. Gray was disappointed by every new set of Dylan originals after *"Love and Theft,"* while Heylin thought the critics had overrated even that album. "We've all had to watch this extraordinary process whereby he's sort of become this can-do-no-wrong figure, at the precise point when he does nothing *but* wrong," Heylin said. He gave Dylan credit for moments of magnificence on *Modern Times* in 2006. But he had a hard time hearing fans rave about some recent concert performance of "Like a Rolling Stone," as if it had been even a shadow of the howling wonder from the 1966 live shows. Those people needed "serious remedial care," in his opinion. "The '66 version is one of the greatest things ever. And this"—Late Dylan in concert—"is beyond embarrassing, you know? The band stinks, Bob doesn't know the words, he can't sing for shit. Which bit of it is fantastic?"

To Heylin, argument was sport, his preferred method of communication. Even when he recounted a fact, he loaded it with an opinion, the opinion being that somebody else had it wrong. The man could launch a debate in an empty room. He was the kind of bully you could come to love if you didn't take whatever came out of his mouth to heart. Face to face, he could be charming and approachable. In his fifties, he still had a boyish face and a bottomless enthusiasm for music.

Heylin first saw Dylan during his return to England for a six-night stand at Earls Court in 1978. He was eighteen, and already a major fan and bootleg collector. (It was never *just* Dylan; he was also a punk music fan.) The concerts sparked a resurgence of interest, and soon the country's fans were coming together for Dylan conferences to trade tapes and talk about his music. At one of these the idea for a "Bob Dylan Information Office" came up, and in 1981, Wanted Man and its newsletter, the *Telegraph*, were born. Heylin was involved from the beginning. Later, the fanzine would evolve into a critical journal, but he always considered its main purpose to be historical. Let somebody else figure out what "Visions of Johanna" really meant. He wanted to dig for intel, and tapes. He was driven by the sense that the world, at that time, had forgotten how important Dylan was, and by the need to get the facts documented before they were lost or buried.

In his late twenties, Heylin quit his family's insurance brokerage to become a writer full-time. He would go on to publish many Dylan books: a detailed timeline of Dylan's life through 1995, assembled from articles, books, interviews, and whatever other records he could find; one book detailing Dylan's recording sessions; three editions of a biography; and a song-by-song breakdown in two volumes. Add to that two others involving Dylan, plus guides to Dylan's unreleased recordings and many articles, and you begin to wonder how he had time for the dozen-plus other books he's written about music. Writers like Heylin battled against a culture of silence among those close to Dylan. This was a man who once said he felt the same way about people who sat for interviews with biographers as Civil War generals did about infiltrators in their ranks. "They're spies," Dylan said with a sneer. "All informers should be shot."

Heylin aimed to be a rock historian; he had two history degrees, and he considered himself "a scholar who prides himself on getting things right." He had his detractors, who called him a train spotter obsessed with facts and dates, or who charged him with making unsupported assumptions and getting minor details wrong. ("We all get things wrong. I've never claimed I'm infallible," he said. That's why he kept digging. That's why he revised his editions over the years.) But it is impossible to deny the importance of his work on Dylan. Even Gray recognized that. "His knowledge is immense, his research formidable, and his prose prolific," he wrote in *The Bob Dylan Encyclopedia*. "He has unearthed so much of the information we have about Dylan's recordings and his life, and has interpreted that information so forcefully, that had Heylin never interested himself in these subjects, the whole face of Dylanology would be different." And, Gray added, "less combative." Heylin is well-known for hammering anybody and everybody in print. He is quick to attack other Dylan writers for their faulty reasoning and flawed scholarship, and one of his books was famously "NOT dedicated to Jeff Rosen," manager of the singer's business and publishing operations. Andy Muir, who counts Heylin as a friend, said it is no surprise that this was the sort of biographer Dylan would attract: spiky and abrasive. "He torments people for fun," Andy said with some admiration.

Even Dylan himself is not safe from Heylin's barbs. He counts the singer as an artistic genius, of course. And yet he's like the brother who can't bring himself to say a kind word without pairing it with a dig. "Mr. Heylin seems to feel himself in competition with his sub-

ject," the *New York Times* wrote about his biography, "making gratu-
itous and unsupported *ex-cathedra* pronouncements on the relative
merits of Mr. Dylan's songs, career choices and romantic involve-
ments. These seem designed, finally, to leave us with the impression
that Mr. Dylan's life and career would have gone much better if he
had only let Mr. Heylin run it for him."

How could he have considered the last assertion an insult? His
entire career had been built around the idea that *of course* he could
do it better. Once, during a 1993 show in London, Heylin took
out a newspaper and ostentatiously started reading. "I had just had
enough," he says. "I'd been there six nights, he was playing the same
songs every night, he was *murdering* them every night, and I'd had
enough." For years he had considered Dylan the world's greatest
live performer, and as late as 2000 the singer was still capable of
thrilling the biographer. But after 2003, Heylin had all but stopped
going to the shows. "From a critical perspective, I have to step back
and say, 'Look, trust me, it's worthless. Why are you listening to it?'
Unless you're writing a book on the decline of Bob Dylan creatively,
it's a total waste of time." He wondered whether Dylan kept going
just to see who would last longer, him or the fans. "He's winning,"
he says. "Trust me."

The sense that the train could go off the tracks was always a key
part of Dylan's appeal. When he showed up at Gerde's Folk City or
the Gaslight in the early 1960s, he would do Chaplinesque comedy
routines on the stage, looking like a rank amateur, and then the
next minute he'd deliver something breathtaking. The Never Ending
Tour had a similar dynamic. People went to shows for years in the
hopes of hearing something rare and wonderful, a moment when
suddenly Dylan came alive and gave a song some new twist. "The
ability to fly by the seat of your pants is what defines him as a performance artist, and in order to do that you have to be prepared to

fail," Heylin says. Moments like those seem to be missing from Late Dylan. There is no longer that element of surprise, the sense that you might see something you'd never seen before and wouldn't see again. "I don't think I have any illusions about what I expect for the remainder of the Never Ending Tour," Heylin said. "And as Bob himself has said, it has to end. None of us are immortal."

In 1992, he went to a show at a music festival in the South Florida Fairgrounds, which did not sound to Heylin like a particularly appropriate venue for a living legend. Instead of wandering around and eating corn dogs, the nuts stood outside for six hours to make sure they got up front. It was unpleasant, but when the show started, Dylan came on and did something Heylin had never seen him do before: He played the harmonica on the first nine songs, sometimes giving the audience three solos in a single song. For Heylin, it made the entire day worth it.

But well into the third decade of the Never Ending Tour, he thought it highly unlikely that Dylan would do something as unpredictable and exciting and *great* as he had that night in Florida, and many other nights on the road.

"That's not going to happen," Heylin said. "Is it sad? Well, you know, it happens to us all."

8

ON THE RAIL

At a general-admission concert, the way to score a spot at the foot of the stage is to be one of the first people in the door. Getting "on the rail," as the regulars put it, was a practical matter for Charlie Cicirella. He was barely five feet tall, and since he wanted a clear line of sight, he went early and stood in line. He had very simple ideas about this. Everything flowed from one basic rule: Do the time. He was uncompromising about the people who gamed the system by coming late and cutting ahead. Pile a sleep deficit atop his usual ornery streak, and Charlie could be a monster. "I've got a reputation, and part of this reputation is irascibility," he admitted. He wore it proudly. Whenever he made it to the rail, you could be sure he had earned it. "That's why we get there early. We work for it."

Trouble broke out on every Dylan line. People cut in and refused to move. Sharp words were said, elbows thrown. But this week's run of general-admission shows was in Manhattan, and Charlie was preparing for more difficulty than usual. New York City fans had a cutthroat reputation. During a multiple-night stand at the Hammerstein Ballroom in 2003, it seemed like nobody got along. Fans walked outside after the encore and lined up immediately for the next night's show, twenty-two hours off.

This time Dylan was playing a trio of concerts at a club in Hell's Kitchen called Terminal 5. The first show was on the Monday before Thanksgiving, November 22, 2010. Charlie made plans to fly in from Cleveland on Sunday, but he was having some anxiety. He no longer had a driver's license, and he didn't know what airport security would do. But they waved him past and he made his flight. In New York, he took a taxi to the hostel where he was staying, dropped off his bag, and went directly uptown to the venue. He hoped to be first in line.

Charlie arrived around ten P.M. and found a red chair by the door with a note taped to its back. Beautiful. Someone had the nerve to lay claim to the first spot without even being there. The trickster did not show up for hours, and when she did, around six A.M., Charlie challenged her claim and she immediately backed down. Obviously, this man wanted it more than she did.

In the morning, cars poured off the West Side Highway, piloted by commuters wearing business suits and dresses. Some glanced over at the clutch of men and women loitering on the sidewalk, and you could almost see thought bubbles appear above their heads: *When did the homeless shelter open up next to the Infiniti dealership?*

People flew in from all over the world to see the shows. There were fans from Norway and Italy, from Montana and California. They came because it was New York, the city where Dylan invented himself. But there was nothing at all romantic about this grimy sidewalk where two dozen people killed time in front of unmarked metal security doors.

They milled around, read trashy magazines, did a little work, tried to sleep on the sidewalk.

Suddenly, in the middle of this calm, Charlie started going ballistic. "We're fucked!" he cried. "We're fucked!"

Security was saying they were going to let in the first 250 people to mingle in a rooftop bar. A while later, they would guide the crowd downstairs to the stage. Charlie could see only disaster. It would be a free-for-all. The people who had waited all this time would have no advantage. They would have to fight for their positions against fans who had arrived a few hours before the doors opened—people who had not paid their dues like he had.

Charlie marched around back and tried to talk the security chief, a man named Stephan, out of this terrible plan. Stephan wore a black jacket, a spotless Yankees cap, and diamond earrings. He stood at attention, the classic bouncer's pose: eyes forward, his back straight, chest puffed out. He towered over Charlie, whose floppy gray hair looked disheveled from his all-nighter.

Politely, Charlie pleaded for Stephan to help preserve the line order.

"The people that's in front will be the first ones in," Stephan promised.

"I've seen this go *soooo* wrong," Charlie countered.

"It goes right."

"Yeah," Charlie said, "but you haven't seen Bob fans."

2

In 2010, it was business as usual for Dylan. He was performing about as many concerts as he had when the Never Ending Tour began two decades earlier. If you waited outside a medium-size venue anywhere in the world, he was bound to stop by sooner or later. He played

Tokyo in March, Athens and Istanbul in May. He started the month of June in Bucharest and he ended it in Bordeaux. He played a festival in England, then roamed through the Great Plains. Austin in August was sweltering. A few fans passed out from the heat waiting for him to come on in Lincoln.

Two days later he played the world's biggest biker rally, in Sturgis, South Dakota. The stage sat in the middle of a massive campground that looked like one of Dylan's phantasmagoric songs brought to life. It was the freak-show circus from "Ballad of a Thin Man," the outlandish world of "Desolation Row," the set for "Tombstone Blues." The Buffalo Chip had a pool bar sponsored by Hedonism II, the racy Jamaican resort. It had a mechanical bull. It had a firing range. Bikers could ride right up to the stage and rev their motors. Women wore body paint instead of clothes; some men sprouted devil's horns. The Coors spokesmodel was there, and so were the US Air Force recruiters. "It's fucking insanity!" screamed a Dylan freak who had driven eleven hours from Winnipeg. "What *is* this place?" Before Dylan went on stage the mob saw a twenty-one-gun salute, a prowar rant by actor Lorenzo Lamas, and a scantily clad acrobat riding a motorcycle on a high wire. Two minutes after Dylan finished his act, ten women in string bikinis gyrated onto the stage to impress the clipboard-wielding judges of the Miss Buffalo Chip Beauty Pageant, followed shortly after by Kid Rock. The smattering of Dylan fans were wigged out by the scene but they thought their man put on a great show. The badass bikers from the Sons of Silence Motorcycle Club (motto: *Donec Mors Non Separat*, "Until Death Separates Us") did not seem impressed. Dylan looked like he enjoyed himself.

The Peripatetic One played his sixty-third show of the year at Seattle's Bumbershoot Festival in September. On the last leg of the year, he'd do seven weeks of dates in college towns from Florida to Wisconsin, followed by the three shows in New York and a couple of casino gigs. When the shows were announced, Charlie mapped out a trip that would have him looping through the Midwest in late October and early November: Ann Arbor, Kalamazoo, Chicago, Indianapolis, Akron, Columbus. Six shows in ten days, more than a thousand miles round trip from his home outside Cleveland. He didn't have much money in his bank account, but Charlie thought he could pull it off. If he was lucky, he'd catch the New York shows, too.

Charlie was intense, conspiratorial, a bit pushy in a disarmingly self-conscious kind of way. The first time we spoke on the phone, he suggested I fly him to New York so he could show me how serious tourgoers did the line. He was full of confidence, almost bluster, but at the same time he could be sensitive. "If you talk to me for twenty minutes, not to blow my own horn, I think it could be more interesting than two other people you talk to for two hours," he said. "Or maybe I just think I'm more interesting than most other people do, and in that case don't tell me because it will really let me down."

He started writing poetry at fourteen, and reciting it soon after. After a little while at community college, he left home and followed a girl to Columbus, where he read his poetry on Mondays at a bar that hosted slams, Larry's. It was the center of the little countercultural community in the city. The wooden tables were graffiti-scarred. Velvet Underground was on the jukebox. Word was that Dylan once overnighted in the apartment upstairs. A guy he met at Larry's, impressed with Charlie's stuff, introduced him to a man who could help him get published. The man was Jim Shepard, a lo-fi legend in underground music circles who founded a series of experimental rock bands—V-3, Vertical Slit—and made records largely outside of the studio system. Shepard also had a publishing outfit. The young poet handed him a manila folder filled with writing, and next thing he knew he had two chapbooks out.

Shepard was the first person who made Charlie see that he could really be an artist. "With Shepard, all things were possible," he said. "He pulled me off the street when I was having some problems. He turned me on to music and poetry and books. And he was like, 'You want to be an artist, just go for it.'"

They became friends and sometimes performed together. "Being on a stage with him was like being onstage with a caged panther," Charlie wrote later. "He was manic—maniacal—incendiary." Shepard was as outside the mainstream as anyone could be. One guy who knew him said that the best steady job he could remember him having was jukebox routeman. Shepard once told an interviewer, "I don't watch the news. I don't read the papers. I'm not really in touch with society. I was born. I'm here, but I don't believe any of it."

Charlie tried to internalize Shepard's philosophy, which was to work as if he had six months to live. That meant using his time to create, not sitting in some office cubicle or standing behind a retail counter at the mall. Charlie always had some creative project going. He produced a radio show and posted it online for friends—Radio Ether, he called it. He recorded his poems and uploaded them to a blog. Some pieces he did with musician friends, who improvised behind him on guitar or ukulele or cello or flute. He had a band, Root Cellar, that played sporadically. "I sing," Charlie said. "I scream, actually." They did a song called "Danger Pussy." Often when Charlie made something, he didn't do anything with it. "Mostly," he said, "it goes into a drawer."

He could throw himself into all kinds of complex creative projects, but the mundane matters of life left him stumped. He didn't know where to start. How did you get a driver's license? What was the best way of buying a car? He thought his head would explode if he tried to do things like that. "My brain doesn't work that way," he said. "You want me to go out and get a job and work? I'll do it. I'm going to have to do it sometime. Sometime soon. But that doesn't make *sense* to me. I have to really feel something. It has to feel right."

He'd held down his share of jobs. He learned tarot so he could work a psychic call line at seven dollars an hour. For four years he managed a college bar in Columbus, but when that ended, he said he stopped caring about finding something else. He went numb.

Jim Shepard killed himself in 1998, at age forty. Charlie hit rock bottom a few years later. On the verge of being evicted, he moved to Oxford, Mississippi, to live with a girl he had met through Dylan fan circles. That lasted four months. Out of options, he moved back home to Cleveland. His last steady gig was at a Starbucks in the mall across the street from his mother's home in Lyndhurst, Ohio, where he had been camped out on the couch for years. He drew unemployment for a while.

But despite his bleak financial situation, he still found ways to see Dylan shows. By the time October arrived, he had tickets for the six Midwest concerts and a ride with a friend in Chicago. He planned to crash wherever he could and tap his limited funds for food and incidentals. It felt like a minor miracle to be able to go back on the road.

Ann Arbor sucked. Kalamazoo was great. He thought Chicago was out of this world. "Just the way he said 'para-*lyzed*' during 'Positively Fourth Street'—it was just unbelievable," Charlie said over dinner the next night in Indianapolis, a few hours before another show. "He spit it out. But he didn't. He put it out there a little bit, and it was dangling off his tongue, and then he pulled it back in and then he pushed it out. Like a piano out of a window. Then it just came down"—Charlie smacked the table—"and it lay there on the sidewalk. He did 'Positively Fourth Street' like he wrote it seven minutes before he walked out on stage."

"Like he was angry?" someone asked.

"No," he said. "Like he was *resigned*. Like I just know how you are and you're never going to fucking change and I'm on to you. And your little dog."

Charlie had arranged to eat at the kind of place where he thought he might run into Dylan, a restaurant called Maxine's Chicken & Waffles that was attached to a Citgo gas station. Charlie struck up a conversation with one of the waitresses, whose name was Jolene.

"That's funny," he said. "We're going to see Bob Dylan, and he does a song called 'Jolene.' Has he ever eaten here?"

"Bob Dylan?" Jolene asked. "If he has, I missed him."

As a teenager Charlie didn't have a lot of friends. He wasn't comfortable in his own skin. He remembers walking home from school with kids who obviously didn't want anything to do with him. But then one day he put on *Highway 61 Revisited*, which he had checked out of the library but was long overdue. The second time he listened to "Like a Rolling Stone," something clicked. It was the first time he could ever remember not feeling alone. He never forgot how that comforted him as a teenager. "Somebody spoke to me," he said. "Somebody understood."

So count Charlie among the people who wanted to meet Dylan one day. "I think he would think I was funny," he says. "I really believe I could be the one guy who could talk to him without bullshit. He needs another Jewish poet now that Ginsberg is dead."

3

He'd made it to New York, and now the concert was close. The sky grew dark and the white garage doors swung open and the venue lights flickered to life. At five P.M., the line was getting tense. Charlie had not been able to get the security man to change his plan, and he was edgy. More ticket holders arrived. Friends let latecomers break rank. Charlie mistakenly went after a woman who had been there all day.

A reporter from Radio Ireland walked around sticking a microphone in people's faces. "Have you seen Bob Dylan before?"

"Seventeen times," someone answered. "This will be eighteen, nineteen, and twenty."

"There *is* treatment for that," the radio man said before moving down the line to the next willing interviewee. "What does Bob Dylan mean to *you*?"

Security opened the gates and everybody rushed up to the third-floor bar. But instead of looking for beers, they turned around at the door and immediately stacked up a new line, which stretched up a set of stairs and around a balcony. Charlie salvaged the first spot.

A woman who hadn't waited long slipped in near the front, and someone started shouting, "Don't talk to her!" as if by ignoring her they could make her disappear.

A few minutes later they were off. Grown men and women dashed down the stairs, jog-walking like kids at a pool who didn't want to be busted for running. They ran a few steps, walked, ran a few steps, looking around for guards all the while, and then sprinted for the promised land.

When they got there, everyone suddenly became calm and quiet. It was like they'd shot the rapids and made it to the calm water below.

After forty-five minutes, incense poured out of the tin buckets onstage—fans knew the brand, Nag Champa—signaling that Dylan was coming soon. At 8:04, amid a steady clapping from the crowd, he appeared from behind a curtain.

The crowd hooted and screamed and throbbed as Dylan strode up to his organ with a disjointed lope, a walking jog. He wore the

Late Dylan dress code: a black coat with white trim along the collar and cuffs; a white tuxedo shirt open at the collar; a bolo tie with a fancy slide, a shimmering eagle in flight on a pearly backdrop rimmed in silver; black pants with a stripe down each leg; a flat-brimmed hat with a brown feather in the band; boots that glittered silver in the lights; and gleaming gold-and-diamond bands on both his left and right ring fingers.

Dylan settled in behind the organ and the band launched into the first song. "I'm gonna change my way of thinkin,' make myself a different set of rules," he barked. "Put my best foot forward, and stop being influenced by fools." The song came from his first gospel album, *Slow Train Coming*, but Dylan had rewritten it in the ensuing thirty-one years. The original lyrics decried sons marrying mothers and fathers turning daughters into whores, and paraphrased Christ's warning: "Watch therefore, for you know neither the day nor the hour in which the Son of Man comes." Late Dylan was less Bible-thumping, and he sang a different version in New York. Where the old song lamented that "you forgot all about the golden rule," now he flipped it: "We living by the golden rule, whoever got the gold *rules*." Despite the retooling, he still sounded like a true believer. "Oh, Lord, I have no friend but you," he yowled. He sang that "Jesus is coming." The "storms on the ocean, out on the mountain, too," evoked Jesus walking on water, Moses receiving the Ten Commandments on Mount Sinai. But at the moment, nobody was thinking about any of that. "Gonna Change My Way of Thinking" was no Sunday-morning hymn, no prayerful meditation; it rocked. Heads bobbed. Someone took a hit off a glass pipe, and a man in a fedora gripped the rail, rocked back, and started to boogie.

At intervals, Dylan picked up a harmonica and went out to center stage, only a few feet from his rapt fans. He is not a tall man, but from the foot of the stage he towered over the crowd. Dylan performed "Tangled Up in Blue" this way. His kaleidoscopic song from *Blood on the Tracks* is about being on the road and still wondering about the woman he left behind. He preened a bit as the band started in, then stepped up and sang. His face was always in motion—a grimace, a baring of the teeth, a flash of the tongue. Something resembling a smile crossed his face, but it looked intentionally fake. He had begun to do a number of songs like this each night, out from behind the piano, pacing around. Between lines he would shrug his shoulders as if trying to adjust the suit coat. He would tug at his lapels. He would turn his back, wait for the moment, then face front and blow his harp, bent at the waist, one hand outstretched. He would strut around like a marionette street hustler, all jerky juke and jive.

A few months earlier he'd turned "Lay, Lady, Lay" into a lascivious come-on for some woman in the front row. He threw his arms wide and grinned. He laughed, turning back to look at his drummer as if they shared an inside joke, like they had been talking about this woman earlier. He posed, a peacock, and then flipped sweaty gray curls off his neck. He shot his leg out like a runway model and tried to croon. Years earlier, he'd said that when he was up onstage with the crowd looking back at him, he couldn't help but feel like he was in a burlesque show. By 2010, he was playing the part.

The band played a gentle version of "Desolation Row" and charged through "Highway 61 Revisited," where the promoter is cooking up a world war. But Dylan did not lean on nostalgia. He played his later songs as well, and they were fresher, more suited to his band and his rasp. Those songs swung, or settled into melancholy shadows, or skulked down dark streets. "Ain't Talkin,'" from *Modern Times*, felt like a long creep through a desecrated Garden of Eden, a Cormac McCarthy novel in F minor. No one would argue the concert was classic Dylan. It wasn't 1966, or even 1995, but up front, with the amps at 10 and the players so close they seemed larger than life, a kind of hypnosis set in. *This* was the drug the rail chasers were after.

Then it was over, and Dylan came to center stage and stood with the band. He bowed, stone-faced, and walked off. Beyond introducing the musicians, the Sphinx hadn't said a word. He exited a side door and stepped into an idling SUV before the house lights came on. The crowd started to file out, but the fans who had waited on the sidewalk all day weren't ready for it to end. They milled about, chattering while the crew worked on the stage. Charlie debated whether to go sleep at the hostel or stay out all night. *Get the hell to bed*, his friends insisted. He relented. But he still planned on returning at four A.M. Five hours to go.

First he needed a late dinner, and he walked to a deli down the street. He had discovered the joint the night before and immediately fallen in love. Waiting for his sandwich, he started breaking down the show. "Unbelievable. Look, I was crying. I don't know if it was because of the Nag Champa or the sleep deprivation. I'm sure not sleeping kicks it in. The whole show was great—but those first two or three songs were just, oh my God, they were out of the box.

"It's watching a man do what he loves, and it really reaffirms for me: Do what you love. I'm not saying you'll be Bob Dylan, but just do what you love.

"The best 'Desolation' I have ever heard. Now, I know when he does that weird singing thing, that staccato, it can be annoying, but this time it worked. I'll tell you why. He was stepping *into* the microphone for the lyrics. And he was fierce tonight. He *knew* he was in New York City. This show tonight was something special.

"I was right where he looks when he's singing on the keyboard, and I'll tell you this—even though it will sound crazy. It's happened enough and it happened tonight. I'll start screaming at important moments, and he'll start responding to that. During 'Thunder in the Mountain' I started saying *Go! Go! Go!* And he just kicked it in. I know, I know. I sound like a crazy fan, but who knows?"

He stopped talking and took a bite of his sandwich.

"By the way," he said. "I'm not getting there at four. I'm getting there at three."

4

It was four A.M. on Wednesday now, thirty hours later, and the mysterious fan I came to think of as the Man in the Fedora hadn't slept. For the third straight night he was on the sidewalk out in front of Terminal 5. He'd been front and center Monday and Tuesday. Last night, he and Charlie had drinks and dinner with a friend, and he invited Charlie to crash at the place where he was staying. But as soon as they got there, the Man in the Fedora decided that if he went to sleep, the alarm would go off just as he achieved rapid eye movement. He would have been shattered coming out of it. So instead of climbing into bed he showered, put on a pink shirt under a pinstriped suit, slipped a purple feather into the band of his hat, and hailed a cab. He left Charlie sleeping on the floor.

They had met a few weeks earlier and spoken a lot in the line over the past two days. The man had spent the year seeing as many Dylan shows as possible, and he'd made it to upward of seventy of them, including Istanbul. He was friendly but cagey. (He insisted his name not appear in print. He had a good reason for it, he promised.) He spoke a lot but gave up little. He said he was a successful businessman who made enough money to retire early, and he was treating life as an adventure. "People who say there's nothing to do, that freaks me out," he said. He first saw Dylan in 1978. That year, an estimated two hundred thousand fans flocked to an airfield forty miles outside London to see Dylan. With his beads and top hat and leather jacket, "he was just the essence of a *god*," the Man in the Fedora said. "Some kind of deity. It was like some sort of religious experience."

At three A.M., Charlie's cell phone alarm trilled. Finding his friend gone, he hailed his own cab. Pulling up, he stepped out and asked, "Is Bob Dylan playing here tonight?" It seemed really funny at the time.

Cold wind whipped off the Hudson, picking up speed through a tunnel down the street and then jetting across the line like ice water from a spigot. Charlie was wearing a flimsy coat and a thermal T-shirt. He sat down and leaned his head against the cold frame of the garage door. "I'm going to sleep in line," he said. He knew he wouldn't really be able to do it. "I slept in Columbus and a puddle of water passed by. I moved over and fell asleep again." He was quiet for a minute or two. Then he picked his head up off the wall. "You know, after three nights of this, I won't be able to feed myself." Sleep deprivation was making him introspective. "How do we do this?" Charlie asked himself. "*Wooooo*. There are waves. In Detroit in '05, I started to have a nervous breakdown. 'Why am I such a mess? Why is my life such a mess?' But once he started to do 'I'll Remember You,' I felt that rush. You *feel* it. For me, part of it is I want to see if I can do it. Plus, whenever you get to the rail and he's singing, it's worth it. Just the moment it connects for you. Whatever happened during the day—if you're tired or you're hungry—it doesn't matter."

By six A.M. the sky had gone from black to blue. The Man in the Fedora, standing and looking dapper, asked the assembled, "Does anybody else think the version of 'Jolene' was the best ever?"

Charlie had done enough to establish his position at the head of the line, and he stood up and walked around the block to the corner store, which had coffee, water, egg breakfasts, soups, sandwiches, and, crucially, toilets. He had insisted that I meet him out front early and spend all day in line. By dawn, I was ready to surrender. "You've got to take it in stages," he said. "Right now we've got to get food. There have been good shows, and tonight is going to be a mother-fucking barn burner. Because he *knows* he's in New York City. The one thing you cannot do is think about how many hours are left." I'd already done it: fourteen.

When Charlie returned, the line had grown but his spot was safe. Fourth in line was a sixty-five-year-old woman who had arrived around five. She zipped herself in a sleeping bag, which was inside a trash bag, and lay down atop a flattened box. She didn't mind sleeping on the street. She was with family. "I'm close to all these people," she explained. "Even if we only see each other five times a year, we take care of each other. It's such a stressful situation. You're bonded in blood. In friendship and trust and Bob."

A woman with a thin face, an easy smile, and long gray hair appeared at intervals, sipping coffee and smoking cigarettes. She was a computer programmer in Norway who had flown off for these shows without telling her boss. She would wait in line for a while, slip away to her hotel and write code, then come back and make sure she hadn't lost her spot. She had to be close to the stage. "You get addicted," she said. "Once you've been up there, you don't want to go back."

Dylan's days as a heartthrob were long gone, but still, a good number of the fans charging the rail every night were women, some of whom sought to position themselves where they could make eye contact. One of them had theories about the attraction. "He's this elusive, mysterious, unavailable guy, and I think women in partic-ular are drawn to that," said Elizabeth Wolfson, a psychotherapist and clinical psychology professor in Santa Barbara. "That's just my psychological interpretation. It's like the elusive other that is so compelling you want him to draw you in. You want to make that connection."

At the shows, she added, the male fans were more interested in what song Dylan was going to play, or they were busy documenting it.

"Women aren't doing that," she said. "They're looking at his boots."

And they're asking themselves questions: Why those pants? Did he just look at me? Is he married now? When Dylan began to wear bands on his ring fingers, the women were the first to notice. Wolfson knew she was generalizing. But those thoughts flashed through her own mind, much as she hated to admit it.

When Dylan first arrived in the Village in 1961, emaciated and boyish, women reacted maternally. Wolfson still sensed that vibe from the women who waited in line. He looked fragile, vulnerable, almost elfin onstage. "You want to take care of him," she said. "He's so small up there, and he can be so awkward. There's a Charlie Chaplin aspect to it."

All that said, the music was what kept Wolfson returning every night. "To the nondiscerning eye it looks the same night after night, but not to me. To me it's different." He might alter a phrase, change the intonation of a syllable. She might get a different feel from the band or the crowd. "I guess it's like having sex," she said. "Is it the same? Yes. But it's always different. Are you going to stop because you did it before? If you find something in life that you enjoy and you're passionate about, why would you stop?"

The hours passed slowly on the third day in front of Terminal 5. People returned to hotel rooms to nap. They fetched coffee and lunch. Random conversations percolated here and there down the line. And then, finally, we had made it to seven P.M. again. The crowd massed at barricades as the venue prepared to open the doors.

Security looked over the bedraggled mob, amused. "Who's number one here?" asked a plainclothes cop wearing a leather coat and a brush cut.

"I am," Charlie said.

"When did you get here?"

"Three fifteen."

"Whoa. You must be exhausted. I don't have time for this sort of thing."

"We have jobs, too," a woman said.

"We're not homeless," said another.

"We just look that way."

"Who came the farthest?" another cop asked.

"She came from Oslo."

"Ireland!"

"Wales!"

"You must *really* like Bob Dylan."

The crowd rushed up to the bar and prepared for the dash downstairs. The fans were amped. I had been getting advice about how to claim and keep a spot on the rail. "Don't let anybody push you," one woman told me. "They're all *jackals*." I felt like I was an offensive lineman in the tunnel, bouncing around, pounding on my teammates' shoulder pads, preparing to rush out onto the field and blow some defensive tackle off the line. "When you get down there, get big!" the sleeping-bag lady told me. She had ditched her parka, slipped into a frilly black cocktail dress, applied glittery eye shadow, and daubed gloss onto her lips. "Twenty dollars a tube," she informed me. "We call this the Slutty Grandmother look."

The Man in the Fedora turned to me. "The excitement and anticipation could be measured on a Richter scale," he said.

"Can you imagine someone trying to get in front of this group now?" Charlie asked. He cackled.

"Walk! Walk! Walk!" security said as they sent the crowd downstairs. "You're the first ones in the club. Walk!" The rail in front of the piano was wide open, and I went for it and spread out my arms. The Man in the Fedora slid in next to me, and he made space between us for another guy who had been in line all three days. Charlie, a few spots down the rail, sent a text. "No matter what DON'T GIVE ANYONE UR SPOT EVEN FOR A SONG! No one is ur friend we're in the heart of darkness and the ONLY SUN is up there on that stage. U know u worked 4 it so enjoy ur spoils!"

Like the first night, the new material kept the concert afloat. "Beyond Here Lies Nothin'" (2009) was a dance song for anyone but the most sclerotic souls. If you'd read Scott Warmuth's blog and you remembered where the lyrics came from, "Tweedle Dee & Tweedle Dum" (2001) was a chain of flashing images—New Orleans and Lewis Carroll and Henry Timrod. On "Can't Wait" (1997), the band played a bluesy stop-start groove for all it was worth.

Halfway through the show Dylan stepped out to center stage and took the mic. "Forgetful heart . . . lost your power of recall," he sang over a quiet violin and the thrum of a stand-up bass played with a bow. "Every little detail . . . you don't remember at all." This was Late Late Dylan. He had released "Forgetful Heart" the year before on *Together Through Life*, and onstage it had grown into as gripping a song as any, filled with ache. He lost the woman, but at the end he realizes that the affair may have always been an illusion: They never had a chance. Dylan wailed a spooky harmonica solo and as the song evaporated in the air he stepped forward and reached out his arms, as if the women up front were fading ghosts. They swooned. A thought crossed multiple minds up front: "That was for me."

The stage went dark and Dylan put down the harp and jog-walked back to the piano as the band launched into a rocking song from *"Love and Theft"* called "Honest with Me." Glaring at the same women, he spat out the opening couplet. "Well, I'm stranded in the city that never sleeps, some of these women they just give me the creeps." As if to say, *Pull yourself together. That, a minute ago? That was just an act.*

The show ended earsplittingly: "All Along the Watchtower" was the sound of a band trying to blow apart a room. The drums were as deafening as a firing squad. It was music for the Second Coming, and it was with this song that Dylan sent his followers back to the streets, as he had many times before. They walked out with their ears ringing and fateful lines ("The hour is getting late") circling in their brains.

"God bless ya, Bobby!" the Man in the Fedora yelled.

Charlie was equal parts exhilarated and worn-out. Three days of anxiety and total joy were written on his face. He went back to the same deli, one last 10:30 P.M. meal. He was already thinking about tomorrow: subway, airport, plane, home. The noise would be rattling around in his brain for days.

5

When she was in her twenties, Elizabeth Wolfson went to California on a vacation. She rented a car and drove up to Malibu to see Dylan's house with the onion dome. She knew it sounded like stalking, but she was not the first nor the last person to make that pilgrimage. She got lost but she didn't give up. She wanted to find the place so desperately that she picked up a hitchhiker and asked for directions, and he knew the way.

Soon she found herself walking through the gate and into the dirt back lot, past the decrepit vehicles and the empty guard shack and right up to the door. It was open.

As she considered whether to cross the threshold or not, a guard showed up.

"You have to leave," he said.

Now she was in her mid-fifties, and she had had a perfectly happy life, a great love, two children, a rewarding career. Two things were left on her life list: to write a book and to meet Bob Dylan. The book she could write. But she couldn't figure out how she would meet Dylan. She was a goal-oriented person, and this drove her crazy. "Look, I've been listening to him since I was fifteen years old. That's a lifetime. The passion has never wavered." *Blood on the Tracks,* the record he wrote while his marriage disintegrated, was the soundtrack to her first breakup. *Time Out of Mind,* the 1997 album soaked in regret, appeared as her own marriage fell apart. ("It was so potent I could barely listen to it.") "Forgetful Heart" appeared just as another relationship was ending. In between, there were all the songs about unrequited love.

"He and I have been through a lot together and *he doesn't know it,*" she said. "He doesn't know I exist. Can you see how that would be frustrating? I don't have any grandiose idea that because he's affected me he's going to care. I just think it's not fair that it's a one-way relationship." She wasn't delusional. She didn't think he was going to ask her out on a date, or invite her to his home. But if he did she would have to drop everything and go. "I don't think he's Jesus, I don't think he's the messiah. He's just a human being. But he's filled with poetry."

Years ago, a writer asked Dylan about the people who made pilgrimages to see him at shows and wanted to meet him. What did he have for these fans? "In India," he answered, "they have men that live in the Himalayas, and people make long journeys to sit at their feet.

And what happens when they sit at their feet? Nothing. Nothing happens. They're usually given a big dose of silence."

Once, Dylan and Elizabeth did communicate, wordlessly, from the rail to the stage. As he was taking his bow at the end of a concert in 2011, she gave a thumbs-up and he stuck his thumbs down. Was he not happy with the show? She gave two thumbs up, and he followed suit.

Two thumbs up. It was a start.

MIRRORS

In 2009, a very long entry appeared on a blog called Radioactive Dylan. The author called it a "prematurely published Dylan obituary." He explained that, listening to the radio one night, he heard a talk show playing "Like a Rolling Stone," and for whatever reason he thought the host was going to say that he had queued up the song because Bob Dylan was dead. Just the idea of Dylan's passing sent the writer to his keyboard, where he let loose a torrent of prose. The bulk of the post's thirty-five thousand words was one uninterrupted paragraph—its multihued text the only aid to readers—documenting his half of an imaginary conversation with a newcomer to Dylan fandom. He expounded on Dylan's magnificence, and argued that while he knew about all the other great artists of history, Milton and Mozart and Melville, he had concluded that none of them outshined his hero. "Indeed, Dylan's career stands as the strongest case for Artist of the Millennium."

The author was Bryan Styble, founder of the first Dylan fanzine, *Talkin' Bob Zimmerman Blues*, and the man involved in acquiring the "armpit tape" copy of Dylan playing in the St. Paul attic apartment in 1960. Back then he went as Brian Stibal. He changed his name because he was tired of people mispronouncing it, though others thought he did it because those *y*'s gave him and Dylan something in common. Bryan was a self-described math nerd with Asperger's. He could talk about almost any topic for hours, uninterrupted. (Later, he would be a radio host and a *Jeopardy!* contestant.) He was imposing, boisterous, very loud. He was aware of this. He knew it made people uncomfortable, that it made people misunderstand him. "I'm an intense person. That's why people don't like me."

When he was in his twenties, Bryan spent a lot of time listening to and thinking about Dylan. The singer had cautioned his fans not to conflate the music and the man. "I'm not the songs. It's like somebody expecting Shakespeare to be Hamlet, or Goethe to be Faust," he said. But Bryan thought Dylan was wrong. "It is my profound belief that more than any other artist in any medium in any era, Dylan blurs the line between art and artist," Bryan told me once. "These songs were so personal that he *couldn't* be telling stories." This became the insight that propelled him: To understand the songs, he needed to know the man, *personally*. He needed to locate Dylan, and he needed to talk to him.

In 1980, Bryan was hoping to break into television or radio broadcasting, and he faced a choice: New York or Los Angeles? He moved west, and he would be lying if he didn't acknowledge that part of the reason was that his hero lived there. When he got to LA, he began driving past Dylan's Santa Monica rehearsal space two and three times a week. If there was anything going on—players milling around, music blaring from open windows—he would stop and hang around. Later, he would make a point of driving past Dylan's

As soon as they learned the title of the album and its track list, fans flew into action. First off, *The Tempest* was believed to be the last play that Shakespeare wrote on his own. Was this a hint that Dylan was ready to hang it up? One digger didn't even wait for lyrics to begin looking for appropriations: He found the title of the opener, "Duquesne Whistle," in a 1933 *Time* magazine reference to the Pennsylvania city's steelworks. (In the song, it turned out, they were train whistles.) On the album cover, the title was written in bright red cursive, and the capital *T* looked a lot like a cross, so students of Dylan began flipping through their Bibles for references to the song titles. Someone discovered that the cover image—of a woman in rapture—was taken at a fountain in front of the Austrian Parliament building in the center of Vienna, and that was parsed for meaning.

Critics and fans lavished *Tempest* with praise. A few made silly comparisons—best Dylan record since 1976, one critic declared it—but even Clinton Heylin and Andy Muir found a lot to like. After walking out of the Roundhouse in 2009, Andy had come back around on Dylan. Strangely, he fell back in love while listening to the record of Christmas songs Dylan released later that year. Somehow the man sounded so much more authentic croaking "O Little Town of Bethlehem" than he had in years. Andy had hoped he would find a way back into the fold, and sure enough, the next few times he saw Dylan in concert he enjoyed himself. When *Tempest* landed, Andy was his old ecstatic self again. He loved "Long and Wasted Years" so much that he put it on a continuous loop for a while and reveled in the glorious feeling of appreciating new Dylan.

Scott Warmuth listened to that song and found that some of its words came from *Talk That Talk: An Anthology of African-American Storytelling*. Dylan borrowed from a tale of a buzzard who fools a rabbit and a squirrel into riding on his back so he can smash them to the ground and devour them. A monkey turns the tables on the bird. There they were again: tricksters. Tricksters tricking tricksters, in fact.

Dylan sat down with *Rolling Stone* for the One Big Interview and spent some time launching attacks on anybody who had ever tried to figure him out. He and the interviewer, Mikal Gilmore, spoke about how Dylan changed after the motorcycle wreck in 1966. At one point, Dylan pulled out a paperback, the autobiography of infamous Hells Angel Sonny Barger, and insisted Gilmore read aloud from a passage about a motorcycle-club president who died in a wreck in the 1960s. The man's name: Bobby Zimmerman.

Dylan told Gilmore that the book opened his eyes. He suddenly and finally knew why he was so different from other people. He must have undergone a "transfiguration," Dylan said. "So when you ask some of your questions, you're asking them to a person who's long dead. You're asking them to a person that doesn't exist. But people make that mistake about me all the time. I've lived through a lot. Have you ever heard of a book called *No Man Knows My History*? It's about Joseph Smith, the Mormon prophet. The title could refer to me."

The whole routine almost seemed like a send-up of the crazy efforts by critics, writers, and fans to explain Dylan. They poked and prodded at his songs, his biography, and his interviews, hoping these things would give up, finally, the secrets of his inner being. Gilmore played the straight man, as every journalist must, and tried to move the conversation onto safer, established ground. He returned to Dylan's own crash in 1966. "Afterward, with the music made in Woodstock with the Band, and with *John Wesley Harding* and *Nashville Skyline*, some were bewildered by your transformation," Gilmore said. "You came back from that hiatus looking different, sounding different, in voice, music and words."

Dylan pounced. "Why is it when people talk about me they have to go crazy? What the fuck is the matter with them?"

So these things happened, he continued. "So fucking what? They want to know what can't be known. They are searching—they are seekers. Like in the Pete Townshend song where he's trying to find his way to 50 million fables." In the song, the Seeker looks for answers from all his idols—Bob Dylan, the Beatles, Timothy Leary—and he gets nowhere. He's bound to die searching. "Why are they doing this? They don't really know. It's sad. It really is. May the Lord have mercy on them. They are lost souls."

Later in the conversation, he griped about the army of annotators trailing behind him. "There's a whole world of scholars, professors, and Dylanologists, and everything I do affects them in some way. And, you know, in some ways, I've given them life. They'd be nowhere without me."

A week before *Tempest* arrived in record stores, the tour passed through a little venue north of New York. The Capitol Theater in Port Chester was an old movie house that had been converted into a concert hall with room for eighteen hundred. The place had fallen into disrepair, but new owners restored it and booked Dylan for the grand reopening. Port Chester was only forty minutes by train from Manhattan, and all the regulars trekked up. Mitch Blank sat in the balcony. Jeff Friedman taped the concert. In the lobby, Nina Goss and Charlie Haeussler ran into Lucas Stensland, who had recently returned to New York from Minnesota.

As the crowd waited for Dylan to come on, they noticed something new on the stage. There were five large mirrors facing out toward the crowd. They were round, oval, and rectangular, in beautiful frames, large enough to hang on a wall at home. One floated in front of Dylan's keyboard, one was propped inside the open lid of a trunk, others leaned against pieces of stage gear.

What were these doing there? Were they some kind of deterrent to surreptitious paparazzi? Dylan had long insisted that no photographs be taken at his concerts, and he could be camera-shy offstage. "Cameras make ghosts out of people," he said. But the dictum had long been ignored by fans, and it was impossible to enforce in the smartphone age. Perhaps the mirrors were there to annoy the annoying. Their flashes would shoot back into their own eyes. Nobody could say for sure.

But after his fuming comments in *Rolling Stone* appeared a week later, it didn't seem unreasonable to ask if the mirrors were meant to send a sharper message to the audience at his feet: *Take a look at yourselves, would you please?*

What must it be like to be Dylan, music writer Paul Williams once wondered, and carry around "the half-formed dreams of millions on your back"? Dylan always had been afraid of his followers, and Williams could understand why. "Their relationship with him is so intense, they expect so much, and more than once over the years they've turned really nasty when he chose to deliver something other than their notion of who 'Bob Dylan' should be." Williams wrote that in the aftermath of the first gospel concerts in 1979, but he just as easily could have said it after *Another Side* in 1964, Newport in 1966, *Nashville Skyline* in 1969, Live Aid in 1985, or London in 2009. So many controversies. So much disappointment. Dylan acted entirely unfazed: "Oh, I let you down? Big deal," he said once. "Find somebody else." More than one fan really did wish he had died in the motorcycle wreck in 1966. It would have been better that way. He'd have been frozen in his glory. Instead he got old. He kept putting out new records and doing shows. He kept confounding.

The audience always wants to see the *real* Bob Dylan. Whoever that is. As if that would even be possible. After he traveled in the Rolling Thunder caravan with Dylan in 1975, playwright Sam

Shepard wrote that "fans are more dangerous than a man with a weapon because they're after something invisible. Some imagined 'something.' At least with a gun you know what you're facing."

Dylan preferred to keep the myth alive. He preferred to leave people wondering. He preferred the mask. You could even argue that Dylan considered the mask the point of the whole enterprise. "There's nothing to figure out," said a musician I met at Zimmy's. "Same thing with the Mona Lisa smile. She was smiling because everybody's trying to figure out why she was smiling."

In 1978, music critic Jonathan Cott tried to ask Dylan about some of the new songs on *Street-Legal*, and the singer batted around the questions briefly before finally balking. "I'm the first person who'll put it to you and the last person who'll explain it to you," he said. "Those questions can be answered dozens of different ways, and I'm sure they're all legitimate. Everybody sees in the mirror what he sees. No two people see the same thing."

Maybe that was the point of the stage mirrors. Maybe, for the thousandth time, Dylan was saying, *Stop expecting answers from me*. You should come up with them for yourself. The point of the songs wasn't what they said *about him*. The point was what they said *to you*.

Maybe. Or maybe not; no explanation was forthcoming, anyway.

The mirrors were one more mystery for the tribe. Before his followers figured out why they were there, they would be gone.

AUTHOR'S NOTE

Every new work about Dylan stands on the shoulders of the many volumes that came before. This book is no exception. To complement my reporting on the lives of Dylan's followers, I consulted hundreds of sources about the man: books, fanzines, films, newspapers, magazines, and blogs. What follows is not a comprehensive bibliography, but a selection of sources I relied on most.

The most thorough and informative biography is Clinton Heylin's *Behind the Shades*; a third edition was published in 2011. Others include Anthony Scaduto's *Bob Dylan* (1971); Robert Shelton's *No Direction Home* (1986); Bob Spitz's *Dylan* (1989); and Howard Sounes's *Down the Highway* (2001). Dylan's own words can be found in his memoir, *Chronicles: Volume One*, as well as *Bob Dylan: The Essential Interviews*, edited by Jonathan Cott, and *Every Mind Polluting Word,* a massive fan-produced assemblage of his interviews over the years for magazines and newspapers. Dylan's songs are compiled in *Lyrics*; newer compositions are posted on bobdylan.com.

Just Like Bob Zimmerman's Blues: Dylan in Minnesota by Dave Engel; *Highway 61 Revisited*, edited by Colleen J. Sheehy and Thomas Swiss; and *Positively Main Street* by Toby Thompson shed light on Dylan and Hibbing. Martin Scorsese's *No Direction Home* is the authorized look at Dylan's early years. *A Simple Twist of Fate* by Andy Gill and Kevin Odegard delves into *Blood on the Tracks*. Heylin's *Revolution in the Air* and *Still on the Road* take readers through Dylan's musical career song by song. The spiritual elements of Dylan's work are considered in *Dylan—What Happened?* by Paul Williams; *Dylan Redeemed* by Stephen H. Webb; *Bob Dylan: Prophet, Mystic, Poet* by Seth Rogovoy; *The Gospel According to Bob Dylan* and *Tangled Up in the Bible* by Michael Gilmour; and *Restless Pilgrim* by Scott M. Marshall.

Highlighting the evolution in thinking about Dylan over the years are *Bob Dylan: The Early Years*, edited by Craig McGregor; *The Bob Dylan Companion*, edited by Carl Benson; *The Dylan Companion*, edited by Elizabeth Thomson and David Gutman; and *Bob Dylan by Greil Marcus: Writings 1968–2010*. Michael Gray's *Bob Dylan Encyclopedia* is a helpful aid to researchers. Stephen Scobie's clear-eyed *Alias: Bob Dylan Revisited*; Andrew Muir's *Troubadour*; Mike Marqusee's *Wicked Messenger*; and *Dylan at Play*, edited by Nina Goss and Nick Smart, offer new ways of thinking about songs, as do two classics of Dylan studies, Christopher Ricks's *Dylan's Visions of Sin* and Gray's *Song & Dance Man III: The Art of Bob Dylan*.

Heylin's *Bootleg* tells the story of the underground record industry, and his *Bob Dylan: The Recording Sessions* is a helpful source about Dylan's studio work through 1994. More information about sessions and performances can be found in Glen Dundas's *Tangled* and Michael Krogsgaard's *Positively Bob Dylan*. Olaf Bjorner tracks Dylan's work online at www.bjorner.com/bob.htm.

Other accounts about or by Dylan's fans include: *On the Road with Bob Dylan* by Larry "Ratso" Sloman; *My Life in Garbology* by A.J. Weberman; *The Ballad of Bob Dylan* by Daniel Mark Epstein; *Razor's Edge: Bob Dylan and the Never Ending Tour* by Andrew Muir; *Encounters with Bob Dylan: If You See Him, Say Hello*, edited by Tracy Johnson; *Touched by the Hand of Bob* by Dave Henderson; *Confessions of a Dylanomaniac* by Marcel Levesque; *Bobcat Nation* by Adam Selzer; *How Does It Feel: Reflections on Bob Dylan*, edited by Joe Ladwig; and two documentary films, *How Many Roads*, produced by Jos de Putter, and *The Ballad of A.J. Weberman* by James Bluemel and Oliver Ralfe. Fanzines and journals past and present—the *Telegraph*; the *Bridge*; *Judas!*; *Homer, the slut*; *Freewheelin'*; *ISIS*; *Look Back*; *On the Tracks*; and *Montague Street: The Art of Bob Dylan*—transport readers into hidden corners of Dylan obsession. Articles from the *Telegraph* are anthologized in *Wanted Man: In Search of Bob Dylan*, edited by John Bauldie, and *All Across the Telegraph*, edited by Bauldie and Gray. *ISIS: A Bob Dylan Anthology* and *Bob Dylan Anthology Volume 2: 20 Years of ISIS* are edited by Derek Barker.

Of the dozens of Dylan Internet sites, Expecting Rain (expectingrain.com), ISIS (bobdylanisis.com), and the examiner.com Bob Dylan blog by Harold Lepidus are the best places for up-to-the-minute Dylan news, while BobLinks (boblinks.com), the Never Ending Pool (theneverendingpool.org), and John Baldwin's Desolation Row Information Service keep the world current on road news. The archives of rec.music.dylan are filled with nuggets of intel. EDLIS Café on Facebook brings some anarchy to Dylan fandom.

While the book draws frequently on this vast library of all things Dylan, certain details come from other sources not cited in the text. In chapter one, I relied on interviews by the *Star-Ledger* of Newark, New Jersey, and *Good Morning America* to describe Dylan's encounter with police in New Jersey, and the *Winnipeg Free Press* for details about his visit to Neil Young's childhood home. I found a description of Dylan at Sun Studio on the A.V. Club website. In chapter two, I turned to the Greenwich Village Society for Historical Preservation and Dave Van Ronk's *The Mayor of MacDougal Street* for background on the neighborhood. Some details about the Forest Hills show in 1965 came from Daniel Kramer's *Bob Dylan*, Greil Marcus's *Invisible Republic*, and the *Village Voice*. Detail on Woody Guthrie comes from Ed Cray's *Ramblin' Man*. Weberman's thinking is drawn from his books, *Dylan to English Dictionary* and *Right Wing Bob*.

In chapter three, I drew from a profile of Bob Fass in the *New Yorker*, and from pieces in the *New York Times*, the *Washington Post*, and *Time* about 1970s spiritual movements. I also relied on a *Village Voice* interview with Sandy Gant. In chapter four, details of George Hecksher's collection came from Morgan Library press releases. A Ron Rosenbaum piece in the *New York Observer* described the obsession with the *Blood on the Tracks* notebook. In chapter five, I used details found in Bauldie's *Diary of a Bobcat*, an Adrian Deevoy story in *Q* magazine, and pieces about an accused serial killer in the *Guardian* and the *San Francisco Chronicle*.

In chapter six, I referenced postings on rec.music.dylan and Eyolf Østrem's website, dylanchords.info. I used details from a *Wall Street Journal* story about Chris Johnson and a *New Yorker* piece about yakuza. In describing the debate about Dylan's borrowings, I relied on an essay by Robert Polito for the Poetry Foundation and quoted from a paper delivered at a conference in Austria by Stephen Scobie, *Plagiarism, Bob, Jean-Luc, and Me*. Details about the Cramps came from the *Washington Post*, the *Los Angeles Times*, and *Plazm* magazine. Joni Mitchell's comments were drawn from an interview transcript posted on jonimitchell.com. Larry Charles's comments appeared in the Minneapolis *Star Tribune*.

In chapter seven, I drew on the *Biograph* liner notes, a Michael

Gray review in the *Daily Telegraph*, and a piece by Wes Stace in the *Times Literary Supplement*. In chapter eight, I used details from the *Columbus Dispatch, Rolling Stone*, and a blog called Word Riot.

The central figures in this book put up with countless phone calls, visits, and e-mails from me, and I'm grateful to all of them for their time and their trust. In particular, Mitch Blank and Glen Dundas generously helped this book in more ways than I can count. They opened doors, shared material, confirmed details, and became invaluable advocates.

Many others helped me navigate this subculture. Bob Levinson introduced me to my first crop of fans through his Dylan class in New York. Jeff Friedman, Larry Hanson, Clinton Heylin, Andrew Muir, Stephen Scobie, Wes Stace, Lucas Stensland, and John Stokes shared old fanzines and other materials.

I spoke to more people than I ever could have included in the final cast. For every story in the book I had ten more I wanted to include. Don LaSala invited me into Big Pink for a beer. Christopher Ricks gave me a private class in Dylan studies. C. P. Lee showed me the Free Trade Hall in Manchester. Unfortunately, those and many other scenes didn't find a home in these pages. But every interview helped color the book. Thanks to Scott Alarik, Ian Alderson, Wyatt Alexander, Stephen Hazan Arnoff, John Baldwin, Gordon Ball, Eugen Banauch, Renardo Barden, Derek Barker, Frank Beacham, Sarah Beatty, Christian Behrens, Janena Benjamin, Ray Benson, Bob Bettendorf, Bill Biersach, Damon Bramblett, Aaron Brown, John Bushey, Hans Peter Bushoff, Jean-Martin Büttner, Leslie Carole, Bill Carpenter, Andy Carroll, Daniel Cavicchi, Christine Consolvo, Edward Cook, Chris Cooper, Roy Cougle, Becky Dalton, Pat Dean, Butch Dener, Arie de Reus, Madge Dundas, Olivier Durand, Monte

Edwardson, Jonathan Eig, Al Eldridge, Jack Evans, Lisa Finnie, Susan Fino, Jim Fox, Gregg French, Nelson French, Eleanor Friedberger, Benedict Giamo, Joel Gilbert, Stu Gilbert, Michael Gilmour, Jeff Gold, Andy Goldstein, Michael Gray, Keith Gubitz, Colin Hall, Heather Haroldson, Brian Hassett, Benjamin Hedin, Dennis Hengeveld, Mark Hime, Sissel Høisæter, Mikhail Horowitz, John Howells, Gary Ivan, Masato Kato, John Keis, Roy Kelly, Terry Kelly, Joe and Mary Keyes, Dan Klute, Nick Kostopoulos, Michael Krogsgaard, Seth Kulick, Kenn Kweder, Jim LaClair, Elliott Landy, Kim Larsen, John Lattanzio, David Leaver, Dan Leighton, Harold Lepidus, Jonathan Lethem, Mary Pauline Lowry, Alex Lubet, Martin MacKinnon, Angel Marolt, Bev Martin, Zainab McCoy, Dennis McDougal, Simon Montgomery, Jules Moore, Karen Moynihan, Elliott Murphy, Jan Murray, Abe Nahum, Josh Nelson, Tom Noonan, John Nye, James O'Brien, Barry Ollman, Richard Oppenheimer, Andrea Orlandi, Barb Pagliocca, Tom Palaima, Susan Paraventi, Paul Penn, Mel Prussack, Walter Raubicheck, Dave Rave, Ike Reilly, Martin and Teodora Ricketts, George Rothe, Kait Runevitch, Carole Sass, Mike Sawatzky, Caroline Schwarz, Hans Seeger, John Sipowicz, Brian Slattery, Larry "Ratso" Sloman, Al Small, Nick Smart, Ross Smith, Howard Sounes, Bob Stacy, Nat Stensland, Thomas Storch, Mike Sutton, Thom Swiss, Richard Thomas, Toby Thompson, David Tracer, Mike and Pam Turnbull, David Vidmar, Glenn Warmuth, Stephen Webb, Rob Whitehouse, John Wraith, Paul Wultz, Amy Young, Larry Yudelson, and all those shady types who only wanted to help on the sly.

Several people read drafts and saved me from errors major and minor: Tom Moon, Craig McCoy, Mark Sutton, Mick Gold, Bill Reynolds, Harry Green, Jonathan Schuppe, Jeanne Villahermosa, and Geoff Ross.

My agent, Larry Weissman, made it happen again, and with

Sarah Self put together the film deal for *The Big One* that gave me breathing room to take on this project. For the second time, my editor, Jofie Ferrari-Adler, saved me from myself. This book would be far weaker if not for his keen eye, his patience, and his unflagging enthusiasm. Thanks also to Jonathan Karp, Anne Tate Pearce, Richard Rhorer, Dana Trocker, Ed Winstead, Maggie Higby, and the staff at Simon & Schuster.

I'm grateful to Cindy Tobisman and Nicole Pearl, Gene La Fond, Chris Hockenhull, and the Dundases for putting me up on the road, and to *Big One* fans Graham, Stephen, and Michael Stiles for much-needed invitations to fish and watch baseball.

I owe my parents for everything, and my brother, Jim, for leaving that copy of *Biograph* behind, and my kids, Jane and Owen, for putting up with more Bob Dylan than is recommended by pediatricians. I couldn't have done a book like this without my wife, Monica. Whatever doubts she harbored about where the project was heading as it stretched from one year into several (and many thousands of miles), she kept them mostly to herself. If she had ever told me what she was really thinking, I might never have had the nerve to finish.